The Cambridge Companion to Willa Cather

The Cambridge Companion to Willa Cather offers thirteen original essays by leading scholars of a major American novelist. Willa Cather's luminous prose is 'easy' to read yet surprisingly difficult to understand. The essays collected here are theoretically informed but accessibly written and cover the full range of Cather's career, including most of her twelve novels and several of her short stories. The essays situate Cather's work in a broad range of critical, cultural, and literary contexts, and the introduction explores current trends in Cather scholarship as well as the author's place in contemporary culture. With a detailed chronology and a guide to further reading, the volume offers students and teachers a fresh and thorough sense of the author of *My Ántonia*, *The Professor's House*, and *Death Comes for the Archbishop*.

THE CAMBRIDGE COMPANION TO

WILLA CATHER

EDITED BY

MARILEE LINDEMANN

CAMBRIDGE UNIVERSITY PRESS
Cambridge, New York, Melbourne, Madrid, Cape Town, Singapore, São Paulo

Cambridge University Press
The Edinburgh Building, Cambridge CB2 2RU, UK

Published in the United States of America by Cambridge University Press, New York

www.cambridge.org
Information on this title: www.cambridge.org/9780521527934

First published 2005

Printed in the United Kingdom at the University Press, Cambridge

A catalogue record for this book is available from the British Library

Library of Congress Cataloguing in Publication data
The Cambridge companion to Willa Cather / edited by Marilee Lindemann.
p.   cm. – (Cambridge companions to literature)
Includes bibliographical references and index.
ISBN 0-521-82110-X – ISBN 0-521-52793-7 (pbk.)
1. Cather, Willa, 1873–1947 – Criticism and interpretation – Handbooks, manuals, etc.
2. Women and literature – United States – History – 20th century – Handbooks, manuals, etc.
I. Title; Companion to Willa Cather.   II. Lindemann, Marilee.   III. Series.
PS3505.A87Z59155   2004
813'.52 – dc22   2004051820

ISBN-13 978-0-521-82110-0 hardback
ISBN-10 0-521-82110-X hardback
ISBN-13 978-0-521-52793-4 paperback
ISBN-10 0-521-52793-7 paperback

In memory of
Susan J. Rosowski
1942–2004

CONTENTS

CONTENTS

ILLUSTRATIONS

NOTES ON CONTRIBUTORS

JONATHAN GOLDBERG is Sir William Osler Professor of English at The Johns Hopkins University. He is the author of *Willa Cather and Others* (2001) as well as of a number of books on early modernity and sexuality, including *Sodometries* (1992) and *Desiring Women Writing* (1997). He is the editor of *Queering the Renaissance* (1994) and *Reclaiming Sodom* (1994). His most recent book is *Tempest in the Caribbean* (2003).

ANNE E. GOLDMAN is associate professor of English at Sonoma State University. She is the author of *Take My Word: Autobiographical Innovations of Ethnic American Working Women* (1996) and *Continental Divides: Revisioning American Literature* (2000). She is co-editor of a volume of critical essays, *Maria Amparo Ruiz de Burton: Critical and Pedagogical Perspectives*, forthcoming from the University of Nebraska Press. Her current project considers Jewish American cultural studies from 1990 to the present.

MARILEE LINDEMANN is associate professor of English and director of Lesbian, Gay, Bisexual, and Transgender Studies at the University of Maryland. She is the author of *Willa Cather: Queering America* (1999) and of numerous essays on American women writers and queer literary history. She has also edited *Alexander's Bridge* (1997) and *O Pioneers!* (1999) for Oxford University Press.

MARK J. MADIGAN is associate professor of English at Nazareth College of Rochester and has published widely on Cather, Dorothy Canfield Fisher, and other American writers. He is the editor of *Keeping Fires Night and Day: Selected Letters of Dorothy Canfield Fisher* (1993), as well as of Fisher's *The Bedquilt and Other Stories* (1997) and *Seasoned Timber* (1996). He is the volume editor of *Youth and the Bright Medusa*, forthcoming in the Willa Cather Scholarly Edition. He was a Fulbright Scholar at the University of Ljubljana, Slovenia, in 2004.

LISA MARCUS is associate professor of English and chair of Women's Studies at Pacific Lutheran University. She has an essay on Cather in *Willa Cather's Southern Connections* (2000); an essay on Pauline Hopkins in *Speaking the Other Self: American Women Writers* (1997); and numerous essays on feminism and feminist studies in *The Women's Review of Books*. She is completing a book, *Tricky Magic: Slavery and Female Fictions of America*.

RICHARD MILLINGTON is professor of English at Smith College. He is the author of *Practicing Romance: Narrative Form and Cultural Engagement in Hawthorne's Fiction* (1992), and of essays on Hawthorne and Willa Cather. He co-edited *Hitchcock's America* (1999), which includes his essay on *North by Northwest*, and edited *The Cambridge Companion to Nathaniel Hawthorne* (2004).

SHARON O'BRIEN is John Hope Caldwell Professor of American Cultures at Dickinson College. She is the author of *Willa Cather: The Emerging Voice* (1987), *Willa Cather* (1994), and many essays on Cather, biography and autobiography, feminist theory, and depression. She also edited *New Essays on* My Ántonia (1998) and the three-volume Library of America edition of Cather (1992). Her most recent book is *The Family Silver: A Memoir of Depression and Inheritance* (2004).

GUY J. REYNOLDS is a professor of English at the University of Nebraska-Lincoln. He is the author of *Willa Cather in Context: Progress, Race, Empire* (1996) and *Twentieth-Century American Women's Fiction* (1999), as well as of a number of articles on American literature.

ANN ROMINES is professor of English and director of graduate studies at George Washington University. She is the author of numerous essays on Cather and other American women writers and of two books: *The Home Plot: Women, Writing and Domestic Ritual* (1992) and *Constructing the Little House: Gender, Culture, and Laura Ingalls Wilder* (1997). She is editor of *Willa Cather's Southern Connections: New Essays on Cather and the South* (2000) and of the forthcoming Nebraska Scholarly Edition of *Sapphira and the Slave Girl*.

SUSAN J. ROSOWSKI was University Professor and Adele Hall Distinguished Professor at the University of Nebraska-Lincoln. She was the author of *Birthing a Nation: Gender, Creativity, and the Significance of the West in American Literature* (1999) and *The Voyage Perilous: Willa Cather's Romanticism* (1986). She was also general editor of the Nebraska Scholarly Edition of Willa Cather and editor in chief of *Cather Studies*.

LEONA SEVICK earned her doctorate in English at the University of Maryland, where she wrote a dissertation on Cather and antimodernism. She has published articles on Cather and is currently at work on a book on Cather and the Arts and Crafts movement. She teaches world literature at McDaniel College.

JANIS P. STOUT is professor of English emerita at Texas A&M University. Her most recent books are *Katherine Anne Porter: A Sense of the Times* (1995), *Through the Window, Out the Door: Women's Narratives of Departure* (1998), *Willa Cather: The Writer and Her World* (2000), and *A Calendar of the Letters of Willa Cather* (2002).

JOHN N. SWIFT is professor of English and Comparative Literary Studies at Occidental College in Los Angeles. A past president of the Willa Cather Foundation, he has written numerous articles on Cather and other modern writers and is co-editor of *Willa Cather and the American Southwest* (2002).

JOSEPH R. URGO is professor and chair of English at The University of Mississippi. He is the author of *Willa Cather and the Myth of American Migration* (1995) and, most recently, *In the Age of Distraction* (2000). He also edited the Broadview Press edition of *My Ántonia* (2003).

ACKNOWLEDGMENTS

"Willa was just plain Billy to all of us," remarked one of Willa Cather's classmates in the prep program at the University of Nebraska in the early 1890s in commenting on how the mannishly dressed, intelligent, and highly unconventional young woman from Red Cloud was received by her peers. (The comment is reprinted in James Shively's *Writings from Willa Cather's Campus Years* [Lincoln, NE: University of Nebraska Press, 1950], p. 122.) This book is for all the students, teachers, fans, and admirers of "just plain Billy," who know well that there is nothing simple about her "plainness" and much to enjoy in the limpid prose of one of the finest stylists the United States has yet produced.

I am grateful to my friend and colleague Robert S. Levine for cajoling me into taking on this project and to Ray Ryan of Cambridge University Press for seeing to it that I got it done. Jennifer Landon was an intrepid research and technology assistant whose work on the chronology saved me from pulling out my hair. Her help was invaluable. My thanks and admiration to the volume's contributors, who produced excellent work in a timely way and made this a book that will be worth reading for years to come. I note with sorrow that one contributor, Susan J. Rosowski, did not live to see her fine essay on Cather's comic spirit into print, as she succumbed to cancer while the book was in production. Sue was one of the best friends that Billy and many a Cather scholar ever had. Her years of extraordinary dedication to Cather studies and the community that surrounds it helped to create the varied audiences for this book, and so I am pleased to offer it in her memory.

Finally, Martha Nell Smith is the best friend and more that *this* friend of Billy ever had. I embrace you, darling, as Latour embraced Vaillant, "for the past – for the future."

1873

December 7   Wilella Cather is born in Back Creek Valley, near Winchester, Virginia in the home of her maternal grandmother, Rachel Boak. Named after a deceased aunt, she is the eldest child of Charles and Mary Virginia (Jennie) Cather. Nicknamed "Willie" by her family, she will rename herself "Willa."

Brothers and sisters: Roscoe (b. 1877), Douglass (b. 1880), Jessica (b. 1881), James (b. 1886), Elsie (b. 1890), and John (Jack) (b. 1892).

1874

Fall   Willa's parents move the family to Willow Shade, home of her paternal grandparents, William and Caroline Cather. Willow Shade is located between Back Creek Valley and Winchester.

1877   William and Caroline Cather move to Nebraska, joining a son and daughter-in-law who are already farming there.

1883

February   Willow Shade sold after the sheep barn burns down.

April   Charles and Jennie Cather move the family, including Grandmother Boak, to Catherton Precinct, Webster County, Nebraska.

Fall   Willa attends the New Virginia country school.

1884   Willa's family moves to Red Cloud, after her father decides to give up farming and open a real-estate and loan office.

1886   Cather cuts her hair short, takes to wearing boys' clothes, and calls herself "William Cather." She will sustain this public stance of radical gender nonconformity through to 1892.

1890

June   Gives the commencement speech, "Superstition vs. Investigation," at her high-school graduation in Red Cloud.

September Enrolls in the Latin School (University Prep) in Lincoln, Nebraska.

1891

March 1   *Nebraska State Journal* publishes Cather's essay on Carlyle, which was submitted by her teacher, Ebenezer Hunt, without her knowledge.

September Enters the University of Nebraska. Begins relationship with Louise Pound, a student three years ahead of her in school who was a brilliant student and an accomplished athlete.

November *Nebraska State Journal* publishes Cather's essay on Hamlet.

1892

May   First fiction published. "Peter," a story submitted by Professor Herbert Bates, is published in *The Mahogany Tree*.

June   Poem, "Shakespeare: A Freshman Theme," published in the University of Nebraska student newspaper, *The Hesperian*. In a passionate letter to Louise Pound, she declares that it is unfair that "feminine friendship" should be regarded as unnatural.

Fall   Becomes the literary editor of *The Hesperian*.

1893   Becomes a regular contributor to the *Nebraska State Journal*; reviews plays and writes a Sunday column.

1894   Publishes a satirical piece about Pound's brother Roscoe in *The Hesperian*, ruining her relationship with Louise and the entire Pound family.

1895

June   Graduates from the University of Nebraska. Works for the Lincoln *Courier*.

1896   Publishes stories in *Overland Monthly* and *Nebraska Literary Magazine*.

June   Moves to Pittsburgh, PA, to edit *Home Monthly*.

October   Contributes drama criticism to the *Pittsburgh Leader*.

1897

January–June	Contributes column to the *Nebraska State Journal*. Still edits *Home Monthly*. Returns to Red Cloud in June.
July	*Home Monthly* sold.
September	Returns to Pittsburgh with job on the *Pittsburgh Leader*. Works on the telegraph desk and writes play and book reviews. Sends "Passing Show" column to the Lincoln *Courier*. Continues to write "Helen Delay" book column for the *Home Monthly*.

1898

February	Spends a week in New York, has lunch with Modjeska; may have contributed a review or reviews to the *New York Sun*.
May	Visits her cousin, Howard Gore, in Washington, DC.

1899

	Meets Isabelle McClung, daughter of a prominent Pittsburgh judge, Samuel McClung, and wife Fannie. Cather and McClung form an intense, life-long friendship based in part on their mutual interests in the arts. Cather would later claim that Isabelle was the one person for whom all her books had been written.

1900

	Resigns from Pittsburgh *Leader*.
Fall	Moves to Washington, DC. Secures a part-time job editing translations.
November–December	Article about Nevin appears in the *Ladies Home Journal*. Writes a Washington column which appears in the *Nebraska State Journal* and *Index of Pittsburgh Life* until March, 1901.

1901

March	Returns to Pittsburgh and moves into the McClung residence on Murray Hill Avenue. Teaches Latin and English at the Central High School.
June	Story, "El Dorado," appears in *New England Magazine*.

1902

April	Last contribution to the Lincoln *Courier*.
June–September	Goes abroad with Isabelle McClung. "The Professor's Commencement" appears in *New England Magazine*. Weekly columns about her trip appear in the *Nebraska State Journal*. Articles also appear in the Pittsburgh *Gazette*.

1903

January "A Death in the Desert" appears in *Scribners*.

April Publishes a book of verse, *April Twilights*.

May Meets S. S. McClure, editor and publisher of *McClure's Magazine*, in New York City; he expresses great enthusiasm for her work.

Summer Vacations in Nebraska, where she meets Lincoln native, Edith Lewis.

1904–5 Teaches at Allegheny High School and freelances. Publishes a collection of short stories, *The Troll Garden*, in May, 1905. Visits Edith Lewis in New York both years.

1906

June Ends teaching career and moves to New York. Joins *McClure's* editorial staff. Lives in Greenwich Village.

1907 Temporarily moves to Boston to research the life of Mary Baker Eddy for *McClure's*. Three stories appear in *McClure's*, one in *Century*.

1908

March Meets Sarah Orne Jewett, accomplished author of regionalist short fiction, and Annie Adams Fields, widow of Boston publisher James T. Fields. Jewett is a crucial source of professional advice as Cather wrestles with the dilemma of how to develop as a writer of fiction while earning a living as a journalist.

April–May Promoted to managing editor of *McClure's*. Goes abroad with Isabelle McClung.

December "On the Gull's Road" appears in *McClure's*. Moves into a Greenwich Village apartment with Edith Lewis.

1909 Saddened by death of Sarah Orne Jewett. Assumes full editorial responsibility for *McClure's* when S. S. McClure travels in Europe.

1910 Travels to London for *McClure's*. Begins work on *Alexander's Bridge*.

1911 S. S. McClure dismissed from magazine. Cather finishes *Alexander's Bridge*. On leave from *McClure's*, Cather and Isabelle McClung rent house in Cherry Valley, NY, for fall.

1912

Winter/spring — *Alexander's Bridge* serialized in *McClure's* under the title *Alexander's Masquerade*. *Alexander's Bridge* published by Houghton Mifflin in April. "Behind the Singer Tower" appears in *Collier's*. On leave from *McClure's*, Cather visits her brother in Arizona and travels extensively in the Southwest. The trip fired her imagination and helped her to make a permanent break from the magazine, though she would collaborate with McClure over the next year on his autobiography.

August — "The Bohemian Girl" appears in *McClure's*.

1913 — *O Pioneers!* published by Houghton Mifflin. Cather moves to an apartment at 5 Bank Street with Edith Lewis. *My Autobiography* by S. S. McClure serialized in *McClure's*, beginning in October. "Three American Singers" published in *McClure's* in December. Wagnerian soprano Olive Fremstad is featured in the article and will enter into Cather's depiction of a singer in *The Song of the Lark*.

1914 — Writes articles for *McClure's*. Begins *The Song of the Lark*.

1915

Summer — Visits Mesa Verde with Edith Lewis, a trip that would later inspire the "Tom Outland's Story" section of *The Professor's House*.

Fall — *The Song of the Lark* published by Houghton Mifflin. Judge McClung dies; Isabelle McClung announces she is to be married to Jan Hambourg.

1916 — Travels to New Mexico with Edith Lewis. Begins *My Ántonia*.

1917 — Receives honorary degree from the University of Nebraska.

1918 — *My Ántonia* is published by Houghton Mifflin in September. Visits Red Cloud, reads cousin G. P. Cather's letters home from the front, and then starts work on her novel of World War I, *One of Ours*.

1920 — Travels to Europe with Edith Lewis. Publishes *Youth and the Bright Medusa* with new publisher, Alfred A. Knopf.

1921	Spends April–July with Isabelle and Jan Hambourg in Toronto. Visits Red Cloud. Finishes *One of Ours*. Begins *A Lost Lady*. Has tonsils removed, hemorrhages and is very ill. Sanatorium stay in Wernersville, PA.
1922 *Summer*	Teaches at Bread Loaf School in Middlebury, VT. Visits Grand Manan Island in the Bay of Fundy. Knopf publishes *One of Ours*.
December	Joins Episcopal Church when visiting parents in Red Cloud for their fiftieth wedding anniversary.
1923	Spends six months in Europe with Hambourgs. *A Lost Lady* serialized in *Century* magazine April–June. Knopf publishes *A Lost Lady*. Warner Brothers buys film rights. Begins *The Professor's House*. Awarded the Pulitzer Prize for fiction for *One of Ours*.
1924	Finishes *The Professor's House*. Edits two-volume edition of Sarah Orne Jewett's fiction for Houghton Mifflin. Meets novelist D. H. Lawrence in New York.
1925	Serializes *The Professor's House* in *Collier's* magazine June–August. Visits Red Cloud and Southwest. Begins work on *Death Comes for the Archbishop*. Knopf publishes *The Professor's House*. Film version of *A Lost Lady* released.
1926	Knopf publishes *My Mortal Enemy*. Cather purchases land on Grand Manan, and she and Lewis have a cottage built there.
1927	*Death Comes for the Archbishop* serialized in *Forum* magazine January–June. Knopf publishes *Death Comes for the Archbishop* in September. Moves with Lewis to Grosvenor Hotel after Bank Street apartment is torn down.
1928 *March*	Father dies. Cather stays in Red Cloud for a month. Mother moves with brother Douglass to southern California.
Spring/Summer	Visits Quebec and spends two months at Grand Manan. Begins work on *Shadows on the Rock*.

1929   Receives honorary degree from Yale. Visits mother in Long Beach, CA.

1930   Visits mother in sanatorium in Pasadena. Visits France. Finishes *Shadows on the Rock*. Receives the gold medal of the American Academy of Arts and Letters for *Death Comes for the Archbishop*.

1931   Receives honorary degree from Princeton. Mother dies. Knopf publishes *Shadows on the Rock*. Cather family reunion in Red Cloud in December (Cather's last trip to Nebraska).

1932   Publishes a collection of short stories, *Obscure Destinies*. Moves to 570 Park Avenue with Edith Lewis. Begins working on *Lucy Gayheart*.

1933   Receives the Prix Femina Américain for *Shadows on the Rock*. Receives an honorary degree from Smith College.

1935   Visits Isabelle Hambourg, who returns to US for medical reasons. Knopf publishes *Lucy Gayheart*.

1936   Knopf publishes *Not Under Forty*, a collection of essays.

1937   Begins work on *Sapphira and the Slave Girl* and oversees preparation of the Autograph Edition of her collected works, which Houghton Mifflin publishes in twelve volumes in 1937–8.

1938   Brother Douglass dies. Isabelle Hambourg dies in Sorrento.

1940   Knopf publishes *Sapphira and the Slave Girl*.

1944   Receives Gold Medal of the National Institute of Arts and Letters.

1945   Brother Roscoe dies.

1947   Dies on April 24 of a cerebral hemorrhage at her apartment in New York. Buried in Jaffrey, New Hampshire.

1948   Collection of short stories, *The Old Beauty and Others*, published by Knopf.

MARILEE LINDEMANN

Introduction

> When we find ourselves on shipboard, among hundreds of strangers, we very
> soon recognize those who are sympathetic to us. We find our own books in
> much the same way. We like a writer much as we like individuals; for what he
> is, simply, underneath all his accomplishments.
> Willa Cather, "Miss Jewett" (1936)

I

Willa Cather had little use for critics, preferring to have ordinary readers
find and encounter her books without the mediating lens of the professional
interpreter. Critics have, from time to time, returned the favor, consigning her
to near-oblivion in the 1930s when they judged her to be out of touch with
the painful social and economic realities of Depression-era America.[1] Today,
fortunately, her reputation with both lay and professional readers is secure,
for she is widely read (the prestigious Library of America has two Cather volumes in its series, and *My Ántonia* has been reprinted in the Penguin Great
Books of the 20th Century series), regularly taught (in a range of undergraduate and graduate courses in American literature, women's literature,
and lesbian/gay/queer studies), and the subject of intense critical scrutiny
and controversy. Those controversies have in recent years landed Cather on
the cover of such influential middle-brow publications as *The New Yorker*
and *The New York Review of Books*, where tabloid-style headlines demand
to know "What have the academics done to Willa Cather?" or proclaim
"Justice for Willa Cather," as if the long-dead writer has been a hostage
or a political prisoner who has finally gained her freedom. Her status in
contemporary popular culture is evident in the fact that three of her early
novels – *O Pioneers!, The Song of the Lark*, and *My Ántonia* – have been
made into movies for television since the early 1990s, featuring such high-
powered stars as Jessica Lange and Jason Robards. In 1999, *My Ántonia* was
even caught up in the rage for mass-media book clubs, as National Public
Radio talk-show maven Diane Rehm selected Cather's 1918 story of life on
the Nebraska frontier for an on-air discussion of what one guest described
as "one of *the* great American novels."[2]

But the most fascinating evidence of Cather's place in contemporary cultural politics may well be that the First Lady of the United States, Laura Bush, featured her work as part of a White House symposium on the literary legacy of women in the American West in September, 2002. Many of the contributors to this volume as well as its editor attended, and one, Cather biographer Sharon O'Brien, was one of the keynote speakers. The event, which was billed as a celebration of the works of three writers (Edna Ferber and Laura Ingalls Wilder as well as Cather) "who happen to have been women," was the third in a series of such symposia hosted by Mrs. Bush. When the *New York Times* reported on the symposia, noting that the First Lady was quietly building "a literary room of her own" within the White House and wondering what her motives might be in doing so, Mrs. Bush disavowed any political intention and declared that "there is nothing political about American literature."[3] The "women of the West" event, however, was attended by Second Lady Lynne V. Cheney, a well-known conservative culture warrior whose tenure as chair of the National Endowment for the Humanities (1986–93) was marked by hostility towards the scholarly projects of multiculturalism and postmodernism.[4] Her mere presence served as a reminder that literature and literary criticism – and the arts and humanities generally – are deeply political, if only because speech, representation, and interpretation always involve human beings in contests for power and authority. Were that not the case, Mrs. Cheney would never have bothered to attack the politics of those scholars in the humanities with whom she disagreed, as she did, for example, in her 1995 book, *Telling the Truth*, which sought to discredit postmodernism by associating it with moral relativism. A few months after the "women of the West" symposium, Mrs. Bush hastily postponed the next symposium, "Poetry and the American Voice," after the event became tangled up in the politics of her husband's plans to invade Iraq (which he did in March, 2003). A number of poets who had been invited planned to present the First Lady with poems protesting against the imminent war. Again, the White House refused to see anything political in its silencing of "the American Voice," steadfastly maintaining that the event was canceled to keep a "literary event" from being turned into a "political forum." It's hard work, apparently, making sure "there's nothing political about American literature."

Willa Cather might well have agreed with Laura Bush's assertion about American literature being apolitical, and she probably would have been delighted to have been read and celebrated in a White House occupied by conservative Texans. She was a lifelong Republican whose fiction avoided overt political crusading and can be construed to uphold a traditional American value system of hard work and rugged individualism. Her novels and short stories are replete with characters such as *My Ántonia*'s Lena Lingard, an immigrant who, through skill, determination, and enterprise, realizes the American dreams of material success and social mobility. In recent years, however, many readers of Cather have sought to situate her work not in the realm of dreams but amid the messier realities she often claimed to be trying to avoid. ("What has art ever been but escape?" Cather mused in a 1936 essay. She goes on to express contempt for the idea that art might help to solve the problems of "industrial life," insisting that "economics and art are strangers."[5]) The essays gathered here tend to read against the grain of Cather's escapism, for they view her not as a crusader but as an acute observer of American life whose deeply felt responses to changing social and demographic conditions are illuminating both for what they celebrate and for what they evade or repress. Thus, we see, for example, in John Swift's essay on *The Professor's House* (1925) an examination of how changing legal theories about property and contract in the early twentieth century feed into the anxieties fueling that fractured, contradictory text. Similarly, Lisa Marcus's discussion of two neglected Cather short stories from the 1910s focuses on how their "geography of Jewishness" fits in with contemporary ambivalence about the waves of so-called New Immigrants – mostly from southern and eastern Europe and often Jewish – that arrived in the United States in the decades before World War I. Taken together, then, the essays in *The Cambridge Companion to Willa Cather* tap into an ongoing fascination with a major American novelist who can be easy to read but surprisingly difficult to understand. The goal of the anthology is to help readers to plumb some of Cather's depths, to get at "what [she] is, simply," and at times not so simply, "underneath all [her] accomplishments."

Cather studies has been revitalized and almost wholly transformed in the last thirty years. She is no longer merely Nebraska's first lady of letters, whose well-wrought paeans to "the American Dream" earned the modestly respectful attention of myth-and-symbol critics and new critics throughout the 1950s and 1960s.[6] In the 1970s, feminist criticism began to create new contexts for reading Cather that made her seem less quaint and more engaged in the rough-and-tumble of the times in which she lived and wrote (1873–1947). The focus on gender and on her place in female literary traditions revealed a feistier Cather whose pioneer heroines defied convention by dressing in men's clothes and performing physical and intellectual work usually considered "masculine." In 1987, with the publication of Sharon O'Brien's psychobiography *Willa Cather: The Emerging Voice*, the lesbian Cather was brought out of the closet after decades of diffident silence, and critics began combing the novels and short stories for evidence of how sexuality is translated into textuality, of how lesbianism is masked or disguised to evade detection and censure. By the late 1990s, the possibilities of the masquerade model were more or less exhausted, but cultural studies and queer studies kept Cather in the eye of several contemporary critical storms. Cather's status in the academy is evident in the attention she has garnered recently from theorists and New Americanists who are not Cather specialists, including Eve Kosofsky Sedgwick, Judith Butler, and Walter Benn Michaels.[7] With studies such as Julie Abraham's *Are Girls Necessary? Lesbian Writing and Modern Histories* (1996), Guy Reynolds's *Willa Cather in Context: Progress, Race, Empire* (1996), and my own *Willa Cather: Queering America* (1999), Cather's relationships to modernism, progressivism, and turn-of-the- century discourses of sex and nation were brought into sharper focus. Also, thanks largely to the University of Nebraska Press's scholarly edition project, which in 1992 began producing meticulous editions of Cather's works, textual and manuscript issues have emerged as a new area of inquiry and debate. With so much going on and so many perspectives in play, it is safe to say that Cather studies has moved into the twenty-first century with the writer hotly but healthily contested and at or near the center of crucial conversations about the politics and the aesthetics of modern American fiction.

Though she is most often associated with the prairie landscapes immortalized in *O Pioneers!* and *My Ántonia*, Willa Cather was actually born in Back Creek, Virginia just eight years after the end of the Civil War, which had divided her family and alienated neighbors from one another throughout the struggle over slavery and secession. (Her father's family were mostly Unionists, except for great-grandfather James, who opposed both slavery and secession but sided with the South over his belief in states' rights; her mother's family were mostly Confederates, though her grandmother Rachel Boak strongly opposed slavery and helped a slave named Nancy escape to Canada on the underground railway.) That Cather was influenced by her childhood in the Reconstruction South is evident in her identification with a maternal uncle, William Seibert Boak, who served in the Confederate army and died at nineteen from wounds received at Manassas. Cather liked to pretend that she was named after this uncle, writing a 1902 poem, "The Namesake," dedicated to his memory and adopting Sibert as a middle name in the early years of her professional career. It was only in her last completed novel, *Sapphira and the Slave Girl*, published in 1940, that Cather drew significantly upon the experiences of those early years in Virginia, but scholars have recently begun to grapple with the importance of her southern origins to Cather's sensibility and her sense of history. While acknowledging that the Great Plains and the Southwest drew the bulk of Cather's imaginative attention, Janis Stout declares in *Willa Cather: The Writer and Her World* (2002) that "the fact remains that she was southern first – and in a very real way, last." Ann Romines's essay, "Willa Cather and 'The Old Story': *Sapphira and the Slave Girl*," offers readers of this volume a sense of how criticism is reckoning with that crucial but under-examined fact.

In 1883, when Cather was not yet ten years old, her family left the comfort and familiarity of Virginia for the open and still largely unsettled spaces of Webster County in south-eastern Nebraska. After just eighteen months on a farm, the family moved into the frontier town of Red Cloud, where Cather's father opened an insurance office. Initially, Cather experienced the vastness of the prairie as inhuman and overwhelming, a feeling eloquently described by the narrator of *My Ántonia*, Jim Burden. Recalling his first ride over the prairie (after a journey, like Cather's, from Virginia to Nebraska), Jim remarks:

> There was nothing but land: not a country at all, but the material out of which countries are made . . . I had the feeling that the world was left behind, that we had got over the edge of it, and were outside man's jurisdiction . . . Between that earth and that sky I felt erased, blotted out. I did not say my prayers that night: here, I felt, what would be would be.[8]

Cather would soon come to love her adopted home with a passion, however, and would remain in Nebraska until 1896, when, a year after graduating from the University of Nebraska in Lincoln, she would move to Pittsburgh to pursue a career in magazine journalism. She had begun writing in college and by the time she left Lincoln had acquired a reputation throughout the Midwest as a lively writer and a tough, audacious critic, particularly of drama. (Janis Stout's essay on Cather and the performing arts explores the lasting importance of this early professional experience, which instilled in the young writer a life-long devotion to theatre and music and influenced the development of her own artistic principles and goals.) Except for a brief stint of high-school teaching in Pittsburgh, she worked in journalism until 1912, ending up in New York City as managing editor of *McClure's*, one of the most influential magazines of the "muckraking" era. *McClure's* was renowned for the quality of its investigative reporting on the kinds of social and economic changes (such as the rise of the city and the emergence of monopoly capitalism) that accompanied America's transition from an agrarian to an industrial economy. During her years as a reporter and editor, Cather's progress as a creative writer was hampered, though her talent was surely nurtured through the discipline of journalism and the range of experiences her profession made available to her. She managed to publish a volume of poetry and one collection of short stories, but with the publication of a novella, *Alexander's Bridge*, in 1912, her lengthy apprenticeship was over and Cather turned full-time to the writing of fiction. By 1918, she would produce three more novels, including the one for which she is best known, *My Ántonia*.

Cather was thirty-eight years old when *Alexander's Bridge* was published. Her forties would be a decade of critical and popular success, capped off in 1923 with a Pulitzer Prize for her novel of World War I, *One of Ours*. Her fifties showed even greater artistic confidence and ambition, resulting in works that many readers consider to be her finest: *A Lost Lady* (1923), *The Professor's House*, and *Death Comes for the Archbishop* (1927). Even a thumbnail sketch of her biography, I hope, elucidates the concatenation of influences and experiences that prepared Cather for this extraordinary period of productivity and achievement. First, she shared with her narrator Jim Burden a sense of having grown up "outside man's jurisdiction" and reveled in the westerner's expansive sense of self and possibility. She took advantage of the comparative freedom of the frontier to experiment with sex- and gender-nonconformity in her adolescence, going through an extended period of cross-dressing when she called herself (and was called by others) William, Willie, or Billy. It should also be noted that Cather could be sharply critical of the provincial character of small prairie towns and of the stifling pressure to conform, yet she herself abandoned the overt gender radicalism of her youth and adopted a more conventional style of dress and appearance as she reached adulthood. The tension between conformity and nonconformity that is evident in her life story and in her contradictory sense of the West is played out over and over again in Cather's fiction as characters struggle to create a sense of self as well as relationships to family, community, and region. Thus, Thea Kronborg in *The Song of the Lark* leaves her hometown of Moonstone, Colorado, bitterly vowing that she "was going away to fight, and she was going away forever" (p. 310), but later, having achieved success as an opera singer in New York, she credits Moonstone for giving her a sense of standards and a "rich, romantic past" (p. 552).[9]

A second salient aspect of Cather's formative experiences is that she was a member of the first generation of college-educated women in the United States to attend public, co-educational institutions such as the University of Nebraska, which was founded in 1869. By inclination and training, Cather was one of the turn-of-the-century's "New Women," fitting to a tee the description offered by historian Carroll Smith-Rosenberg: "single, highly educated, economically autonomous," eager for professional visibility, willing to challenge existing gender relations, yet confident of her "rightful place within the genteel world."[10] Her early fiction in particular contains numerous examples of female characters who are prepared to make their own way and deft at taking advantage of economic opportunities. In addition to the aforementioned Thea Kronborg, the best example of such characters is perhaps Alexandra Bergson from O Pioneers! (1913). She succeeds as a farmer and a landowner by embracing new technologies and taking the risk of buying up land when others are losing their nerve. Crucially, however, Cather was also a New Woman whose primary emotional and probably erotic attachments were to other women, from her college crush on Louise Pound to her life-long passion for the socialite Isabelle McClung Hambourg and her forty-year domestic partnership with Edith Lewis. Cather came of age when the new science of sexology was pathologizing such attachments as unnatural and as signs of "inversion." (Earlier in the nineteenth century, female same-sex attachment had generally been understood within the less threatening [because presumed to be non-sexual] model of "romantic friendship.") That process of stigmatization may help to explain why Cather so zealously guarded her privacy (by destroying letters and putting restrictions on how surviving letters might be used) and why her fiction is generally reticent on the subject of same-sex intimacy. Only Death Comes for the Archbishop, with its lavish attention to the loving comradeship of two missionary priests, comes very close to the subject, but the characters' clear commitment to their vows of celibacy helps to ensure that their devotion to one another is viewed as merely platonic.

Some readers over the years have criticized Cather for seeming to avoid sexuality or for depicting marriage and heterosexuality as institutions that are invariably corrosive and disappointing. It is true that Godfrey St. Peters's sardonic assessment of marriage and adulthood in The Professor's House ("His career, his wife, his family, were not his life at all, but a chain of events which had happened to him. All these things had nothing to do with the person he was in the beginning"[11]) is by no means an isolated instance of domestic disillusionment. One can cite numerous other examples, including the tragicomic marital discord of Wick Cutter and his wife in My Ántonia. Black Hawk's dissolute money-lender is so determined that his wife's family will not inherit his money that he murders his wife and then kills himself in order to circumvent the marriage property laws. But, as Jonathan Goldberg's essay, "Willa Cather and Sexuality," demonstrates, reading sexuality in Cather requires attention to much more than the question of whether the lesbian writer writes from the closet or shows hostility to heterosexuality. Goldberg is drawn to the problematics of identity (and thus of identity terms such as "the lesbian writer") in Cather's work and its links to ambivalence and alterity, or otherness. His concern is not to find the lesbian in the text but, building particularly on the work of Judith Butler, to examine the puzzling cross-identifications that result from the push and pull of desires that may be socially or legally prohibited yet proliferate and subvert those very prohibitions.

When asked about her success, Cather was fond of quoting the French historian Michelet: "Le but n'est rien; le chemin, c'est tout." ("The end is nothing; the road is all.") For all her emphasis on place, which implies rootedness and permanence, Willa Cather was a writer of the road. She was, in other words, as drawn to and defined by themes of mobility and transition as any American writer has ever been, as Joseph Urgo has argued in his book *Willa Cather and the Myth of American Migration* (1995) and in his essay for this volume, "The Cather Thesis: The American Empire of Migration." Those themes, as we have seen, arose out of the facts of her life and of the time in which she lived. Born in the South in the nineteenth century, she would grow up in the Midwest but spend most of her adult life in New York City, the cultural capital of the United States in the twentieth century, which many called in its early years "the American century." The road for Cather is thus a way of linking radically disjunctive geographic and cultural locations: South and North; West and East; rural and urban; Victorian and modern; European and American; romantic friendship and lesbianism. The road may well seem to be "all" to someone who was on it as frequently as Cather was, whether because she was relocating or merely traveling, which she did often and with a sense of adventure. (Cather took long summer trips back to Nebraska, traveled extensively in the Southwest and Northeast, built a summer cottage in Canada, and made several trips to Europe.)

The paradigmatic Cather character is also frequently on the road, which is variously imaged in her fiction as a space of challenge, flux, danger, possibility, and liminality. A conversation on board a train is the narrative set up for *My Ántonia*, for example, as a journey across Iowa prompts Jim and an unnamed narrator to recall their childhoods in Nebraska. Jim Burden, it turns out, has a professional investment in being on the road, for he is a lawyer for "one of the great Western railways" (p. 3). (Jim is not the only Cather character with such an investment. Captain Daniel Forrester of *A Lost Lady* is identified in the opening of that book as "a railroad man, a contractor for the Burlington who had built hundreds of miles of road for the Burlington, – over the sage brush and cattle country, and on up into the Black Hills."[12]) The first book of *Death Comes for the Archbishop* opens with the main character, Jean Marie Latour, wandering on horseback "through an arid stretch of country somewhere in central New Mexico." He must find his way in a region that he experiences as a "geometrical nightmare" because of the oppressive repetition of the "conical red hills" that dominate the landscape.[13] Latour's initial disorientation is important, for it suggests that one of his tasks in the novel is to learn to read the landscape more effectively, to come to see the differences within the apparent sameness of the desert, which he clearly does by the end of the book. Sometimes being on the road is a sign of a character's ambitions, as when Alexandra Bergson spends five days riding in a buckboard to explore farms in the river country to see how prospects there compared to hers on higher land, or when the peripatetic Thea Kronborg goes from Moonstone to Chicago to (after brief stops in Arizona and New York) Germany and finally back to New York in pursuit of opportunities to train and perform. Sometimes being on the road (or on board ship) is a sign of a character's instability or ambivalence, as when Bartley Alexander, the protagonist of *Alexander's Bridge*, moves restlessly back and forth between his wife in Boston and his mistress in London. Even Cather's late, neglected novel, *Lucy Gayheart* (1935), a grim, post-mortem narrative about a young woman with artistic ambition who drowns while ice skating, has recurring images of mobility and travel. Lucy is initially described as "a slight figure always in motion; dancing or skating or walking swiftly with intense direction, like a bird flying home."[14] Neighbors, according to the narrator, "always knew her by the way she moved" (p. 4). Twenty-five years after her death, Lucy's erstwhile suitor Harry Gordon, stuck in a loveless marriage and still haunted by his harsh treatment of her, takes refuge in an automobile: "His farms were scattered far and wide, and he lived on the road. He often went to Denver for the week-end, 'driving like the devil'" (p. 221). In this instance, the tropes of motion are deployed ironically, emblems of romantic aspirations relentlessly thwarted in a novel as cold and bleak as Edith Wharton's *Ethan Frome*. In the end, Lucy is dead, and Harry's life "on the road" is anything but a joyride.

II

Happily for those who undertake the journey, the "road" through Cather's fiction is circuitous but well marked by generations of readers who, like her Professor St. Peter, delight in "the fun" (p. 23) of scholarly work and critical exchange. Thus, in response to the *New Yorker*'s overwrought question, "What have the academics done to Willa Cather?" I am pleased to offer this volume as a way of saying that the patient is doing very well, thank you, and the doctors are justifiably proud of their efforts. Like other *Cambridge Companions*, this one aims to be not an end but a beginning. It is an invitation and a guide to readers interested in exploring the range of critical debates and interpretive possibilities opened up by the kinds of tools scholars and teachers of Cather bring to their work today. It has been a long time since Cather studies had a collection of essays with the breadth of this one. James Schroeter's *Willa Cather and Her Critics* was published in 1967, and John Murphy's *Critical Essays on Willa Cather* came out in 1984. More recent collections have focused more narrowly on particular texts (e.g., O'Brien's

New Essays on My Ántonia [1999]) or on particular themes or issues (e.g., Romines's *Willa Cather's Southern Connections* [2000] and John N. Swift and Joseph R. Urgo's *Willa Cather and the American Southwest* [2002]). Regrettably, constraints of space limited the number of critics whose work could be presented here, but the bibliography at the end of the volume will point readers in the direction of other fine scholarship. In organizing and assembling the book, I have tried to provide both full coverage of Cather's career and detailed analyses of particular texts to help meet a range of readerly needs and interests. Thus, the first section of the *Companion*, "Contexts and Critical Issues," is composed of nine essays that address points of contention or new areas of interest that have emerged in recent criticism. The second section, "Studies of Major Works," has essays focused specifically on the novels that have been most widely read, taught, and argued about in the last several years – *My Ántonia*, *The Professor's House*, *Death Comes for the Archbishop*, and *Sapphira and the Slave Girl*. I recognize that my selections here may cause some controversy or disappointment, as every novel has its partisans and none seems merely "minor." Another editor might have applied the label of "major works" to a different set of texts. Indeed, I myself might have applied it differently at a different time. It is unlikely, for example, that *Sapphira and the Slave Girl* would have made anyone's list of "major works" before Toni Morrison wrote about it in her slim but provocative *Playing in the Dark: Whiteness and the Literary Imagination* (1992). For decades, Cather's last book was largely ignored, written off as a flawed product of the writer's old age, but Morrison's discussion of it suddenly put *Sapphira* on the critical radar screen, provoking broad attention to its troubling racial and gender dynamics. *Sapphira*'s movement from the margin to the center is a useful reminder that designations such as "major" and "minor" are always to some extent arbitrary and subject to change, embedded as they are in the shifting sands of taste and critical trends. Nevertheless, I apply the label of "major works" to four texts in order to create a space for sustained attention to the books that have mattered most in recent years – and invite readers to make their own interventions into the mattering process by endeavoring to do for *Lucy Gayheart* or *Shadows on the Rock* what Toni Morrison did for *Sapphira and the Slave Girl*.

One of the pleasures of preparing a volume like this one is having the opportunity to listen in on the serendipitous conversations that arise between and among the essays as contributors develop their ideas. I might have constructed an entirely different table of contents that foregrounded those conversations by grouping the essays according to the approaches, assumptions, or issues they had in common, which would have resulted in a tripartite organizational structure along the following lines: Part I. Politics and Culture; Part II. Psychology and Biography; and Part III. Genre and Aesthetics. This introduction has already touched upon several essays that would be at home in the first category, including those by Swift, Marcus, Urgo, and Goldberg (though the latter's emphasis on desire and identification suggests that its interests are psychological as well). To those might be added Guy Reynolds's discussion of Cather as a progressive, which examines how the prairie populism of the 1890s influenced the development of what he terms her "midwestern radical vision." Reynolds reads Cather's supposed nostalgia not as a retreat from modernity but as a critique of the drive towards a standardized and increasingly centralized culture that accompanied the development of modern industrial capitalism. Cather's regionalism, according to Reynolds, is a protest against the loss of the kinds of folk cultures and communities she depicts in her early immigrant and pioneer fictions as well as in her later explorations of tribal cultures in *Death Comes for the Archbishop* and *The Professor's House*. Far from a reactionary or a nativist, Reynolds's Cather is "a midwestern Atlanticist, a cosmopolitan, a pro-European American" who embraces diversity and pluralism as an alternative to the increasing homogeneity of modern American culture.

A second cluster of essays takes up questions that are chiefly psychological or biographical in nature, though even the life and mind of the writer have a way of getting tangled up in politics these days, as the essays by Sharon O'Brien and Leona Sevick demonstrate. In "Willa Cather in the Country of the Ill," O'Brien turns to issues and materials that did not enter into her study of the early stages of Cather's career, *The Emerging Voice*. Her analysis of Cather's responses to age and illness suggests that the author experienced repeated episodes of what is now called depression in the second half of her life. (As O'Brien points out, in Cather's day the term of art for such a condition was "nerve exhaustion" or "neurasthenia.") O'Brien's essay raises important new questions about Cather's creative process and the representation of illness, disability, and the mind/body problem in her fiction, but it also makes clear that Cather's personal experiences of illness were ideologically inflected and mediated by powerful cultural imperatives – such as the assumption, so pervasive in American culture, that illness is a sign of weakness, a failure of the individual will to pull the self up by the bootstraps. As if in response to O'Brien's call for further exploration of illness and depression in Cather, Sevick's essay looks at what she calls "the politics of depression" in *Death Comes for the Archbishop*. Depression has a "politics," according to Sevick, because it can be related to the individual's efforts to negotiate a transition from one social or economic order to another. Building upon the work of cultural historian T. J. Jackson Lears, Sevick reads Cather's archbishop as a modern neurasthenic, subject to periods of depression and alienation because his sensitive constitution is upset by the pace and the scale of social and technological change. She sees the novel's fascination with Catholicism as directly related to this psychosocial crisis. Religion had therapeutic benefits, offering the neurasthenic an alternative to the spiritual deadness of secular materialism and holding out the possibility of authentic and meaningful spiritual experience. As Sevick, via Lears, points out, however, religion – and Catholicism in particular – was often as much an accommodation to modernity as a protest against it, aiding and abetting the spread of industrialism, imperialism, and consumerism. Her analysis gets at an ambivalence in Cather that is crucial to understanding some of the key tensions and contradictions that animate her work.

Anne E. Goldman's rereading of *My Ántonia* is also psychological in its approach, though the essay also explores representational choices that help to explain Cather's distinctiveness as a novelist. Like O'Brien, Goldman is interested in the issue of age, but her specific focus is on Cather's representations of middle-aged women, in *Ántonia* and elsewhere. Noting that such women are not typically the subject of art, Goldman sees the resilience and resolute dignity of characters like Ántonia as a chief source of their literary and psychological power. These characters have a quality of receptiveness to new experience and learning that allows them to summon "the courage to try to live well throughout middle age and beyond," according to Goldman. Such qualities distinguish Cather's middle-aged women from her middle-aged men, who tend to bruise more easily and recover more slowly, if at all, from the wounds that life invariably causes. Ann Romines's essay on *Sapphira and the Slave Girl*, which was mentioned earlier in this introduction, grapples with another age-related issue, the complex psychology of going home. Her analysis of Cather's last novel examines the author's profound ambivalence about her Southern origins and the scrutiny of the meanings of "home" and "homecoming" that is woven throughout *Sapphira*, a tale of many layers and multiple, competing perspectives. "Home" in Romines's reading is a repository of personal and cultural memory and a site of both solace and horror, since the pleasant domestic surface of "home" was sustained by the underlying horrors of slavery.

A final group of essays might be made out of those that share an interest in questions related to genre, aesthetics, and literary canons. Janis Stout's discussion of how Cather's fascination with the performing arts informed her artistic principles has already been noted. In her reviews of performances and interviews with artists, Cather shows a preoccupation with "power," by which she seems to have meant, as Stout puts it, "a combination of passionate commitment, intelligent understanding, and personal presence or authority." That preoccupation clearly carried over into her development of fictional characters. The performing artist in Cather's fiction, according to Stout, offers the possibility of transformation and even redemption by breaking out of the constraints of conventionality and daring to achieve great things. Susan J. Rosowski turns in a surprisingly different direction for her discussion of Cather's aesthetic principles. Cather's sense of humor can be hard to detect, but in "Willa Cather and the Comic Sense of Self," Rosowski demonstrates that the classic motivating impulse of comedy – the desire to celebrate life's continuities and the "capacity of human beings to lose themselves in the regenerative and adaptive rhythm of life" – animates much of Cather's fiction. Connecting Cather to Walt Whitman, whose fluid sense of self and joyful freedom from boundaries may be described as comic, and philosopher Henri Bergson, whose *Laughter: An Essay on the Meaning of the Comic* was translated into English when she was starting to work on *O Pioneers!*, Rosowski tracks the movements of the comic sensibility in the first decade of Cather's novelistic career, from *Alexander's Bridge* (1912) to *One of Ours* (1922). Rosowski's emphasis on themes of play and flexibility, self-negligence and sympathetic identification results in a fresh new reading of these early novels that should help to dislodge the misperception that Cather herself was an "earnest American" whose fondness for starched white cotton clothing was more than just a fashion statement.

Cather's literary reputation justifiably rests chiefly on her accomplishments as a novelist, but Mark Madigan's essay, "Cather and the Short Story," offers an important reassessment of her work in another genre. She published sixty-two short stories during her lifetime and three collections, *The Troll Garden* (1905), *Youth and the Bright Medusa* (1920), and *Obscure Destinies* (1932). A fourth collection, *The Old Beauty and Others* (1948), was published a year after her death. Her ongoing engagement with the form suggests that Cather was drawn to the short story by more than economic necessity or as a way to practice the craft of fiction. Madigan explores the significant thematic and stylistic continuities between Cather's work in the novel and her work in the short story and shows how actively involved the author was in fashioning her reputation as a writer of short stories, even to the extent of rewriting part of her personal history for the dustjacket copy of *Youth and the Bright Medusa*. Madigan also suggests, however, that in some stories Cather consciously wrote against the carefully constructed image of herself as a regionalist writer of the West. In "Coming, Aphrodite!," for example, one of the best short stories she ever wrote, Cather uses New York City as the setting for a sexy and sophisticated story of young artist lovers who quarrel over the meaning of artistic success. The story, which was first published in H. L. Mencken's *Smart Set*, shows that Cather could write convincingly and well in the cool idiom of the Jazz Age and perhaps explains why she was admired and imitated by the younger writer who gave the period its name, F. Scott Fitzgerald. Richard Millington aims to write Cather into the literary history that Fitzgerald has dominated in his elucidation of "Willa Cather's American Modernism." Millington reads "modernism" not as a genre or a literary movement but as a cultural project whose ambition was to subvert an established, still Victorian cultural dispensation by seizing and recasting its characteristic means of expression. Like many other essays in this volume, Millington's argues against the idea that Cather was somehow estranged from her time. He notes the ways in which her texts are energized by contemporary intellectual ferments such as the emergence of an anthropological idea of culture and defines her "modernism" as a resistant and revisionary relation to the novelistic tradition she inherited from the Victorians, resulting in a remaking of the novel that opens up new possibilities of thought and feeling for her characters and her readers.

Often, for Willa Cather's young characters in small, provincial towns, reading is a window that opens suddenly upon a larger, previously unknown world, even as it affords new views of the self and its immediate surroundings. Jim Burden studies Virgil at the university and begins to understand the places and people of his own past as his "patria," the humble neighborhood that is the wellspring of his imagination. Tom Outland, too, studies Virgil, in an intoxicating summer of solitude on the Blue Mesa when the splendors of the *Aeneid* intermingle with the austere, high-desert beauty of the Cliff City. For Claude Wheeler in *One of Ours*, the home of the Erlich family in Lincoln, which is stuffed full of books that looked "interesting and hard-used,"[15] is "a warm and gracious atmosphere, charged with generous enthusiasms and ennobled by romantic friendships" (p. 73). There, he overcomes the reticence of the middle-class farm boy and amazes himself by offering up opinions and "using words that had never crossed his lips before, that in his mind were only associated with the printed page" (p. 41). Books and spirited conversation about culture and ideas help to liberate Claude from the painful self-consciousness of his youth, though it is also arguable that books fuel the naive romanticism that leads to his death in combat, as he commands his men from atop a parapet, believing that "they were mortal, but they were unconquerable" (p. 386).

Like the readers *in* her texts, the readers *of* Cather's texts are encouraged to participate actively in the reading process, which she clearly saw as a dynamic and reciprocal transaction. In her most famous critical pronouncement, from her essay of 1922, "The Novel Démeublé," Cather declared that "Whatever is felt upon the page without being specifically named there – that, one might say, is created. It is the inexplicable presence of the thing not named, of the overtone divined by the ear but not heard by it, the verbal mood, the emotional aura of the fact or the thing or the deed, that gives high quality to the novel or the drama, as well as to poetry itself."[16] Cather's formulation creates a vital and challenging role for the reader, who is called upon to feel deeply, to listen carefully, to be alert to moods, auras, divinations. Her reader is part detective, searching for evidence of things "not named," and part sympathetic friend, sensitive enough to understand feelings that are beyond or perhaps beneath words – there and not there, ineffable yet powerful. It is my hope that *The Cambridge Companion to Willa Cather* will make a modest contribution towards preparing her readers for the arduous and deeply pleasurable tasks the author has put before them.

NOTES

1. For an examination of the vicissitudes of Cather's critical reputation, with particular attention to the gender dynamics of American literary canon formation, see Sharon O'Brien, "Becoming Noncanonical: The Case against Willa Cather" in Cathy N. Davidson, ed., *Reading in America: Literature and Social History* (Baltimore: Johns Hopkins University Press, 1989), pp. 240–58. For primary evidence of Cather's treatment by critics during her lifetime, see Margaret Anne O'Connor, ed., *Willa Cather: The Contemporary Reviews* (Cambridge: Cambridge University Press, 2001).

2. Joan Acocella's "Cather and the Academy" appeared in *The New Yorker* of 27 November 1995 (pp. 56–71), with a cover blurb asking, "What have the academics done to Willa Cather?" An expanded version of that essay was later published as *Willa Cather and the Politics of Criticism* (Lincoln, NE, and London: University of Nebraska Press, 2000), a book that was widely reviewed. A. S. Byatt's review in *The New York Review of Books* of November 30, 2000 (pp. 51–3) is titled "Justice for Willa Cather."

    O Pioneers! was a Hallmark Hall of Fame Production, directed by Glenn Jordan and written for television by Robert W. Lenski, 1992. *The Song of the Lark* was an ALT Films production for ExxonMobil's Masterpiece Theatre, directed by Karen Arthur and written for television by Joseph Maurer, 2002. *My Ántonia* was a USA Pictures production, directed by Joseph Sargent, written for television and produced by Victoria Riskin, 1995. *The Diane Rehm Show* on *My Ántonia* was broadcast on October 1, 1999.

3. See Elizabeth Bumiller, "White House Letter: Quietly, the First Lady Builds a Literary Room of Her Own," *New York Times*, October 7, 2002 (A1).

4. As director of the NEH, Cheney published a series of provocations aimed chiefly at scholarship and teaching rooted in multiculturalism, feminism, and postmodernism, including *American Memory: A Report on the Humanities in the Nation's Public Schools* (Washington, DC: National Endowment for the Humanities, 1987) and *Tyrannical Machine: A Report on Education Practices Gone Wrong and Our Best Hopes for Setting Them Right* (Washington, DC: National Endowment for the Humanities, 1990). A book Cheney wrote after leaving the NEH, *Telling the Truth: Why Our Culture and Country Have Stopped Making Sense – and What We Can Do About It* (New York: Simon & Schuster, 1995), is referred to below.

5. Cather's comments on "escapism" were originally published in a letter to *The Commonweal*. They are reprinted in *Willa Cather on Writing: Critical Studies on Writing as an Art* (1949; Lincoln, NE, and London: University of Nebraska Press, 1988), pp. 18–29.
6. John J. Murphy's collection, *Critical Essays on Willa Cather* (G. K. Hall, 1984), offers a fair representation of both myth-and-symbol and new critical responses to Cather.
7. I refer here to Sedgwick's essay, "Across Gender, Across Sexuality: Willa Cather and Others," *South Atlantic Quarterly* 88.1 (Winter 1989), pp. 53–72; Butler's "'Dangerous Crossing': Willa Cather's Masculine Names" in *Bodies That Matter* (New York: Routledge, 1993); and Michaels's discussion of Cather in *Our America: Nativism, Modernism, and Pluralism* (Durham, NC, and London: Duke University Press, 1995).
8. Willa Cather, *My Ántonia* (1918, rev. 1926; New York: Penguin Books, 1994), p. 13. Future references will be made parenthetically.
9. Willa Cather, *The Song of the Lark* (1915; Boston, MA: Houghton Mifflin, 1983), pp. 310, 552.
10. See Carroll Smith-Rosenberg, "The New Woman as Androgyne: Social Disorder and Gender Crisis, 1870–1936," in *Disorderly Conduct: Visions of Gender in Victorian America* (New York: Knopf, 1985), p. 245.
11. Willa Cather, *The Professor's House* (1925; New York: Vintage, 1990), p. 240. Future references will be made parenthetically.
12. Willa Cather, *A Lost Lady* (1923; New York: Vintage, 1990), p. 4.
13. Willa Cather, *Death Comes for the Archbishop* (1927; New York: Vintage, 1990), p. 17.
14. Willa Cather, *Lucy Gayheart* (1935; New York: Vintage, 1976), p. 3. Future references will be made parenthetically.
15. Willa Cather, *One of Ours* (1922; New York: Vintage, 1971), p. 36. Future references will be made parenthetically.
16. "The Novel Démeublé" was first published in *The New Republic* of April 12, 1922. It is reprinted in Cather's collection of essays, *Not Under Forty* (New York: Knopf, 1936).

I

CONTEXTS AND CRITICAL ISSUES

I

GUY J. REYNOLDS

Willa Cather as progressive: politics and the writer

Cather was a writer who emerged at a transitional moment in the evolution of American culture, and the complexity of her work results from her responses to this shifting historical matrix. Born in 1873, she was an American of the late-Victorian period, and she lived her early life in the relatively provincial backwater of rural Nebraska. But it would be a patronizing mistake to see this historical and geographical context as inevitably quiet or conservative or politically insignificant. This was a time of considerable political ferment, a ferment that was formative in shaping her fiction's social and political dimensions. After the settlement of the prairies and their initial cultivation by American and European pioneers, the later years of the nineteenth century were lean. The 1890s, when Cather was a student in Lincoln and then a fledgling journalist, were a decade of agricultural crisis. Crop failures, drought, and depopulation (as the prairie schooners continued to move westwards, beyond such states as Kansas and Nebraska) heralded a crisis. Then the Panic of 1893, when a London financial firm abruptly crashed, saw British investors pull their money out of the United States, precipitating a three-year depression (and, as we shall see, directly affecting Nebraskans whom Cather knew). The rise in unemployment and strikes was eerily premonitory of the 1930s, and the crisis touched Cather's state too. In 1895 the power company in her hometown of Red Cloud failed; "the town had no electricity for ten years."[1] The decade taught Nebraskans tough lessons about a globalizing economy, about failure as well as success.

And such a context produced a changed political landscape. A major response to this crisis was the formation of the People's Party (also known as the Populist Party), which originated in Ohio but held its first national convention in Omaha, Nebraska in 1892. Populism was a reaction against the excesses of the late nineteenth-century Gilded Age; it sought to return power and economic independence to the people. A reformist movement, Populism was largely rooted in such western States as Nebraska, Kansas, and Colorado. One of its key demands, for "free silver," was based on a campaign against the gold standard and for the unlimited supply of a coinage based on the metal that the West had in abundance. Populism resulted from a groundswell of rural disaffection; it was anti-establishment, rooted in agrarian revolt, resentful of capitalism's impact on the common man. But even though the Democrats adopted part of their program for the Presidential campaign of 1896, and put forward the Nebraskan radical William Jennings Bryan, it was the Republican candidate, William McKinley, who prevailed.[2]

These years left a lasting and powerful mark on Cather, and an understanding of her work in the context of Populism helps us to see how she can be read as a progressive writer. Cather wrote a wry analysis of William Jennings Bryan for the *Library* magazine in 1900 – an essay that saw him as a synthesis of the Midwest, an incarnation of "its inflammability and volubility, its strength and its crudeness, its high seriousness and self-confidence."[3] Here we come to a major contradiction in Cather's career. At certain points she engaged with the political scene in quite a detailed way. And yet by the 1930s many critics thought her disengaged from the modern scene. Cather became the focus of a heated debate about ideology, a debate where she was repeatedly cast as a writer alienated from her age; an author fixated by nostalgia and elegy rather than by the contemporary world. These readings formed part of a larger debate about her progressivism.[4] For leftist critics, she seemed to have little to say in a context formed by the Depression and by radical responses to the decade's crises. She seemed, quite simply, irrelevant because insufficiently progressive. Granville Hicks's 1933 attack on Cather ("The Case Against Willa Cather") was one of a series of impassioned pleas both against and on behalf of her work. In 1932 Archer Winsten published "A Defense of Willa Cather." In 1937 Lionel Trilling lambasted her domestic mysticism. Meanwhile, E. K. Brown produced his 1936 "Homage to Willa Cather" and Robert Footman replied with "The Genius of Willa Cather" in 1938. This run of accounts shows that Cather's work had managed to find a faultline in the literary culture of the 1930s, and that faultline could be said to be "progress." Had Cather simply become, as Hicks implied, an anti-progressive at a time when a progressive vision was a vital response to the nation's ills?[5]

Cather's formative years in the Nebraska of the Populists provides a different pathway into her politics. She was certainly not an urban-industrial radical writer, in the sense that John Dos Passos or Upton Sinclair were. Nor did she share the declarative, polemical voice of a Steinbeck. Instead, her politics were rooted in an older folkway, a rural diagnosis of American democracy that had emerged in the 1890s. Like the Populists, Cather was interested in a "purer" form of capitalism, rooted in community and locality.

Like the Populists, she was suspicious of the increasingly attenuated and mediated forms of modern capitalism. Like the Populists, Cather valorized a regionalist idealism, where integrity and virtue were enshrined in midwestern small towns. Her thought bears a good deal of similarity to that of other radicals from around the United States at the turn of the twentieth century. As Robert L. Dorman has shown, regionalism was a powerful and politically complex movement in the South and West of the United States. By the inter-war period intellectuals had developed that sense of region into a powerful critique of the dominant culture. Dorman's study, an intellectual history of the period 1920 to 1945, positions Cather among a number of regionalists: Donald Davidson, B. A. Botkin, Mari Sandoz, W. P. Webb. She shared the radical provincial interest in what we might call folk culture (usually a pre-industrial, regionalist, locally rooted culture). There is a strong sense of what we might call "restorationism" in her work, a keen awareness that something has been lost. Dorman's provincial radicals presented an alternative to modern America's standardizing drive; they called for a decentralized, local, organic political economy. Dorman notes "three distinct sources for folk values that have commonly been appropriated by participants in the regionalist tradition: pioneer agrarian-republican communities, Indian tribal cultures, and immigrant-borne folk life."[6] All three sources of "folk values" are, of course, central to Cather's work from the immigrant, pioneer fictions (O Pioneers! and My Ántonia) through to explorations of "tribal cultures" in Death Comes for the Archbishop and The Professor's House.

We can build on Dorman's suggestions to present further motifs that mark Cather's distinctive development of a midwestern radical vision. Four characteristics stand out – motifs and themes in her fiction that grow out of broader currents in the Zeitgeist. First, her work is studded with representations of an idealized community that seems to be slipping away into memory and history: the pioneer communities of late nineteenth-century Nebraska; the Mesa communities of the Pueblo Indians; the French Canadian world of Quebec. Cather's oeuvre can be read as an extended exercise in the artistic memory's re-creation of a seemingly vanished, idealized place. This is less an act of retreat (as many critics have suggested) than a form of regionalist commitment (and recommitment) to the American spaces where a "beloved community" once existed. The act of memory then has a civic function in Cather, projecting images of the ideal place, and testing her readers' willingness to see such places emerge again. Second, she traces themes of reform and progress, particularly as they work their way into the texture of her characters' lives. Hence, the interest in progressive farming in O Pioneers! or the quest to create an adaptive and creative church mission in *Death Comes for the Archbishop*. Many of Cather's characters (one thinks of Alexandra Bergson or Father Latour) are thoroughly progressive and pragmatic in their desire to make the best of themselves and their situation. Indeed, *Death Comes for the Archbishop* and *O Pioneers!* turn on acts of progressive determination: the founding of a farm, the founding of a church; the shared vision to leave the world better than one found it. Third, there is in Cather's writing an often withering, satirical assault on the degradations of American business, allied to a veneration of older ways of making money. Fourth, a certain religiosity; Cather was a writer of the Progressive Era who embodied in her work the typical Progressive discourse of a fervent and often religious idealism.

The first of these motifs (the ideal community) exemplifies Cather's highly idiosyncratic progressive fiction. Her ideal communities are informed by an appreciation of local culture's distinctive history, which she derived from new work in anthropology and archaeology then emerging in US universities. Cather shared with another major female modernist, Zora Neale Hurston, a sense of region informed by the emergent scholarship of folk culture; a feminized folkloric fiction was the result.[7] Recent scholarship has demonstrated just how catholic were Cather's readings in these emergent disciplines, notably the anthropology and archaeology of the Southwest.[8] She had visited Arizona and the Southwest in 1912 – a trip associated by her biographers with a revival in her creative energies.[9] These trips also gave her vital intellectual material. For instance, as David Harrell has shown, a trip to Mesa Verde in 1915 might well have led to Cather's reading the work of the Smithsonian archaeologist Jesse Walter Fewkes.[10] She used such reading to shape a very distinctive regionalist politics, suggesting that local folkloric cultures had persisted in America throughout time.

Anthropology and archaeology fed into a highly eclectic sense of the multiple regions of America. Although she is, naturally, usually thought of as a Nebraskan novelist, the regions represented in her fiction conjure up a myriad Americas; she was the most diverse of writers, in terms of the places her imagination inhabited. Although predominantly a western and a southwestern novelist, she stretched an imaginative net towards colonial French America (*Shadows on the Rock*) and the South (*Sapphira and the Slave Girl*); and at the time of her death she had begun work on a novel set in medieval Avignon. If we think through the development of Cather's career after 1922, we see a correlation between the increasing geographical mobility of her work and her anxieties about cultural dislocation. Cather famously wrote in 1936 that the world had "broken in two in 1922."[11] She could no longer map her regionalist progressivism on to the midwestern heartland;

the standardization of American culture meant that this terrain, utterly distinctive in her youth, was now lost. Her fiction then multiplied outwards, as she incorporated a range of imaginative Americas into her work; but she still sought out those idealized progressive places first depicted in the Nebraskan novels. As if in response to what she perceived as the bland conformity of the "standard," Cather's latter career was a defiant exercise in creative pluralism. In place of a single, standardized "America," she offers a pluralistic range of Americas by taking the whole of North America (from Canada to Arizona and Mexico, via Virginia and Nebraska) as her subject. This variety is Cather's answer to a modern American society she felt was becoming "singular" in the worst way: fixated on a single – and narrowly straitened – model of a national culture.[12]

The second strand of Cather's progressivism focuses on motifs of reform. Cather's early life had been played out during the Populist era; but her major work was produced during the so-called "Progressive Era" of the 1910s and 1920s. Progressivism was a broad, diffuse political movement – a politics of national remedy (and, like Populism, a reaction to the degradations of late nineteenth-century capitalism). Progressives emphasized reform, the revival of community, the rooting out of corruption, the revival of democracy, the application of modern managerialism to social problems; they favored regulation rather than revolution in business. Actual Progressive party tickets were advanced in both 1912 (when Theodore Roosevelt lost to Woodrow Wilson) and 1924 (when Robert La Follette lost to Calvin Coolidge). While the Populists wanted to resist the acceleration towards modern capitalism (with its urbanization and industrialism), Progressives sought to remedy and reform this new culture – but fundamentally, they accepted it.[13] Progressivism was an eminently pragmatic political ideology that put its faith in Americans' ability to organize and to manage their way to a better future. Cather's connections with Progressivism were significant. As an editor at *McClure's Magazine*, she would have encountered the "muckrakers" such as Lincoln Steffens and Ida Tarbell, journalists whose attacks on corruption and corporate misdeeds were foundational to Progressivism. S. S. McClure, her mentor and employer at the magazine, used his position to write and to lecture on such progressive issues as municipal reform, nationalization of the railroads and governmental efficiency. She then became the ghostwriter of S. S. McClure's *My Autobiography* (1914), a memoir which has been read as a distinctively Progressive document.[14] In her work at *McClure's* Cather was enmeshed in Progressivism on a daily basis.

And her fiction is in tune with a progressive desire to reform, to manage, to create pragmatic solutions to social and economic difficulties. Take Alexandra's discussion with her brothers in *O Pioneers!*, where a conjunction of modern farming techniques and judicious business sense enables the Bergsons to leap forward. Alexandra's diagnosis of their position blends a Populist's fear of rural ruin with a Progressive's desire to move forward through the application of rationality and scientism. "But as sure as we are sitting here to-night, we can sit down here ten years from now independent landowners, not struggling farmers any longer."[15] Or take the scientific progressivism of Tom Outland in *The Professor's House*, with his design for a jet engine. Or the steady reforming mission of Father Latour in *Death Comes for the Archbishop*. In their different ways, these characters share a central progressive drive. They seek to change a culture (and often themselves) by a decisive progressive act, be it the building of a church or the creation of a new engine or the introduction of new agricultural methods. While these characters emerged from the world of the pioneers and the populists, they now move in the world of the progressives. Such figures as Jim Burden, Neil Herbert, Professor St. Peter are deracinated midwesterners, middle-class professionals who move in a bureaucratic and recognizably twentieth-century world. The melancholy felt by these figures results in part from a massive historical dislocation, as they move from the small-town agrarianism of the Populist era to the modernity of Progressivism. Professor St. Peter is typical: a son of Lake Michigan and a farming family, his days are now spent in the modern university, fighting bureaucratic battles.

Her third progressive leitmotif: a typically reformist attack on corrupt business. Cather's fiction is studded with mocking, satirical images of how commercialism and consumerism undermine the integrity of provincial America. Think of the Marsellus house in *The Professor's House*, with its ludicrous glass knobs; or, in the same novel, the sale of beautiful archaeological relics from the ancient Cliff City. When Fechtig buys the goods, Tom appeals to a sense of the commonwealth of America and to a sense of due inheritance. "They belonged to this country, to the State, and to all the people." After all, "boys like you and me . . . have no other ancestors to inherit from."[16] (As we shall see, such calls for a commonwealth, and for a proper sense of inheritance, echo through Cather's work.)

These characters embody Cather's suspicion of the corrosive impact of acquisitiveness, allied to her wariness about how economic modernism is producing an increasingly consumerist society. In the early fiction, the link between hard work, production, and the distribution of goods is easily identifiable. The farms of Ántonia and Alexandra are forged by the industry of family and community. Goods on the table are the products of one's own labor; there is a valorization of a regionalist economy that enmeshes producers and consumers in a transparent economic relationship. What is interesting about the later, critical representations of business is that the process of capitalist exchange is now more refracted and mediated. Who made the "glass knobs" in the Marsellus house? We do not know. Buying and selling take place increasingly at a distance: when Fechtig gets his acquisitions out of the States, he uses a French boat to take the goods from Mexico City.[17] The process of production is becoming more complex, as the economy moves away from its roots in Jeffersonian agrarianism.

Intellectual historians often find it difficult to position Progressivism as a political ideology; but they note instead a tone that marked Progressive language. Above all, the fervent religiosity of the Progressives draws the historian's eye. Progressives were reformers, imbued with a strong sense of neo-scientific rationality; but they were also idealists, and their language was fervently religious. One commentator notes that the central paradox of Progressivism was that it produced figures who prized rationalism while remaining "moral, religious, spiritual, and even romantically mystical in their public doctrines."[18] Such religiosity and mysticism thread their way into the ecumenical rapture of Cather's work. She was confirmed in the Episcopal Church late in 1922, in Red Cloud. But many readers, encountering *Death Comes for the Archbishop*'s deep engagement with the Catholic mission in New Mexico, imagine that she must have been a Catholic. Although an establishment Protestant, Cather represented a diverse range of religious and mystical experiences, from Latour's Catholic devotions to Tom Outland's new-age pantheism in *The Professor's House* to Thea Kronborg's yearning for the ecstasy of art in *The Song of the Lark*. Repeatedly, a character enters a heightened, rapturous state of mind and being – encountering what Latour beautifully calls a "perpetual flowering."[19] In terms of their basic sensibility, Cather's protagonists epitomize the spiritual idealism that marked the Progressive character.

The template for Cather's ideas about progress – specifically, the progress of American civilization on the Plains – is her 1923 *Nation* essay, "Nebraska: The End of the First Cycle." This essay, Cather's contribution to a series about the various states, distills her distinctive views on the heartland and her sense of the United States's national identity. In order to understand Cather and Progressivism, we must start here, as the established writer (she had just won the Pulitzer Prize for *One of Ours*) takes the long view of her state.

"Nebraska: The End of the First Cycle" opens with a compressed history of the state, taking in environment, early history and the nineteenth-century settlement of the prairies. Essentially, this is a historiographical model familiar from nineteenth-century writing of the West. Civilization progresses through stages; there is an inevitable drive towards "civilization."[20] Cather's essay thus follows the Plains from pre-history through to the heyday of the native Americans and then on to pioneer wagons and the railroads.

The essay is a fine example of Cather's skill as a journalist: her talents for compression and selection; her ability to weave a range of discourses into a seamless prose. "Nebraska" is at once a natural history of the state, a historical account, a travelogue, a personal reminiscence and a thesis about nationhood.

For this is a major statement about how the ideology of progress has animated American civilization, particularly the westward movement of the pioneers. The essay forms, in a way, Cather's reply to Frederick Jackson Turner's frontier thesis. The Wisconsin historian's essay, "The Significance of the Frontier in American History," had originally been delivered at a conference in 1893; but Turner republished this piece, along with other essays on western history, in 1920.[21] Turner created a major historiographical justification for American exceptionalism. At the border between the savage and the civilized, a new being came into view – the American; Turner's potent brew of geographical determinism and crude psychology forged a powerful myth suggesting that a new form of national character, distinct from Europe, was evolving. Cather's essay occupies the same terrain as Turner's analysis; but it comes to very different conclusions.

Cather was an Atlanticist. Indeed, of all the American modernists Cather was perhaps the most fully committed to a model of Atlantic civilization, even if (unlike Fitzgerald, Hemingway, Stein, and the "lost generation") she never lived in Europe. She shared the expatriate writers' interest in European culture (and, if her last novel on Avignon had been completed, would have been the author of two fictions set in Europe). But she also developed a rooted, regionalist modernism that places her next to the defiantly native William Carlos Williams. Cather faces both ways; she created arguments for the interdependence of Europe and America. Cather believed in the interaction between, and linking of, Europe and America. She also had a strong awareness of the diversity of European cultures. Looked at from an American exceptionalist's perspective, Cather's complex Atlanticism lacked a sense of Anglo-Saxonism. In fact, Turner himself castigated Cather for her representations of what he called "non-English stocks," the Scandinavians and central Europeans who fascinated her.[22] Cather articulated her own theory of civilizations – less a clash than a cross-fertilization among the nations of the West. She was a midwestern Atlanticist, a cosmopolitan, a pro-European American. This then led her to call for diversity and pluralism, often rendered in homely images. The "Nebraska" essay replays a favorite metaphor (that culture can be symbolized in terms of food) when she notes that Nebraska has better European pastry than Prague or Vienna. Cather finds on the western prairies transplanted Europeans still imbued with their original culture and qualities – the "cultivated, restless young men from Europe." One might contrast Cather's figures with Turner's moccasin-wearing new Americans. There is, of course, some snobbery in the privileging of the "cultivated" Europeans; but there is also a distinctive theory of cultural connection being advanced here. Cather's work presents her own particular reading of what it means to be "western," not only in the narrowly geographical sense but also in the sense of a theory of the civilization of the West. Cather projects a form of transatlantic progressivism, where the United States and Europe remain closely enmeshed. Thus her computation of the "stock" of Nebraska, where she tells us that the majority of the population (some 75%, in fact) were non-native-born:

> The census of 1910 showed that there were then 228,648 foreign-born and native-born Germans living in Nebraska; 103,503 Scandinavians; 50,680 Czechs. The total foreign population of the State was then 900,571, while the entire population was 1,192,214 . . . With such a majority of foreign stock, nine to three, it would be absurd to say that the influence of the European does not cross the boundary of his own acres, and has had nothing to do with shaping the social ideas of the commonwealth.[23]

Cather's use of the term "commonwealth" in this essay is important. Four states call themselves commonwealths: Massachusetts, Virginia, Kentucky and Pennsylvania. Cather's deployment of "commonwealth" carries with it a specific political tang; "commonwealth" helps to establish this essay's distinctive idealism. "Commonwealth" takes us back to the colonial roots of the United States; and Cather, a native Virginian, would have known the term from her Southern origins. But the ideal of the commonwealth might have had a particular poignancy during the Progressive era. Commonwealth: the common weal, the organization of society for the good of all its citizens. Commonwealth carries an idealistic, deeply democratic connotation; it calls for a *polis* of community and egalitarianism. A commonwealth is the opposite of a plutocracy. As the "Roaring Twenties" took shape around her, Cather explicitly attacked modern business, and particularly high finance, and she simultaneously cast her home state as a lost commonwealth: the place where the common good, honest business, and pioneer virtues were utterly paramount. In her veneration of the Nebraskan commonwealth, Cather articulates a version of that midwestern idealism that runs from the Populists in Omaha in 1892 down to the Progressive Wisconsin heartland of Robert La Follette. But this is an American commonwealth made out of Europeans; it is at once a return to an earlier, Puritan ideal of America and a prescient image of a pluralist community.

"Nebraska" contains her most explicit commentary on the state's politics, when she refers to the turbulent 1890s:

> The rapid industrial development of Nebraska, which began in the latter eight-ies, was arrested in the years 1893–97 by a succession of crop failures and by the financial depression which spread over the whole country at that time – the depression which produced the People's Party and the Free Silver agitation. These years of trial, as everyone now realizes, had a salutary effect upon the new State. They winnowed out the settlers with a purpose from the drift-ing malcontents who are ever seeking a land where man does not live by the sweat of his brow. The slack farmer moved on. Superfluous banks failed, and money lenders who drove hard bargains with desperate men came to grief. The strongest stock survived, and within ten years those who had weathered the storm came into their reward. (p. 238)

This passage encapsulates her complex reading of Nebraska's relative decline in the 1890s. She sees the period as a necessary purgative that helped to finish off inefficient businesses. There is toughness here, and a sense of *laissez-faire* capitalism that might have made a Populist wince; a Populist would also have rejected the latent social Darwinism of her judgment. Yet, in Populist style, her criticisms are directed specifically at the financial com-munity, at money-lenders and banks, rather than the traditional trades and agricultural businesses of the Plains. She seems happy to accept the failure of financiers in the 1890s. It is significant that the symbol for the corrup-tion of Nebraska's pioneer virtue is a medal, an unconscious but powerful echo of the Populists' concern with coinage, perhaps: "there is the other side of the medal, stamped with the ugly crest of materialism, which has set its seal upon all our most productive commonwealths" (p. 238). The Populists rejected the overwhelming importance of gold (and sought a currency based on the silver with which the West was blessed); Cather's imagination, too, configures a civilization in terms of debased coinage. Is it a coincidence that the image Cather should deploy to express the corruption of Nebraska's val-ues should be that of a medal? The image is a classical one, but it carries with it a suggestive echo of the "Battle of the Standards" of 1896, and the arguments over monetary value. The medal "stamped with the ugly crest of materialism" is Cather's answer to Bryan's "cross of gold."

Cather goes on to complain in this essay that "too much prosperity, too many moving-picture shows, too much gaudy fiction have colored the taste and manners of so many of these Nebraskans of the future" (p. 238). Cather was not a socialist; she admired capitalist enterprise and individu-alistic energy too much for that. But she was suspicious of a certain kind of capitalistic excess: the reckless and tasteless materialist culture of display.

Her formulation might be seen as a patrician critique of popular culture (all those films and cheap novels); but it emerged out of a puritan celebration of hard work and achievement. Such an analysis of American capitalism features in the novel that Cather wrote at this time, *A Lost Lady*. In its concision, elegance, and compressed detail, this short fiction has seemed to many readers to epitomize Cather's talents. The tale of a young westerner's fascination with a fading and disillusioned lady, Mrs. Forrester (the wife of a Captain Forrester, a railroad entrepreneur), the novel is suffused with regret, melancholy, and a sense of elegiac loss. With the fading of the Forresters, a purer age is passing away. This is a classic novel of inheritance (familiar from Walter Scott onwards): one class, and its associated social order, gives way to a successor generation (the inheritors) who typically seem to mark a falling-away, as integrity gives way to baser values. We know that Cather based her characters on Silas and Lyra Garber – Garber was one of those ambitous men who had come to Nebraska, and rose to become governor of the state in 1874. The Garbers lived in Cather's hometown of Red Cloud, and they presented her with an image of ambition, ascent, and eventual decline. "Garber's Farmers and Merchants Bank failed in the Panic of 1893," writes Susan Rosowski. "Garber and most of the other stockholders put up their land as security, and the depositors were paid . . . Lyra tried to sell the home place, unsuccessfully until 1910; she rented it out to hog-raisers in the meantime."[24] In other words, the novel emerged out of the crises of the 1890s, the very period that, I am suggesting, should be read as the foundational period for Cather's sense of community and capital. Looking back into her memories of that era, Cather alighted on folk who epitomized the ambition and failure of midwestern entrepreneurialism.

But can the novel be related to the progressive paradigm I have been exploring? The center of the novel is the relationship between Neil Herbert and Marian Forrester, and Cather's prose traces with exquisite and tactful detail the shifting constellation of Neil's feelings; the older woman arouses in him a mixture of fascination, desire, regret, pity, and shame. As important is Cather's tracing of the social and economic context in which this relationship evolves. Captain Forrester is one of the pioneer generation; he staked his claim to a spot of land, built his railroad, became a central figure in the local community. He is a rich man, but Neil sees both the Captain and his wife as inherently democratic and fair. But the Forresters are losing money, and Cather draws a contrast (familiar from the "Nebraska" essay) between the integrity of late nineteenth-century pioneers (with their inherent faith in the "commonwealth") and the moral collapse of the inheritors' generation. The pivotal moment comes when Captain Forrester's bank fails. Note how precisely Cather pinpoints a specific business problem:

The bank, about which Mrs. Forrester knew nothing but its name, was one which paid good interest on small deposits. The depositors were wage-earners; railroad employees, mechanics, and day labourers, many of whom had at some time worked for Captain Forrester. His was the only well-known name among the bank officers, it was the name which promised security and fair treatment to his old workmen and their friends. The other directors were promising young business men with many irons in the fire. But, the Judge said with evident chagrin, they had refused to come up to the scratch and pay their losses like gentlemen. They claimed that the bank was insolvent, not through unwise investments or mismanagement, but because of a nation-wide financial panic, a shrinking in values that no one could have foreseen. They argued that the fair thing was to share the loss with the depositors; to pay them fifty cents on the dollar, giving long-time notes for twenty-five percent, settling on a basis of seventy-five per cent.[25]

In its precision and mathematical detail, this passage recalls the paragraph in O Pioneers! where Alexandra discusses her farm's expansion. Both paragraphs turn with almost pedantic factuality on matters of money-lending and interest rates. Cather, a child of the 1880s and 1890s, understood that entrepreneurialism was forged not only by hard work and thrift, but also by the availability of capital, particularly cheap capital. Once interest rates rise, the house of cards can collapse very quickly indeed. The attack on Cather by leftist critics in the 1930s had the unfortunate effect of masking and marginalizing a central aspect of her achievement as a social novelist: she was an acute analyst of America's business culture. Business, money-making, finance, the distinctive shapes of American capitalism: these seem to be the overt subjects of Upton Sinclair, John Dos Passos, and Sinclair Lewis. But in a more elliptical but none the less telling way, Cather also commands attention as an analyst of how business is shaping society.

Thus, through Neil's eyes Cather presents a waspishly critical account of the moment when the achievement of the railroad pioneers was overtaken by failure; and she framed her fictionalization of this period (A Lost Lady is set in the 1880s and early 1890s) with a keen awareness of class distinctions. The problem with this new generation of businessmen is that division and selfishness supplant earlier Western virtues of solidarity and communality. The younger men constitute a plutocratic oligarchy, marked by conspiracy among themselves and indifference to the broader society. The story lying behind A Lost Lady was one where depositors *were* paid; but as Cather revisited the history of the late nineteenth century, she rewrote history to present a financial culture where the commonwealth had "broken in two."

After this, further decline will take place: Mrs. Forrester slips into alcoholism; Captain Forrester suffers a number of strokes before a premature death. Neil is drawn into becoming Mrs. Forrester's protector, his responses both sexually fascinated and repelled by her flirtations with younger men. It is worth stressing that this personal dynamic, the center of the novel, has been inaugurated by a moment of economic and moral failure, as the new oligarchy of the inheritors comes into view. *A Lost Lady* is perhaps the quintessential Cather novel because in it we see her idealism and progressivism encountering that "other side of the coin" that acknowledged defeat, loss, and failure.[26]

But can an act of memory be a progressive act? This is a critical question when we meditate on Cather's work. Undoubtedly, *A Lost Lady* signals from its title onwards a keen and almost overbearing sense of loss. And Neil will imagine that loss in images saturated in romantic configurations of the late nineteenth-century Plains. "He had seen the end of an era, the sunset of the pioneer," Cather writes. Like a hunter's fire, all that is left is a place where "the ground was warm," where the "flattened grass . . . told the story."[27] But this is more than romantic elegy. For Cather's characters, memory has a civic and progressive function. In returning to that moment of "glory" Neil keeps alive the memory of a golden moment; and through such memories he pledges himself to a vision of the commonwealth. There is a crucial and telling difference, articulated time and again in Cather's work, between memory as escape and memory as an act of civic restitution. It is the latter form of recall and testimony that she prized: in returning to the "flattened grass," the warm ground of the prairies, Cather's characters seek to recover a sense of glory and integrity in an age where materialism and standardization were in the ascendant.

A good number of the characters she developed in her fiction live within this contradictory world. Neil is one of Cather's weary, dogged idealists. He is the confrere of Professor St. Peter (*The Professor's House*) and Jim Burden (*My Ántonia*): the professional midwestern male who carries forward earlier virtues of dignity, hard work, and idealism into an increasingly cynical world. These men – academics, lawyers, architects – seek out work with integrity in order to give a shape and progressive meaning to the world they find themselves in. Cather often counterpoints such characters against the duplicity, triteness, and rapacity that seem increasingly in the ascendant. Tom Outland values the Mesa's relics with passion, while Fechtig covets them materialistically. Neil seeks to hang on to the pure memories of Mrs. Forrester at her best; Ivy Peters's fascination is driven by lust and envy. Each of Cather's idealists seeks to recover a sense of value in a world where value is increasingly scorned. As Neil Herbert ruminates at the end of the novel: "he felt that the Captain knew his wife better even than she knew herself; and that, knowing her, he, – to use one of his own expressions, – 'valued her'."[28]

This is why Neil remains loyal to the memory of Marian: she inspired loyalty, a sense of value, in spite of her triteness and superficiality. The possessiveness that Neil feels at the end of the novel is underpinned by the sense that here, for once in his life, true value was glimpsed.

To address Cather and "progressivism" might seem a perverse task. Her opposition to certain aspects of modern, putatively progressive civilization is well known; she must be one of the few people to have lived in Greenwich Village and rejected Freudianism. As Hermione Lee notes, surveying letters from the 1930s, Cather evinced a "deliberate detachment from the 'progressive' movements of the day – economic and social reform, psychoanalysis and Marxism."[29] Tellingly, the latter two forms of the "progressive" were European movements then taking hold in the United States. Undoubtedly, her mood in the 1930s – partly in response to the attacks upon her – became somewhat reactionary. But to use this later Cather as a rod to beat the earlier writer would be a mistake. She had, in fact, encountered, engaged with, and contributed to progressive thought; but it was a highly distinctive, regionalist model of the progressive that she was interested in: a progressive model forged by the memory of the Nebraska of the 1890s.

NOTES

1. Susan J. Rosowski (with Kari A. Ronning), "Historical Essay," in Willa Cather, *A Lost Lady* (1923; Lincoln, NE, and London: University of Nebraska Press, 1997), p. 192.
2. For accounts of Populism, see John D. Hicks, *The Populist Revolt: A History of the Farmers' Alliance and the Peoples' Party* (Lincoln, NE: University of Nebraska Press, 1961); Norman Pollack, *The Populist Response to Industrial America* (New York: W. W. Norton, 1966); Lawrence Goodwyn, *The Populist Moment: A Short History of the Agrarian Revolt in America* (Oxford: Oxford University Press, 1978); Peter H. Argersinger, *The Limits of Agrarian Radicalism: Western Populism and American Politics* (Lawrence: University Press of Kansas, 1995).
3. Willa Cather, "The Personal Side of William Jennings Bryan" (1900), in William Curtin, ed., *The World and the Parish: Willa Cather's Articles and Reviews, 1893–1902*, 2 vols. (Lincoln, NE: University of Nebraska Press, 1970), p. 789.
4. Cather's place in the canon is a touchstone of recent scholarship. See David Stineback, "No Stone Unturned: Popular versus Professional Evaluations of Willa Cather," *Prospects* 7 (1982), pp. 167–76; Sharon O'Brien, "Becoming Noncanonical: The Case Against Willa Cather," *American Quarterly* 40 (1988), pp. 110–26; and Deborah Carlin, *Cather, Canon, and the Politics of Reading* (Amherst: University of Massachusetts Press, 1992).
5. Archer Winsten, "A Defense of Willa Cather," *Bookman* 74 (March 1932), pp. 634–40. Granville Hicks, "The Case Against Willa Cather," *English Journal* (November 1933), in James Schroeter, ed., *Willa Cather and Her Critics* (Ithaca, NY: Cornell University Press, 1967), pp. 139–47. Lionel Trilling,

"Willa Cather," *New Republic* 90 (1937), in Schroeter, *Willa Cather*, pp. 148–55. Robert Footman, "The Genius of Willa Cather," *American Literature*, 10 (1938), pp. 123–41. E. K. Brown, "Homage to Willa Cather," *Yale Review* 36 (1946), pp. 77–92.

6. Robert L. Dorman, *Revolt of the Provinces: The Regionalist Movement in America, 1920–1945* (Chapel Hill and London: University of North Carolina Press, 1993), p. 10. See also the "essays and commentaries" in Charles Reagan Wilson, ed., *The New Regionalism* (Jackson: University Press of Mississippi, 1998).

7. See Zora Neale Hurston's 1935 text, *Mules and Men* (1935. New York: Harper-Collins, 1990). Hurston collated African-American folk tales and examples of "hoodoo" rituals. We await significant comparative work that would bring together Cather and Hurston.

8. See the essays in John N. Swift and Joseph R. Urgo, eds., *Willa Cather and the American Southwest* (Lincoln, NE, and London: University of Nebraska Press, 2002).

9. For a discussion of the impact of the Southwest on Cather's imagination, see Sharon O'Brien, *Willa Cather: The Emerging Voice* (New York and Oxford: Oxford University Press, 1987), pp. 403–20.

10. David Harrell, *From Mesa Verde to The Professor's House* (Albuquerque: University of New Mexico Press, 1992), pp. 20–4.

11. Willa Cather, *Not Under Forty* (London: Cassell, 1936), p. v. She later changed the title to *Literary Encounters* for her collected works, as if acknowledging that the earlier title had signaled too grumpy a tone. (She declared her work would have little interest for those under forty.)

12. For a discussion of Cather's ideas of a national culture, particularly in relation to language and immigration, see Guy Reynolds, *Willa Cather in Context: Progress, Race, Empire* (New York: St. Martin's Press, 1996), pp. 73–98.

13. For an introduction to Progressivism see Robert M. Crunden, *Ministers of Reform: The Progressives' Achievement in American Civilization 1889–1920* (New York: Basic Books, 1982); Sean Dennis Cashman, *America in the Age of the Titans: The Progressive Era and World War I* (New York and London: New York University Press, 1988); Leon Fink, *Progressive Intellectuals and the Dilemmas of Democratic Commitment* (Cambridge, MA, and London: Harvard University Press, 1997).

14. Robert Stinson, "S. S. McClure's *My Autobiography*: The Progressive as Self-Made Man," *American Quarterly* 22 (1970), pp. 203–12. See Willa Cather, *The Autobiography of S. S. McClure* (Lincoln, NE, and London: University of Nebraska Press, 1997).

15. Willa Cather, *O Pioneers!* (1913), ed. Susan J. Rosowski and Charles W. Mignon with Kathleen Danker (Lincoln, NE, and London: University of Nebraska Press, 1992), p. 65.

16. Willa Cather, *The Professor's House* (1925; London: Virago, 1981), p. 242.

17. Cather, *The Professor's House*, p. 239.

18. Eldon J. Eisenach, *The Lost Promise of Progressivism* (Lawrence: University Press of Kansas, 1994), p. 46.

19. Willa Cather, *Death Comes for the Archbishop* (1927; London: Virago, 1981), p. 256.

20. The classic account of "Stadialism" and the literary imagination remains George Dekker, *The American Historical Romance* (Cambridge: Cambridge University Press, 1987), pp. 73–98.
21. See Frederick Jackson Turner, *The Frontier in American History* (New York: Holt, 1920).
22. Frederick Jackson Turner, Letters of July 16, 1913, and March 7, 1925, in *"Dear Lady": The Letters of Frederick Jackson Turner and Alice Forbes Perkins Hooper, 1910–1932*, ed. R. A. Billington (San Marino: Huntington Library, 1970), pp. 149, 365.
23. "Nebraska: The End of the First Cycle," *The Nation* 117 (September 5, 1923), p. 237. Cather's article was one in a series about different states, and was followed by Arthur Fisher's "Montana: Land of the Copper Collar." Future page references to this essay are given in the text.
24. Rosowski, "Historical Essay," *A Lost Lady*, p. 195. Rosowski's essay gives a careful account of the "Materials and Models" underpinning this fiction.
25. Cather, *A Lost Lady*, pp. 85–6.
26. Cather's imagination was drawn to images of the "other side." She used this phrase in the "Nebraska" essay, and she also deployed it in a comment on *My Ántonia*, a novel she described in an interview as "just the other side of the rug, the pattern that is supposed not to count in a story." Interview with Flora Merrill for the *New York World*, 19 April 1925, in L. Brent Bohlke, ed., *Willa Cather in Person: Interviews, Speeches, and Letters* (Lincoln, NE, and London: University of Nebraska Press, 1986), p. 77.
27. Cather, *A Lost Lady*, p. 160.
28. Cather, *A Lost Lady*, p. 143.
29. Hermione Lee, *Willa Cather: A Life Saved Up* (London: Virago, 1989), p. 328.

2

JOSEPH R. URGO

The Cather thesis: the American empire of migration

"She had heard the new call: 'Go East, young woman, and grow up with the steel and concrete and electric waves.'"

Sinclair Lewis, *Gideon Planish* (1943)

One thing to keep in mind when reading and thinking about Willa Cather is that she was, in both literal and figurative terms, an American pioneer. Her family migrated to Nebraska in the 1880s, a time when people lived in dug-outs and sod-houses (although when young Willa arrived, she had family contacts there to make her settlement relatively easier) and old-timers shared memories of Indian encounters. As an adult, with memories of one uprooting embedded in her consciousness, Cather moved to the Northeast with enthusiasm, finding opportunities for ambitious and intelligent women not in the small towns of Nebraska and the Midwest but in urban centers, amid "the steel and concrete and electric waves" of large cities such as Pittsburgh and New York. There, the figurative pioneer, Cather rose to the top of her field in journalism (in the first decade of the new century she was the editor of *McClure's Magazine*, one of the most famous and widely read magazines in American history) and then abandoned that career to become a novelist. In her fiction she did what is understood to be impossible: she wrote novels embraced as art by critics and read with passion and devotion by the popular reading public.

Willa Cather followed the path of the western pioneer in her lifetime, the path followed by at least half the nation's westward adventurers, though not the one immortalized in American movies and popular culture. In the popular national imagination, pioneers moved west and stayed there, established towns and cities, and expanded American civilization into western territories. Casualties, and there were many in this imaginary scenario, were those who succumbed to illness, madness, or death – death or madness in Indian warfare, death as a result of criminal activities, or illnesses aggravated by living so far from the medical benefits of civilization. What is left out of such popular portrayals for the most part are the stories of those pioneers who decided to turn around and go back east. (A lot more is left out, of course, including mundane matters of work accidents, loneliness, fatigue – not the stuff of legendary tale-telling.) The movement back east, when portrayed at all in popular culture, is often cast as one of failure, cowardice, or comedy. Historically, however, we know that a lot of people tried their fortunes out west and decided that east was preferable; just as millions of immigrants to the United States in the period of the Great Migration (1880–1920) decided that the home country was preferable to America and went back. Statistics show that about half of those who emigrated to America or tried their fortunes out west on the American continent either returned home or went to another location (sometimes trying a series of locations), and for various reasons. The historical record is rarely as simple as the myths it inspires.

Willa Cather was born in Virginia in 1873. In 1883, after the family's barn mysteriously burned down, the Cather family moved to Nebraska, where other family members had emigrated a few years before. Cather's biographers speculate that the barn may have been destroyed by neighbors who held a grudge against the Cathers for their Union sympathies during the Civil War. At the age of ten, Willa Cather undertook a traumatic relocation, one that would affect her profoundly for the rest of her life. Cather's childhood was spent among various dislocated peoples, including Virginians, like herself, but also including German, Swedish, Irish, English, Danish, and Bohemian immigrant settlers in the area. Her family settled in Red Cloud, in Webster County, Nebraska, an agricultural area characterized by miles and miles of wheat and corn – and little else. Land companies advertised aggressively to recruit labor from Europe, enticing emigrants with American dreams of land ownership. However, while the overriding goal of most immigrants was to make a go of their lives in new territories, the trajectory of Cather's career seems, at least in hindsight, to have been characterized by an ambition to return east. She left Red Cloud to attend the University of Nebraska and graduated in 1895. In 1896, she took an editorial job in Pittsburgh and relocated to that city. She would never live in Nebraska again. Ten years later she moved to New York City, where she maintained a permanent address until her death in 1947. While her family stayed in Red Cloud, Nebraska, and went to rest, finally, in the family cemetery plot there, Willa Cather is buried in Jaffrey, New Hampshire, a favorite destination, one used especially for writing, and particularly for writing about western pioneers and their descendants.

As Cather moved east, she brought the West with her, as an idea. Cather traveled often – one might say she traveled incessantly – and took regular trips out west as well as to Maine, New Hampshire, Canada, and other locations. And so while she remained, throughout her adult life, an easterner, and, more specifically, a New Yorker, in terms of permanent residence, in her imagination Willa Cather was a Virginian, a Nebraska pioneer, a southwestern adventurer, a lover of the wilderness seeking refuge from the city.

Those who wish to see where Willa Cather lived, or to answer the question "Where was Willa Cather's home?" must do some traveling. Her birthplace is in Back Creek Valley (near Winchester), Virginia and her childhood home is in Red Cloud, Nebraska; her Pittsburgh apartment was 1180 Murray Hill Avenue; she lived off Washington Square, in New York City, and on Park Avenue; she had regular summer destinations in Jaffrey, New Hampshire, Grand Manan Island in New Brunswick (where she built a small house), and Northeast Harbor on Mount Desert Island in Maine. And then there are the places Cather liked to visit: Walnut Canyon, Arizona; Santa Fe, New Mexico; Boston Garden; Manchester, Massachusetts; Cos Cob, Connecticut; Quebec City; and of course, she went to Nebraska, often. She told a friend once, referring to her travel schedule, that she kept her suitcases under her bed. Like a bee, Cather may be understood to have cross-pollinated ideas from one region to another, carrying the idea of Nebraskan immigrants to New York and transporting a cosmopolitan vantage point to the West, Southwest, and Northeast, never forgetting her origins in the South. But to answer the question "Where was Willa Cather's home?" is no easy one. Perhaps the safest nominative for her is that she was quintessentially American.

The sentence below, taken from the opening paragraphs of Frederick Jackson Turner's "frontier thesis" (published as *The Significance of the Frontier in American History*), delivered first as a lecture at the Chicago World's Fair in 1893, is among the more famous summations in American historiography:

> The peculiarity of American institutions is the fact that they have been com-
> pelled to adapt themselves to the changes of an expanding people – to the
> changes involved in crossing a continent, in winning a wilderness, and in devel-
> oping at each area of this progress out of the primitive economic and political
> conditions of the frontier into the complexity of city life.[1]

Turner argued that westward expansion in United States history was not simply a progressive movement, but constituted "a return to primitive conditions on a continually advancing frontier line," which meant that in American historical experience, progress meant "continually beginning over again on the frontier." As a result, the American character has been constructed by an experience marked by "perennial rebirth," by a "fluidity of American life," and by an "expansion westward with its new opportunities, [and] its continuous touch with the simplicity of primitive society" (p. 4).

"Americanization" is what happens in frontier conditions, according to Turner. The European immigrant arrives on the American frontier, sheds his European traits ("dress, industries, tools, modes of travel, and thought") and adapts to wilderness necessity ("planting Indian corn and plowing with a sharp stick"). The pioneer does not forget his origins in civilization; but at first, the frontier environment is "too strong for the man" and he must adapt or die (p. 5). Nevertheless, over time, he transforms the wilderness in ways that would never occur to the native Indian, and out of the clash of European and Indian, the return of civilization to frontier conditions, emerges the American. "And to study this advance," Turner claimed in 1893, "the men who grew up under these conditions, and the political, economic, and social results of it, is to study the really American part of our history" (p. 5).

Much of frontier history written in the twentieth century amounts to a series of footnotes to Turner, some elaborative, some challenging or revisionist. Women's history has revised the focus on "the men who grew up under these conditions" to include female frontier experience and the domestic adaptations made by mothers, daughters, wives, and independent female pioneers. Ethnic historians have challenged Turner's too-simplistic description of the process by which "immigrants were Americanized, liberated, and fused into a mixed race" (p. 17) in frontier conditions. Social historians have qualified Turner's claim that "to the frontier the American intellect owes its striking characteristics" (p. 27). Turner has subsequently been criticized or amended for the gaps or omissions in his historical method – his use of evidence, for example, and his employment of proof for his claims left much to be desired. Nevertheless, and despite the many faults and omissions of his essay, the Turner thesis remains the single most inspiring and provocative theory in American historiography. In many ways, the entire field of American studies finds its origins in Turner. If Turner was correct, the discipline may be seen as continuing a long tradition of establishing theories of American exceptionalism – how and why it is that the United States is unique among nations because of its historical experience. If Turner was not correct, if he was mistaken, the discipline may be seen as establishing a long tradition of examining how and why it is that Americans think they are exceptional (because of the frontier experience) when in fact they are not. Either way, Turner is at the root of it all.

Willa Cather never responded specifically to the Turner thesis, but as we extrapolate from her life and work, we can adapt Turner's language to formulate what might be called the Cather thesis:

> The peculiarity of American institutions is the fact that they have been compelled to adapt themselves to the restlessness of a migratory people – to the changes involved in crossing and then re-crossing the continent, in spending part of one's life in the wilderness only to return for a while to the city before moving on to another part of the country or to another city, and in influencing at

each stopping point of this crisscrossing memories of someplace else, with ideas brought from another situation, making a frontier out of an established city and establishing a city out of a frontier. Incessant transit makes an American, the seeming inability to stay in one place for very long, or, if rendered stable by circumstances, the desire, nonetheless, to move, or the knowledge that one could have or should have moved.

Frederick Jackson Turner began his thesis about the American frontier by noting a statement from the 1890 Census that declared the absence of any significant large tracts of unsettled lands to report. For the first time in its history, the United States was not in the process of colonizing western territories. The closing of the frontier was a monumental event for Turner, as it was to the existence of the frontier that "the American intellect owes its striking characteristics." Turner enumerated such typical American traits, which he called "traits of the frontier," and listed them as "coarseness and strength combined with acuteness and inquisitiveness; that practical, inventive turn of mind, quick to find expedients; that masterful grasp of material things, lacking in the artistic but powerful to effect great ends; that restless, nervous energy; that dominant individualism, working for good and evil, and withal that buoyancy and exuberance which comes with freedom" (p. 27). Taking its starting point with the passing away of the unsettled lands, Turner's thesis is marked by a kind of nervousness itself, lamenting the disappearance of "a gate of escape from the bondage of the past" (p. 28) and marked by the pervasive sense of ending.

One may wonder what the pioneer and literary artist Willa Cather thought of Turner's assertion that frontier conditions resulted in minds "lacking in the artistic" sensibilities. There is no doubt that Turner was wrong about Willa Cather: it was the experience of frontier conditions in Nebraska, and "that restless, nervous energy; that dominant individualism," characteristic of Cather's intellect, that created the artist herself. Cather's frontier thesis, while not contradicting Turner's, and while not something to which Turner was oblivious by any means, nevertheless refined Turner's focus. It was not the permanent settlers who formed American consciousness – though they certainly contributed to its material basis. Those who left cities to settle in frontier lands, never to return, did important work spreading American institutions by colonization, applying United States law to refine and eliminate primitive conditions, as Turner argued so eloquently. But these settlers did not affect those in the East, those in settled areas, except as the *idea* of progress and empire they represented, as an option, a safety-valve, a possibility of escape for settled Americans. Those who exerted more direct and more immediate influence were those who *did not remain* in the West, but who moved back and forth from one area to another. It is these, the great masses of unsettled people, writers, railroad lawyers, schoolteachers, land speculators, missionaries, fame-seekers, tourists – among many others – who embody Cather's version of the frontier thesis.

Exemplars of the Cather thesis include Jim Burden, the railroad man, born in Virginia, migrant to the Nebraska frontier, best friend to an immigrant woman (through whom he learns to write "The Pioneer Woman's Story," the title of Book IV of *My Ántonia* [1918]), and who, as an adult, "loves with a personal passion the great country through which his railway runs and branches."[2] While Ántonia has remained on the frontier, doing the work required to turn a wild landscape into the domestic basis of civilization, Jim returned east, to study law and then to become a railroad company lawyer. However, Cather makes explicit the debt Jim's intellect owes to the frontier experience, a debt symbolized in the novel by his memory of Ántonia. "More than any other person we remembered," the narrator explains, "this girl seemed to mean to us the country, the conditions, the whole adventure of our childhood" (pp. xi–xii). The country, in the novel, is the Nebraska frontier, what Jim refers to as "not a country at all, but the material out of which countries are made" (p. 7). The conditions were bleak: immigrant families living in dug-outs and sod-houses, men who committed suicide out of despair and loneliness, and a landscape so empty of human signs that Jim reports feeling so "erased, blotted out" (p. 8) that he was not even sure, as a child, whether God would hear his prayers from such exile. Nevertheless, it was "the whole adventure" of his childhood in Nebraska, which formed his eastern, urban, railroad attorney consciousness, that has made him renowned as an entrepreneur, one who "is always able to raise capital for new enterprises" and who has helped others "to do remarkable things in mines and timber and oil" (p. xi). He is, in short, a successful capitalist, with the kind of mind that has driven American expansion for two centuries.

Jim's mind may well be said to be the main focus of the novel. That is to say, while the novel is obviously about Ántonia, it is also quite clearly about Jim's view of her and the influence she has had on his mind – the ways in which she is important to him. At the end of Book IV, "The Pioneer Woman's Story," Jim makes his debt explicit. "The idea of you is a part of my mind," he tells Ántonia; "you influence my likes and dislikes, all my tastes, hundreds of times when I don't realize it. You really are a part of me" (p. 312). The Cather thesis is encapsulated in this moment, when Jim explains that while he did not remain on the frontier, while he returned east to work in New York, he carried with him the idea of Ántonia and all that she had come to mean to him. Jim's possession of the frontier as memory, as a dimension of his consciousness, is the psychic ingredient that makes him the quintessential New Yorker

As we have seen, in her lifetime Cather moved west and she moved east, carrying with her the ideology of migration. In the Cather thesis, movement east, not west, is what strengthens the nation's idea of itself, and, not incidentally, what strengthens the nation's power and establishes the legitimacy of the American empire. Cather's western novels were all written in the East, and mark the infusion of the eastern establishment with western ideals – especially the ideals of expansion and national (as opposed to regional) identity. In her novels, energy flows east, back to such power centers as New York and Washington. And in Cather's prototypically American situations, pre-American loyalties (religion and ethnicity, for example) are supplanted by loyalties enacted by the experience of displacement, a displacement recognized as enabled by national expansion.

Very early in *The Song of the Lark* (1915) Cather makes connections between her main character's ambitions and the nation's movement towards empire. When Thea Kronborg and her friends take a Sunday expedition to the sand hills, a place of "constant tantalization" to Thea,[3] the narrative makes clear what will move east as Thea's career unfolds. She recalls an earlier trip with her father, to a "reunion of old frontiersmen" in Wyoming, when she came upon a site marked by the pathways of migratory pioneer wagon trains. Thea recalls being moved to tears when she saw the dozens of crisscrossing ruts,

> deep furrows, cut in the earth by heavy wagon-wheels, and not grown over with dry, whitish grass. The furrows ran side by side; when one trail had been worn too deep, the next party had abandoned it and made a new trail to the right or left. They were, indeed, only old wagon-ruts, running east and west, and grown over with grass. But as Thea ran about among the white stones, her skirts blowing this way and that, the wind brought to her eyes tears that might have come, anyway. (pp. 47–8)

The furrows are evidence of continuous movement "running east and west" carrying settlers to the frontier and carrying restless people, their ideas as well as material goods and wealth, back east. *The Song of the Lark* will go on to suggest a parallel between Thea Kronborg's individual ascent (and her movement from a small western town to the cultural centers of the East and of Europe) with the progress of the American empire. Cather grounds Thea's consciousness thoroughly in "the spirit of human courage" that "seemed up there with the eagles," making the artist's story an epic of imperial significance as well as an individual story of great success. In *The Song of the Lark*, as in *My Ántonia*, Cather demonstrates essential links between what seem to be highly individualized traits of character and large, abstract historical movements. When Jim Burden takes the idea of the pioneer woman, Ántonia, back east to his railroad development office, he contributes one tiny element to what we call a historical force. When Thea Kronborg carries her great talent from Moonstone to New York and then to Paris, she also contributes to (and in her case, symbolizes) the movement of power from West to East.

American expansion moved west throughout the nineteenth century, transporting energies, resources, and labor to develop and settle new towns, cities, and states. At the same time, or as a result, the idea of an American empire moved east. As the West became settled, as the economic effects of Great Plains agriculture and livestock production became apparent, as gold and oil reserves were developed, as mines began to produce, and as populations soared, the ideas, the wealth, and the power generated by expansion flowed back to urban centers in the East. We know the story of the West. American pioneer tales, from James Fenimore Cooper's nineteenth-century Leatherstocking Tales through the western novels and movies of the twentieth century, Americans have provided themselves and the rest of the world with a steady supply of stories about "how the West was won," how pioneers overcame adversity, lawlessness, and countless challenges in order to bring American civilization to the frontier. Willa Cather was certainly interested in this idea, and she either told or referred to it in many of her novels. Nevertheless, another story captured her imagination, relayed intimately to it, but not as commonly told in her time.

It may be that the one obligation possessed exclusively by a country's literary artists is to render the story of the nation into poetic form. Willa Cather wrote her novels between 1913 and 1947, precisely the years in which the position of the United States as a world power solidified. Her life spans the close of the western continental frontier and the opening of the global imperial frontier, from the settling of the American continent to the height of what has been called the American Century. Of all her great contemporaries, however – including Faulkner and Hemingway – Cather alone confronted the poetic potential of a transnational, American empire in the process of formation. Although William Faulkner projected a global, indeed cosmic, scope in *A Fable*, the emphasis of his work overall is on relations within a fixed and established American national state. And while Ernest Hemingway sought to link continents in his fiction, portraying the fate of Americans in Europe socially and at war, a conception of the nation itself as a developing force was not foremost in his narrative purposes. Willa Cather, however, set about a serious project of writing that depicts a burgeoning American presence on the face of the earth as a historical force of spiritual dimensions.

One of Ours (1922) and *Death Comes for the Archbishop* (1927) are two novels most directly concerned with transforming the American empire into epic material. In both, the movement of ideas, power, and resources is to the East from the West. In *One of Ours*, a conquering army is raised among the millions of sons of western pioneers and settlers, and transported east for battle. The young male soldiers (and female missionaries) in this novel symbolize and embody the empowering of eastern urban centers with energies and lives originating in the West. In *Death Comes for the Archbishop*, the strength of the Catholic Church is enhanced by the claiming of western souls into its faith – as Archbishop Latour moves west, the souls he nourishes look east to the Roman church for salvation. In its plot development, the novel parallels the expansion of the nineteenth-century American empire with the spread of Christianity in pre-medieval Europe. The implied narrative correspondence in both novels suggests that the strength of empire depends on its people's possessing an idea that they can carry with them. The essential benevolence of this empire, or the potential evil within it, was beside the great fact of its presence; it was, simply, a force to reckon with in art. In Cather's vision empire requires motion, expansion, and restlessness; the American empire depends on a population convinced that it holds something transportable and, when as individuals they travel, they will take the idea with them as they move around the nation and the world, immune to local or native forces that may challenge their idea of themselves and their value. *One of Ours* focuses on an individual American man and demonstrates how the logic of empire – or its ideology – informs private decisions and makes sense of private dilemmas. What distinguishes Cather in these novels is that she takes empire as a political fact and depicts life within the context created by that historical contingency. The scope of her literary vision, while often grounded in very specific places, is consistently global in its projection of a spatialized and dynamic conception of history.

The cultural logic of imperialism suggested by Willa Cather implicates every American gesture towards individual distinction as contributing to American empire. Every act of immigration, every continental migration (east and west, north and south), each man and woman's attempt to succeed by endorsement, critique, or attack on the social order or its ideology, is in and of itself an advance of the national culture as a whole towards an imperial position. Thea Kronborg, for example, is thinking not only of the purity of art as she advances her career. She is not committing herself solely to beauty or to voice or even to song. Her ambitions are clearly animated by such aesthetic devotions, but Cather explains that it is much more than this that motivates Thea Kronborg. Thea is rising from nowhere, from the comically named, lowbrow midwestern town of Moonstone, a few generations away from the frontier, from a preacher's family that, in Cather's treatment, is a prototype for Sinclair Lewis's more baldly satirical depictions of the Midwest. But Thea draws strength from the old faces of withered and wasted immigrant men and women at her father's church, faces that are "mysteriously marked by destiny" (p. 115), and which she will carry with her as ideas in her rise to prominence. In the same way that Alexandra Bergson, in *O Pioneers!*, was the first to look on the Great Divide and see agricultural wealth, Thea's is the first face to look on those "who have worked hard and who have always been poor" (p. 113) and see cultural wealth, her own potential for greatness, and the seeds of empire.

The final section of *The Song of the Lark* is titled "Kronborg," suggesting that Thea has become an icon, a great fact. She speaks, in her final textual appearance, with unchallenged authority. She has dwarfed her mentor, Howard Archie, she has withstood with unparalleled dignity the affair with Fred Ottenberg, and she has survived a near marriage to Nordquist. As an artist and as the textual personification of empire she is untouchable. She has become her own reason for being, and by each word uttered and with every gesture committed she articulates and defines what greatness is. Thea decides as well what she will remember and what she will discard, recalling only what contributes to her ascendancy, forgetting the things that may drag her down. At one point, earlier in the novel, she induces fear in Fred Ottenberg by the "elevation" in her eyes, a look described by Cather as one that "had no memories" but was purely "unconscious" (p. 314). As a woman of tremendous power and effect, Thea, as depicted in the novel's epilogue, has returned to Moonstone as an abstraction – she has become an icon in Moonstone, bringing comforting, compensatory memories to the old, and to the young dreams. The product of imperial forces, Thea brought the idea of the West through her tremendous voice east, emerged as a great force, and returned west as an idea to inspire others. In Thea's story is invested considerable value, and on her example is built a social system that implicitly rewards mobility, provisionality, and mutability. Traditional homage to home, fidelity, and stability are voiced as compensation for losses, but these notions hold little value to the ambitious. The successful ones at all levels, from simply "staying afloat" to world domination, move away from these values as easily as they migrate away from their sources – origins, families, and "permanent" residences.

Thea's angst at the end of the novel is real enough, but it is not the stuff of melancholy or regret. The fulfillment that her performances bring to others is "the only commensurate answer" to the question of her purpose or value. Outside of that function, she may indeed wonder about "the good of it all" (p. 399). At the novel's close she serves on the stage the same idea that had motivated her and those who produced her in the past, the idea that "closed roads" are to be opened and "all the gates dropped" (p. 398) that stand between stasis and movement. *The Song of the Lark* may be read as the story of female empowerment and voice, but only narrowly. In the context of the Cather thesis, the success story of individual eastern-moving female ambition becomes an imperial gesture, a definition of how and why out of this country and at this time greatness emerged, and the attention of the world is focused on an American voice.

In a novel at once very similar (in terms of its style and aspects of its form) and, in content, wholly distinct from *The Song of the Lark*, *One of Ours* traces the historical logic that follows when the destination country of the immigrant becomes an economic and military world power. The novel's context is the tremendous productivity of the United States: wheat-fields that feed the world, industries that power machines for domestic consumption and international export, and the main focus, a culture that produces eager, devoted soldiers willing to die for all that it produces, maintains, and symbolizes. The novel is a very political book for its concentration on the American turn, in 1917, towards active, global militarism. The wheat-fields over which Jim Burden rhapsodizes in *My Ántonia* are depicted now as having produced a world power; the "feeling of empire" at the core of Thea Kronborg's ambition in *The Song of the Lark* transfixes the nation; thousands of Thea-like women and men restlessly conceive the world as their personal theater of operations – the globe, in short, has become an American possession in *One of Ours*.

Claude Wheeler moves east to fulfill his destiny in an average sort of way. He is a Thea Kronborg mass-produced in wholesale quantities. He possesses none of her individual talent or genius but all of her dissatisfaction with the midwestern, provincial status quo. He feels that he deserves something more than his middlebrow, farmer-class origins can deliver. He is a small man with big plans, a limited, conventional mind with delusions of greatness. He is also, however, in command of tremendous resources. He has a very wealthy national benefactor known affectionately as his Uncle Sam, who finds him "worth the watchfulness and devotion of so many men and machines, this extravagant consumption of fuel and energy."[4] Multiply Claude Wheeler by hundreds of thousands and extend his mind to the national culture as a whole, and what emerges is a clearly articulated sense of Cather's frontier thesis: moving east from the frontier, the birth of empire, the spread of US ideals on an international scale, packaged and delivered like canned goods across oceans and continents.

One of Ours situates itself on a liminal moment in American history and on a central dilemma in its culture. The moment is when the nation made its turn away from hemispheric isolation towards involvement in a major European war, thus introducing the term "world war" into the international vocabulary. Historically the process extended from the era before the Great War until the eve of World War II, continually refining and expanding the application of American interests abroad. Nevertheless, the terms of the transition are laid out clearly in the novel. These terms involve the unsolved "question of property" (p. 68) and the closing of the American frontier (p. 100), as Claude realizes. Also involved in the transition is the adaptation in the United States to the conditions of "the great argument" of German expansion: "preparation, organization, inexhaustible resources, inexhaustible men." What Cather centers on is not simply a historical moment but also a recurring dilemma in American culture. What is the global role of the nation of immigrants? Is the United States a safe refuge from the world or the next stage in world development? From the former come the American isolationists; from the latter emerges the American mission. In isolation one may cultivate the arts of music and agriculture as ends in themselves, but a nation with a mission knows music as something to march to and knows its farms as the wheatfields and cornfields that feed the world. The Cather thesis, extended to the global stage, is not so much concerned with the question whether the United States is exempt from historical forces or representative of the course of future development. In either case, having produced a migratory consciousness out of its own frontier development, the nation is not constrained by past examples of imperial excesses or failures. As depicted in the scenes of Claude in France, American soldiers march confidently over the ruins of a succession of historical empires.

To anyone raised on American wars, with no conception of a United States without a mobilized army, navy, air force, marine corps, CIA, or NASA, *One of Ours* can hardly be read without some sense of bewilderment. The novel's conclusions are not surprising. From our present vantage point, the entire history of the nation, from Indian-hating Puritans to the war on terror of the twenty-first century, has been a relentless expression of firepower. The historians who have written the story of America in this way were born in the middle of the last century, after global conflict had become a thoroughly naturalized structuring metaphor of American existence – the world's peacekeeper, mediator, and police force. However, Cather's novel reminds us that what appears to be a fact of existence in the present era came about as a result of historical choices, and the particular construction of the American national state. In other words, the national history as we know it today has been written by the heirs of Claude Wheeler, by historians who have written under the sound of the guns. Millions of Americans have since shared the sentiment of Claude's orphan friend, Albert Usher, that "the U.S. Marines are my family. Wherever they are, I'm at home" (p. 229). In the context of *One of Ours*, the American military is among the culture's most profound ideas. It is often at the forefront of social change, as seen later in the twentieth century, in the Civil Rights era. Its weapons research has poured into the marketplaces a steady flow of consumer goods and services, including internet technologies, microwave ovens, and mobile phones. Historically, it is difficult to find a great change in the United States that did not either result from or coincide with war-making of some sort: national independence, frontier settlement, the emancipation of slaves, women's suffrage, racial justice, civil rights.

Cather's novel projects a culture that is moving towards a conception of war as the ultimate articulation of national purpose, a conception as strong as any spiritual orthodoxy. This conclusion (which will be extended further in *Death Comes for the Archbishop*) is reached on numerous levels – economic, religious, social – that converge in the fate and figure of Claude Wheeler. To Claude, enlistment appears like a vision: it is a natural, salvational gesture on his part. After the war the efforts of soldiers were granted mythic significance by post-war initiatives that continued throughout the twentieth century with no signs of weakening. Yellow ribbons, heroes' welcomes, – such are the common aftermath of military service. The sacredness of war participation has become an indispensable component of American culture, embodied in public monuments, holidays, and civic rituals of remembrance and re-creation. In many ways, Cather's novel is concerned with the origins of this phenomenon as a national movement, and as the logical result of the frontier experience.

One of Ours turns directly to the production of American soldiers in the service of empire. Metaphors of harvest abound in the novel, suggesting that raising an army is an organic product of the culture as a whole. The section of the novel entitled "The Voyage of the Anchises" is a meditation on the movement of American minds from one way of thinking to another, from a variety of former occupations to soldiers. The ones who cannot make the transfer do not survive the passage. Cather employs the metaphor of illness, or fever, a common usage of her time for what happens to the world when it goes to war. The metaphor serves another purpose, which is to cast the transformation of the idea of the United States from refuge to empire in naturalistic terms. Throughout the novel the dominant sense is that this metamorphosis is a kind of fulfillment, a harvesting, a logical culmination of the social order and an answer to the dilemma it had produced for itself. Claude articulates the national mission: "I've left everything behind me. I am going over" (p. 251). The descendant of pioneer settlers who left everything behind to go west, Claude, exemplar of the Cather thesis, heads east now, in full possession of a mission to conquer the world, or, in his case, to die in its accomplishment.

Cather's novel is thus a classic study of war culture from the citizen's perspective. College students who accept army reserve commitments in return for college tuition; criminal adolescents given the choice of prison or army enlistment; women and minorities expecting equal (and therefore relatively preferable) treatment under the auspices of the military code; the use of American soldiers in providing natural disaster relief, quelling urban rioting, or feeding starving people around the world – in each of these examples, the American military expands to encompass the culture. None of these examples represents an evil; on the contrary, each of them illustrates a version of the good. It was also good that Claude found service in the army, for otherwise he might have spent his life alone in his honeymoon house waiting for Enid to return, living a long life as a local oddity rather than a short one as a national hero. Nevertheless, what attracts Cather's attention is not the military per se but the conditions that have evolved to authenticate the military alternative as redemptive, and as the deepest and most profound expression of American ideals.

More than soldiers crossed the ocean in 1917; the very idea of America undertook a reverse migration. The immigrant nation returned east from its incubation in the West, where the same ethnic groups at war in Europe were working towards a relatively peaceful and benign domestic American "melting pot." The concept of ideas in transit, the mechanics involved in the projection and migration of an idea across an ocean and a continent, and the relationship between consciousness and materiality are central concerns of Cather's greatest novel of empire, *Death Comes for the Archbishop*. With her missionaries, Cather writes of intellectual colonists: Latour and Vaillant wish to plant ideas and colonize the minds of the Mexicans, the Americans, and (to a lesser extent) the indigenous peoples. The troopships in *One of Ours* embodied the idea of the United States evolving from nation to empire, returning to Europe as the force that would shape the destiny of the world throughout the twentieth century. In the same way, the thousands of immigrants who have come to the United States have embodied the idea that no particular place is necessarily or inevitably home to any human being and that as a species, human beings are movable and take well to being transplanted. The idea of movement is the idea of America as represented by the eagle, the bird of prey that will make its home on any rock high enough to provide a clear view. The eagle settles on the rock only to await its next move. An empire of migratory values, of transactions of power and focus, and of the adaptation of old ideas to contemporary necessity is of major concern to Cather's novel about an itinerant French bishop sent to the Spanish

American Southwest by French and Italian cardinals to spread the faith of Rome in the New World.

Death Comes for the Archbishop opens in 1848, a pivotal year in the territorial expansion of the United States, and concludes near the end of the century, at the close of the frontier. But Cather is not concerned with the usual take of homesteads, forts, Indian wars, and gold rushes – although these material phenomena all figure in the background to the novel's events. Rather, *Death Comes for the Archbishop* centers on the business of transmission, the ways in which intellectual capital – ideas, spirituality, modes of thought – is carried from one place to another. Latour teaches his people, used to living in an isolated region, or as settlers in new territories, to face their minds and their souls east, back to the center of Catholicism and to the authority of Rome. It is out of the movement of ideas, from the structures that allow and foster intellectual and spiritual migration, that empire emerges. Throughout his career in the Southwest, Latour has moved from one place to another representing his faith. He is far from his origins in Auvergne, France, and far from his first position as parish priest on Lake Ontario. His career, as much as his preaching, is testimony to the idea that it does not matter where he lives; he is a missionary, he makes his home where he happens to be. His mobility, his missionary journeys and the simple fact that his faith is transplantable, contributes to the destruction of the indigenous cultures of America as much if not more than the Word he carries of Roman Catholicism.

In terms of the Cather thesis, one recognizes that America is settled by minds in which stability is an abstraction, in which national origins, religious faith, and ethnic identities are traded over time. A tremendous migration of human beings occurred in the nineteenth century, from east to west, from the Old World to the New. These human beings, emigrating from particular places in the eastern hemisphere, came to a new place that did not know their history and were inhabited by sparse populations without the means to hold this great migration at bay. The one common denominator to all emigrant groups was the fact of migration itself. Mobility has passed into the culture of the United States as a great fact of its national existence, a cornerstone to its ideology. As movement becomes a quality of mind, all ideas and belief systems are leveled by the common experience of crossing, of having let go of some prior idea and moved to embrace another. As a French Catholic missionary in the Spanish American frontier, Latour embodies the principle of transitory ideas and mutable belief.

The faith that emerged from the experience of the American frontier, according to the Cather thesis, held that within the very quality of movement there exists an inherent progression of the human condition. "We're over," as the soldiers say in *One of Ours*, we have come here, and because we have crossed over, we achieve authenticity. The idea of America is accomplished through migration from one place to another, intellectually, physically, spiritually; Archbishop Latour is its patron saint. When Thea Kronborg thinks of herself in her relation to others, she imagines that "each of them concealed another person in himself, just as she did," and that everyone had "to guard them fiercely." The sense of spatialized multiplicity, allowing transactions among various potential selves, characterizes a culture of movement and migration. Thea considers her life progress "as if she had an appointment to meet the rest of herself sometime, somewhere. It was moving to meet her and she was moving to meet it" (p. 189). At the end of his life Archbishop Latour, "soon to have done with the calendared time," is described as being situated, spatially, "in the middle of his own consciousness; none of his former states of mind were lost or outgrown."[5] Even Claude Wheeler, before dying, articulates a sense of "beginning over again," possessing another life as a soldier in the Grand Army of the Republic (p. 322). The Cather thesis encapsulates one of the great paradoxes of American history, that out of the nation's great effort to settle the West emerged the idea that settlement itself was antithetical to human experience. While millions of human beings moved west to settle, it was the incessantly migratory American who brought the news that the West had been won. Moving east, back along the furrows of the wagon-ruts, is this new concept of rootedness, not in place, but in the experience, memory, or legacy of having traveled far and having grown up with the country.

NOTES

1. George Rogers Taylor, ed. *The Turner Thesis: Concerning the Role of the Frontier in American History*, third edition (Lexington, MA: D. C. Heath and Co., 1972), p. 3. Future references will be made parenthetically.
2. Willa Cather, *My Ántonia* (1918; Boston: Houghton Mifflin, 1988), p. xi. Future references will be made parenthetically.
3. Willa Cather, *The Song of the Lark* (1915; New York: Penguin, 1991), p. 40. Future references will be made parenthetically.
4. Willa Cather, *One of Ours* (1922; New York: Vintage Classics, 1991), p. 230. Future references will be made parenthetically.
5. Willa Cather, *Death Comes for the Archbishop* (1927; New York: Vintage Classics, 1991), p. 288.

3

RICHARD H. MILLINGTON

Willa Cather's American modernism

In the "Hired Girls" section of *My Ántonia*, just after her move to town, Ántonia tells the following story of country life. It is threshing time, and a tramp emerges from the intense heat, thirsty and looking for beer. Trading places with one of the men, he gets on the threshing machine, and begins to work: "He cut bands all right for a few minutes, and then, Mrs. Harling, he waved his hand to me and jumped head-first right into the threshing machine after the wheat. I begun to scream, and the men run to stop the horses, but the belt had sucked him down, and by the time they got her stopped, he was all beat and cut to pieces. He was wedged in so tight it was a hard job to get him out, and the machine ain't never worked right since." In the dead tramp's pocket they find an old penknife, "the wish-bone of a chicken wrapped up in a piece of paper, and some poetry" – "The Old Oaken Bucket," cut out of a newspaper.[1] One glimpses in this arresting moment some of the distinctive interests and attitudes of Cather's fiction: its emphasis on the *making* of meaning, on the gestures, like the tramp's wave, that produce significance in a world cut loose from overmastering explanatory narratives; its careful attention to ordinary life and work as the field in which such meanings emerge; its tolerance for the inconclusive, suggested by the resonant inconsequence of the contents of the tramp's pockets.

Had the literary history of twentieth-century America unfolded somewhat differently, Ántonia's story of the tramp in the machine might have come down to us, along with, say, the description of the "valley of ashes" that swirls under the gaze of Dr. T. J. Ecklesberg in *The Great Gatsby*, as one of the classic moments of American modernist fiction. In attempting to think about Cather as a modernist, to describe and define the elements of her work that fit that elusive label, I shall in part be supplying a piece of an underwritten literary history: one will look in vain for Cather's name in the index of most accounts, whether new or old, of the nature and history of Anglo-American modernism.[2] Still, for its own sake the question whether or not Cather was *really* a modernist scarcely matters: while the academy has

51

RICHARD H. MILLINGTON

been inordinately slow in recognizing Cather as an indispensable twentieth-century writer, that recognition has now been achieved. Yet defining the terms of that recognition, describing her work and its value, remains an alluringly incomplete enterprise. Asking the question implied by the term "modernism" – "What is the specific relation between a writer's artistic practice and her historical moment?" – will be worthwhile if it enables us to see and to describe her fiction in a new and revealing way.

When scholars have written about Cather's modernism, they have tended to follow one of two routes. Some, such as Phyllis Rose in her remarkable essay "The Case of Willa Cather," have emphasized the formal qualities of her fiction: its affinities with the aesthetic ideals of particular modern artists ("the literary equivalent of an Arp, a Brancusi, a Moore"); its "abstract" conception of character; its unobtrusive but bold recasting of narrative elements.[3] These writers will think of modernism as an aesthetic category, definable mainly by the artist's deployment of his or her medium. Scholars following the second route, which emerges powerfully in recent "historicist" criticism, are interested less in the formal qualities of Cather's fiction than in the relation between the *content* of that fiction and the *context* of her society and culture, and they valuably work to specify the nature of her engagement with the definitive experiences and ideological movements of twentieth-century life – migration and immigration, nostalgia, Progressivism, the emergence of a fully fledged culture of consumption, and so on. Their work thus tends to emphasize the historical resonance of a theme or episode, or what is representative about a particular character's behavior.[4] What I want to propose – and practice – here is, simply, a combination of these approaches. How, we might ask, does Cather *write* her engagement with her era? How does her relation to her times find expression in the artistic practices and aesthetic commitments of her fiction?

Let us begin with history. If we are to understand in any deep way Cather's encounter with American life in the first several decades of the twentieth century, we need a clear description of the kind of cultural transformations under way in the United States as she did her work. In "Towards a Definition of American Modernism," the cultural historian Daniel Joseph Singal valuably suggests that, in defining "modernism," we think of it neither as a set of historical data – distinctively "modern" events and technologies, say – nor as a collection of compositional techniques or ideas about art, but as a "full fledged historical culture" – that is, "a constellation of related ideas, beliefs, values, and modes of perception."[5] If we do the kind of thinking that Singal recommends, we see that "modernism" must be defined over against "American Victorianism," its precursor culture, the dominant value system

52

in America from the 1830s to the early twentieth century. Here, at some length, is Singal's lucid description of that Victorian culture.

> At the core of this . . . culture stood a distinctive set of bedrock assumptions. These included a belief in a predictable universe presided over by a benevolent God and governed by immutable natural laws, a corresponding conviction that humankind was capable of arriving at a unified and fixed set of truths about all aspects of life, and an insistence on preserving absolute standards based on a radical dichotomy between that which was deemed "human" and that regarded as "animal." It was this moral dichotomy above all that constituted the deepest guiding principle of the Victorian outlook. On the "human" or "civilized" side of the dividing line fell everything that served to lift man above the beasts – education, refinement, manners, the arts, religion, and such domesticated emotions as loyalty and family love. The "animal" or "savage" realm, by contrast, contained those instincts and passions that constantly threatened self-control, and which therefore had to be repressed at all cost.   (p. 9)

In Singal's view, then, American Victorian culture built its sense of stability and morality upon a set of clear, simplifying oppositions. As he also points out, this dichotomizing habit of mind applied to people as well as values: "Victorians characterized societies as either civilized or savage, drew a firm line between what they considered superior and inferior classes . . . divided races unambiguously into black and white" and placed the sexes in "separate spheres" based upon a now familiar set of supposedly "natural" characteristics (pp. 9–10).

Modernist culture, Singal proposes – from popular culture, to science, to art – was defined by the way it contested these characteristic dichotomies, joining together what had seemed opposed or boldly recasting value-laden Victorian concepts. Thus in intellectual life the new physics dismantled the certainties of Newtonian order, and Boasian anthropology deconstructed the boundary between civilized and savage, while in popular culture, new dances such as the shimmy, borrowed by middle-class whites from African American culture, let the body speak in a stunning way. For Singal, American modernism emerges, via its criticism of Victorianism, as its own "world view":

> It begins with the premise of an unpredictable universe where nothing is ever stable, and where accordingly human beings must be satisfied with knowledge that is partial and transient at best. Nor is it possible in this situation to devise a fixed and absolute system of morality; moral values must remain in flux, adapting continuously to changing historical circumstances. To create those values and garner whatever knowledge is available, individuals must repeatedly subject themselves – both directly and vicariously through art – to the trials

of experience. . . . In its ideal form at least, Modernism – in stark contrast to Victorianism – eschews innocence and demands instead to know 'reality' in all its depth and complexity, no matter how incomplete and paradoxical that knowledge might be, and no matter how painful.   (pp. 15–16)

If Singal's account gives us a sense of the way modernism might be understood historically, as a view of experience shaped by its modes of opposition to the culture that precedes it, what about our second question: "How might the behavior of Cather's art relate to the contest of values we have been describing?" To Singal's description of the contest of cultures we might propose the following addition: this Victorian sense of the world is implemented and sustained by narratives, by the stories about life that put its interpretations of experience into force and proclaim their explanatory power. American Victorian culture was a profoundly and characteristically *allegorical* culture, committed to grand narratives that reached both out into the social and political world and inward into the self: outward-turning storylines such as "the march of progress," the benevolent triumph of the civilized, the noble mission of educating the savage; and inward-turning storylines such as the narratives of maturation, disciplined self-recognition, interior enlightenment via difficult experience – which we recognize as the plotlines most dear to the Victorian novel.

For a writer such as Cather, whose medium *is* narrative, modernism will especially take the form of challenging or recasting the big narratives that produce and sustain the Victorian sense of the meaningful. Or, to put this another way: artists are likely to experience or express a combat between eras or, in Singal's terms, historical "cultures," as a combat between artistic forms. The energizing target of Cather's fiction is not just the Victorian culture so richly evoked in Singal's essay, not just the orthodox life narratives I have described above, but the deep ideological assumptions and formal procedures of the nineteenth-century novel, the literary form that has preeminently deployed, evoked, and tested those Victorian values.

Let us return, by way of an initial example, to the moment from *My Ántonia* that began this essay. How might Ántonia's story of the tramp, in its form as well as its content, contest the narrative culture of American Victorianism? I have already mentioned some of the features that seem to put this story in accord with our working description of modernism. First, the jaunty wave the tramp delivers as he jumps into the machinery (we might think of this scene as the darker precursor of another classic modernist episode, the tramp's descent into the machine in Chaplin's *Modern Times*) is meaning made on the spot: we are aware, as an aspect of the odd beauty of this moment, of the free-standing, unsponsored quality of the tramp's gesture.

This is a form of meaning that neither depends upon some overarching moral allegory nor issues forth in principles that might guide one towards wisdom or goodness. Our attention is drawn, rather, to the act of meaning-making itself, to the production of the momentary but complete gesture in which the value and beauty of this act inhere.[6] Perhaps most telling of all, though, is the relation between this independent act of storytelling and its narrative surroundings. Ántonia's story of the tramp is told after her arrival in the town of Black Hawk, a place that Cather renders as governed by a kind of compendium of the played-out narratives of a prudential and self-denying Victorian culture. Here is Jim Burden's description of town life:

> The life that went on in [the houses of Black Hawk] seemed to me made up of evasions and negations; shifts to save cooking, to save washing and cleaning, devices to propitiate the tongue of gossip. This guarded mode of existence was like living under a tyranny. People's speech, their voices, their very glances, became furtive and repressed. Every individual taste, every natural appetite, was bridled by caution . . . The growing piles of ashes and cinders in the back yards were the only evidence that the wasteful, consuming process of life went on at all.   (p. 164)

Like the other autonomous stories that disrupt the flow of My Ántonia's maturation plot, the story of the tramp renders as narrative an alternative to the prudential allegories that give their tedious shape to Black Hawk life. The story of the tramp in the threshing machine is there not to be moralized upon or applied as a life lesson; it is there to be witnessed, a modernist exemplification of meaning's creation rather than a Victorian espousal of a moral truth. And in so presenting itself to us, it opens up for us as readers the new possibilities of awareness and feeling that might make us modernists too.

As our brief discussion of the tramp story suggests, one route to the understanding of the distinctive nature of Cather's modernism would be to begin with "form," with the ways her fiction behaves, and go on to ask how its deployment of the elements of narrative resonates historically – how her remaking of the novel opens up the new possibilities of thought and feeling that constitute its modernism. Accordingly, I want to look at three formal aspects of Cather's fiction – its choice of subjects, its way of attending to character, and the nature of its plots – asking in each case about the historical force of its recasting of the novelistic tradition.

Subjects

While Cather may always be fixed in our minds as a Nebraska writer, the subject-matter of her fiction is, in fact, astonishingly various: the prairie country and polyglot culture of Nebraska, yes, but also the American South-west (both prehistoric and contemporary), colonial Quebec, antebellum Virginia, and the suburban Chicago of the 1920s. Is there a logic, a form of interest, that links together the disparate materials of Cather's fiction, that determines who and what qualifies as an object of her novelistic attention? I think there is, but we shall need to turn back to early twentieth-century intellectual history to see what it might be.

In the first three decades of the twentieth century, as Cather's career as a novelist was itself unfolding, a group of related ideas that came to be called "cultural relativism" emerged in the work of the anthropologist Franz Boas and his students at Columbia University and became widely influential among American intellectuals. There are two crucial conceptual elements to this new science of anthropology, both of which have striking affinities to the way Cather's fiction comes to define its sense of the interesting. First, the concept of "culture" is broken free from its static and honorific association with the refined arts that signify genteel cultural authority. Rather than representing what "civilized" European nations have and "primitive" people lack, "culture" refers, more descriptively and objectively, to the interconnected and particular ways distinct communities construct meanings for the individual lives that unfold within them. "Culture," this is to say, becomes an object of study and interest rather than a marker of hierarchical distinctions, and this redefinition of the term equips one to realize that modern American lives, no less than supposedly "primitive" ones, are deeply shaped by distinctive customs. Along with this sense that different cultures – the plural is crucial – comprise distinctive meaning-systems comes a revolutionary claim of their equivalence in value. Thus in *The Mind of Primitive Man* (1911) Boas demonstrates the capacity of putatively savage people to think abstractly, to discriminate aesthetically, and to inhibit impulse, while featuring the irrational customs, prejudices, rituals, and taboos characteristic of genteel Europeans and Americans. Some of Boas's students, especially, used cultural comparisons to overturn customary Victorian hierarchies altogether, arguing that "primitive" cultures made possible much more satisfying and creative individual lives than did American industrial society, as in Edward Sapir's *Dial* essay (1919) on "genuine" and "spurious" cultures, with its contrasting figures of the "telephone girl" and the American Indian spear fisherman and its analysis of the spiritual hunger characteristic of twentieth-century consumer culture. The works of Boas and his disciples, then, identified "culture" as the central arena of human meaning-making, suggesting new kinds of interest in daily life, more capacious notions of imaginativeness and creativity, more pointed criticisms of orthodox American culture.[7]

My suggestion here is not that Cather was a committed Boasian, but that her work is animated by the kind of perspectives the new anthropology made available. Still, there is every reason to believe that anyone as actively engaged in New York intellectual life as Cather was during the early decades of this century would have encountered the ideas I have been describing. A number of Boas's students made the new anthropological perspective, with its witty lampooning of customary cultural hierarchies, available in widely read magazines or in strikingly popular "crossover" books, such as Margaret Mead's *Coming of Age in Samoa* (1928). Moreover, Cather's experience of growing up in Nebraska, with its striking mix of ethnic communities, might be said to have furnished a rich field for the kind of pointed comparisons that delighted Boas's students. She might have been alerted to the force of Boas's work when, during her editorship, *McClure's* published an extensive account of his studies of immigrant skull sizes, an important early attack on theories of racial determinism. Perhaps an informal interest in the imaginative life of distinctive communities was heightened or made self-conscious by following her friend Louise Pound's work on Nebraska folklore and folk music. One certainly sees this affinity in Cather's extraordinary essay on Nebraska for *The Nation* in 1923, where she contrasts the "cosmopolitanism" of the immigrant prairie towns with the "pale proprieties, the insincere, conventional optimism of our [American] art and thought" and laments, in a manner reminiscent of Sapir's criticism of modern American life, the substitution of a denatured, national culture of buying for a distinctive and local culture of making.[8]

What did this anthropological sense of culture – whether derived from the intellectual atmosphere around her, or generated by her own experience, or both – give to Cather's fiction? In several senses, it gave Cather her subject: her sense of who or what might qualify as a plausible object of fictional attention, and the set of characteristic attitudes she brought to the treatment of that material. First, and foundationally, the democratization of cultural value implicit in cultural relativism – the sense that there is no central culture, towering above all others, but that all human communities are alike engaged in making meaningful lives for their inhabitants – underwrites the realization Cather describes in "My First Novels [There Were Two]" that, rather than attempting to reproduce a novel of manners in the tradition of James or Wharton (as she had in *Alexander's Bridge*), she might write about the places and people that mattered to her, as she did in *O Pioneers!* – however "déclassé" Nebraska had seemed as a literary setting.[9] As Cather tells the story of her early career, she becomes herself as a writer at the moment when she gives up her ambition to inherit the tradition of the nineteenth-century novel from its most powerful early twentieth-century practitioners, and turns definitively towards a class of materials that would have been invisible to the novelistic tradition that James and Wharton represent.

But if this anthropological idea of culture, however she came to possess it, freed Cather to recast her sense of who and what belongs in the novel, it also identified for her what would become, in a different sense, the central subject-matter of her fiction: the making of meaning itself. As *My Ántonia*'s tramp story has already begun to show us, Cather found her own way as a writer by finding the making of meaning *in itself* a fully adequate and continually absorbing subject for novelistic attention. An explicit acknowledgment of her commitment to this sense of the writer's subject comes in a letter to Wilbur Cross, thanking him for a sensitive review of *Shadows on the Rock*. Here is her account of that novel's subject: "An orderly little French household that went on trying to live decently, just as ants begin to rebuild when you kick their house down, interests me more than Indian raids or the wild life in the forests . . . And really, a new society begins with the salad dressing more than with the destruction of Indian villages. Those people brought a kind of French culture there and somehow kept it alive on that rock."[10] Cather is adopting here an anthropological view of meaning, in which objects are indeed symbolic of cultural values (the "salad dressing"), but not by symbolizing something other than themselves, and, as she does so, she notes her fiction's lack of interest in the kinds of big events ("Indian raids") that would usually furnish the materials of such settlement narratives. While this is an arresting statement of her principle of selection, the kind of "anthropological" interest referred to is to be found everywhere in Cather's fiction: in the culture of storytelling and storytellers in *My Ántonia*; in *Shadows on the Rock*, of course, a book given over to the sustained observation of a year's work of culture-making; in the recurrent visits paid by her texts to the ancestral puebloan ruins of the American Southwest; in her treatment of the material culture of daily domestic work itself, as in "Old Mrs. Harris"; even in the very careful attention paid to the operation of consumer culture in *The Professor's House*.

This sense that the construction of meaning per se might newly define the object of the novelist's attention, moreover, seems to account for still another aspect of Cather's sense of her subject, her fondness for building cultural comparisons into the fabric or structure of her novels. Such comparisons – whether on a "local" scale such as the visit to the Catholic Fair in *O Pioneers!*, or when they become a structural feature of the novel, as when "Tom Outland's Story" of the discovery of the ruins at Mesa Verde intersects, in its complex way, with the consumeristic domesticity of *The Professor's House* – necessarily put before us the different kinds of meaning different communities make possible for their members. In the light of this definitively modernist interest in cultures rather than Culture, what has often been regarded as "nostalgia" or "escapism" in Cather's work – her tendency, later in her career, to write about distinctively located historical cultures such as the Quebec of *Shadows on the Rock* or the New Mexico of *Death Comes for the Archbishop* at their moment of establishment – is better understood as an "anthropological" interest in the ways people have constructed meaning in particular places at particular times.

Throughout her work, then, Cather has accomplished a significant reconception of the subject of the novel, and that reconception has necessarily freed the novelist and her reader to find forms of meaning unconfined by the customary trajectories of novelistic interest. When the making of meanings and the work of local cultures become the subject of fiction, a new kind of responsiveness – a reader's modernism, if you will – becomes possible: a more open definition of the interesting emerges, and new forms of attention and feeling identify themselves and begin to hold sway.

Characters

Cather's treatment of her characters – our second constitutive element of novelistic form – is no less revisionary than her choice of subjects. In thinking about the ways Cather's conception of character might exemplify a modernist recasting of the interests and categories of Victorian fiction, we shall focus on two questions. First, who gets admitted to the world of Cather's fiction? And second, how are those personages treated by the texts in which they appear? What is it about them that is thought worthy of interest, attention, and observation?

Scholarly definers of literary modernism have noticed as definitive textual features both the prominence of art and artists and what Michael Bell has described as "the elision of the category of the aesthetic into a life term."[11] The making of meaning – art's central activity – and the maker of meaning – the artist – get taken by many modernist writers as "central" or representative figures of the human. In the absence of compelling or convincing systems of belief that might bequeath a sense of meaning to us, we are – or we mean – because we make. Cather exemplifies this pattern, but with a difference. She does indeed write explicitly about artists or conventional culture-makers in her stories, in *The Song of the Lark*, and in *The Professor's House*, but more characteristic, more interesting, more generative is her interest in "local," vernacular makers of meaning: in the many storytellers of *My Ántonia*, the anonymous makers of the cliff city at Mesa Verde, the constructors and preservers of French culture in *Shadows on the Rock*. Indeed, a roster of "central" men and women in Cather's fiction would need to include figures such as Otto Fuchs of *My Ántonia* – not only a storyteller but a character, his scarred face inscribed by his own life narrative, who seems an incarnation of the meaning-maker's artisanal work – and Old Mrs. Harris, whose unobtrusive daily life, as the long story Cather names after her unfolds, accrues a kind of beauty that is the modernist equivalent of holiness. Like the array of interests that generate the subject-matter of her fiction, Cather's sense of character seems to have been inflected by the values articulated in Boasian anthropology, with its redistribution of the prestige of the artist to the ordinary person, engaged in the task of making daily meaning.

No less striking than this democratization of the figure of the artist is Cather's interest in characters placed at foundational or transitional moments in a society's history – figures such as Archbishop Latour, who claims New Mexico for imperial Catholicism, or Pierre Charron in *Shadows on the Rock*, who seems to embody the emergence, in French Canada, of a Canadian, rather than a French, identity. These are figures who represent culture-making writ large and seen as a historical process. Though Cather was a fierce critic of an emerging American consumer culture, this interest in founding moments may explain her notable friendliness towards the early, "creative" phases of capitalist development, evident in her treatment of the railroad magnate Captain Forrester in *A Lost Lady* or the admiration expressed for Jim Burden's encouragement of western entrepreneurs in *My Ántonia*. But Cather is just as interested in the characters who are the revealing casualties of these moments when societal meanings shift – Marian Forrester and Niel Herbert of *A Lost Lady*, Henry Colbert in *Sapphira and the Slave Girl*, Godfrey St. Peter in *The Professor's House*.

Who, then, can get into a Cather novel? Just as the subject-matter of Cather's fiction is held together by an interest in culture, as modern anthropology was coming to redefine that term, so for Cather characters seem interesting in so far as they are themselves culture- or meaning-*makers*, or as they represent strategies of meaning-making, or crises in or transformations of the possibilities or conditions of meaning at a particular moment in history. And how do those novels instruct us to be interested in the lives they present us? While Cather's characters do have psychologies and inner lives, for the most part our interest in them is neither psychological (What explains their actions?) nor ethical (How should we judge their actions?) but observational: not what but *how* do their lives mean?

Plots

If we are correct in our account of the kind of interest that shapes Cather's invention of her characters, we still need to ask how these characters are treated in the fictions they inhabit. Here, in thinking about the revisionary relation to the novelistic tradition that defines Cather's modernism, we need to bring together two kinds of questions. First, what is distinctive about Cather's deployment of plot? What constitutes a significant event in her fiction? What arguments about experience are implied by their trajectories? And second, what happens to Cather's characters as they encounter the plot-lines that shape her narratives?

In these interconnected realms of character and plot, Cather's fiction is remarkable for its resistance to the related ideas of "depth" and "development," definitive elements of the conception of experience native to Victorian novels. For most of the characters in Cather's fiction, the questions that go with a "depth" or "developmental" model of character – What is a character's deeper or self-obscured motivation? How has a character matured or moved towards self-understanding or self-recognition? – seem irrelevant at best and fatuous at worst. What could be more fruitless than to psycho-analyze Ántonia or Old Mrs. Harris, or to posit elaborate schemes of self-recognition or transformation on behalf of any of the characters in *Shadows on the Rock*? Rather, during the course of a narrative, Cather's characters are likely to make evident or transparent their natures, or to come to express or see their lives in a definitive or characteristic way.

Cather's deployment of plot in most of her novels is no less reticent, no less oblique and surprising in its relation to novelistic custom. The key moments or events in a Cather text are more likely to be acts of heightened or illuminated witnessing – a scene that etches itself into the mind, the observation of a particular quality of light, the accruing apprehension of a meaning as it is gathered up by an object or a ritual – rather than climactic life events such as the marriage or romance plots dear to traditional fiction. Even texts that seem to bring character and plot together in more conventional ways turn out to have a surprising or subversive relation to the traditional novel's developmental storylines. Thus the bloody adultery plot of *O Pioneers!* – a classic novelistic routine – is curiously "islanded" within a narrative committed to survival and daily continuity; thus *My Ántonia* turns out to be much more of an anti-maturation narrative than a coming-of-age story, as Jim Burden recommits himself at the book's end to the people and values of his childhood; thus in *The Professor's House* Godfrey St. Peter's crisis of meaning climaxes in his near asphyxiation in his attic study, an ambiguous form of action that is both accidental and suicidal, and yields only a muted determination to carry on.

What is the goal of Cather's apparent recasting of the modes of attention and action that belong to the Victorian novel? I think it must be this: she sets out, as it were, to free her characters from the forms of emplotment that the tradition of the Victorian novel had designated for them. In so doing she frees her fiction – and its readers – from the values, the stories, and the repertoire of emotions that have constituted the ideological "package" of the novelistic tradition she inherits. What does she put in the place of novelistic action, as traditionally conceived? Something like this. In *Shadows on the Rock*, Cecile Auclair returns to the city of Quebec from a brief voyage to the nearby Ile d'Orleans. As she reenters her own house and begins the work of making dinner, she comes to the following realization:

> As she began handling her own things again, it all seemed a little different, – as if she had grown at least two years older in the two nights she had been away. She did not feel like a little girl, doing what she had been taught to do. She was accustomed to think that she did all these things so carefully to please her father, and to carry out her mother's wishes. Now she realized that she did them for herself, quite as much . . . These coppers, big and little, these brooms and clouts and brushes, were tools; and with them one made, not shoes or cabinet-work, but life itself. One made a climate within a climate; one made the days, – the complexion, the special flavour, the special happiness of each day as it passed; one made life.[12]

This, then, is Cather's version of the climax of a novel, the coming together of character and action to produce a moment of insight. Yet this coming together yields no self-defining decision, no lucid and authoritative moral truth. Instead, what Cecile achieves is an instance of the very kind of alertness – not to maturity, or depth, or morality, but to the fact that meanings are made and to the value of the daily work of making them – that Cather's fiction has all along been recommending to us. What Cecile has experienced in this moment of epiphany is the generative insight that has given us Cather's modernism.

We are ready now to draw together our observations of the strikingly "anti-novelistic" behavior of Cather's novels into a claim about the nature of her modernism – about the way the formal renovations we have been specifying might yield the kind of cultural, intellectual, and emotional renovation that modernism promises. What, then, is the experience of reading that Cather's fiction creates for us? What does it refuse to give us? What does it offer us instead? And what is the historical force of this remaking of novelistic possibilities?

I have been suggesting, in this account of Cather's recasting of the novel, that one of the most interesting things about her fiction is what it does *not* find interesting. We have been discovering, as we have examined the characteristic behavior of her fiction, that Cather's modernism is, in part, a project or practice of "disinvestment." By withdrawing its interest from the psychological conceptions of character and the moralizing trajectories of action that underwrite Victorian narrative, Cather's modernist fiction frees its readers, no less than its characters, from a customary repertoire of response, from the habits of feeling and judgment, from the pathways of attention and interest that belong to the Victorian novel and to the cultural dispensation such novels spoke so powerfully for. But her work is also an invitation to "reinvestment": by directing its interests elsewhere, to acts of making and forms of feeling cut free from the depth-seeking, ending-hungry, explanation-driven trajectories of Victorian culture, Cather's novels invite us towards new forms of thought and feeling, towards a new sense of the sources of meaning and value, towards a new repertoire of response.

Let us consider a final example. Late in her career, around the time she was working on *Shadows on the Rock*, Cather wrote a very long story – or a very short novel – called "Old Mrs. Harris." The story records the last days of its title character. It interests itself in the way her labor-laden days unfold, in the material culture of this ordinary life – where Mrs. Harris sleeps, what she covers herself with at night, what she does to care for the family's children – and in the feelings that take shape within and around this family's domestic space. Its low-key array of main events includes the death of the family cat and Mrs. Harris's securing of a college loan for her granddaughter Vickie with the assistance of their cosmopolitan neighbor Mrs. Rosen. At the end of the story, Mrs. Harris dies. Here are some of the things in which the story is not interested: crediting itself for its notably enlightened treatment of the Jewish Rosens; executing any of the other "judgment" plots the story's narrative materials seem to invite – such as the condemnation of the exploitation of Mrs. Harris by her self-involved daughter (indeed, what interests the story is the cultural antecedents of the lack of resentment Mrs. Harris feels); and investing itself in any very enthusiastic way in the successful rescue of Vickie's ambitions. A significant part of reading this story, I am suggesting, is the experience of "disinvestment" – of the story's palpably *not* moving in the directions in which the same materials would lead a Victorian novelist or a judgment-seeking reader.

To what kind of experience does the story invite us instead? Here is a representative passage.

Sometimes, in the morning, if her feet ached more than usual, Mrs. Harris felt a little low. (Nobody did anything about broken arches in those days, and the common endurance test of old age was to keep going after every step cost something.) She would hang up her towel with a sigh and go into the kitchen, feeling that it was hard to make a start. But the moment she heard the children running down the uncarpeted back stairs, she forgot to be low. Indeed, she ceased to be an individual, an old woman with aching feet; she became part of a group, became a relationship. She was drunk up into their freshness when they burst in upon her, telling her about their dreams, explaining their troubles with buttons and shoe-laces and underwear shrunk too small. The tired, solitary old woman Grandmother had been at daybreak vanished; suddenly the morning seemed as important to her as it did to the children, and the mornings ahead stretched out sunshiny, important.[13]

We can certainly see unfolding here the array of interests that we have proposed as defining Cather's modernism: the location of the field of art in the terrain of the everyday, in the world of broken arches and the vicissitudes of laundry; the notation of meaning's local emergence revealing itself as fiction's supreme subject ("she . . . became a relationship . . . suddenly the morning seemed . . . important"). But what is still more striking about this moment and the story that enfolds it is that, these brief remarks notwithstanding, it leaves us with nothing to say. Faced with a passage like this, we do not judge, we witness. And in that shift from interpretation to observation, from allegory to "anthropology," Cather sets the novel and its readers free.

We are now taught to value novels for writing more richly the history of their era or, more radically, for exposing, intentionally or not, the embedded and contradiction-ridden histories that eras prefer to hide from themselves. But Cather's novels achieve their modernism most powerfully not by bringing a history to light – though that is one of the things they necessarily do – but by recasting the affective lives of their readers. In this sense, they do not write history; they make it.

NOTES

1. *My Ántonia* (1926; New York: Vintage, 1994), pp. 134–5. Subsequent citations will be indicated in the text.
2. For a fuller account of the history of Cather's literary reputation see Sharon O'Brien, "Becoming Noncanonical: The Case against Willa Cather," *American Quarterly* 40 (1988), pp. 110–26.
3. "The Case of Willa Cather," in *Writing of Women: Essays in a Renaissance* (Middletown, Conn.: Wesleyan University Press, 1985), pp. 136–52. See also Jo Ann Middleton, *Willa Cather's Modernism: A Study of Style and Technique* (London and Toronto: Associated University Press; Rutherford, NJ: Fairleigh Dickinson University Press, 1990).
4. For valuable examples of this historicist strain in Cather criticism see Guy Reynolds, *Willa Cather in Context: Progress, Race, Empire* (New York: St. Martin's Press, 1996); Joseph R. Urgo, *Willa Cather and the Myth of American Migration* (Urbana and Chicago: University of Illinois Press, 1995); and Leona Sevick, "Nervous Priests and Unlikely Imperialists: Willa Cather's *Death Comes for the Archbishop*," *Willa Cather Pioneer Memorial Newsletter and Review* 46 (Summer 2002), pp. 13–17. For discussions of Cather's fiction that more fully

connect formal and historical questions, see Chip Rhodes, *Structures of the Jazz Age: Mass Culture, Progressive Education, and Racial Disclosures in American Modernism* (London: Verso, 1998), ch. 2; Sarah Wilson, "'Fragmentary and Inconclusive' Violence: National History and Literary Form in *The Professor's House*," *American Literature* 75 (September 2003), pp. 571–99; my own "Willa Cather and 'The Storyteller': Hostility to the Novel in *My Ántonia*," *American Literature* 66 (1994), pp. 689–717, and "Where is Cather's Quebec?: Anthropological Modernism in *Shadows on the Rock*," *Cather Studies* 4 (1999), pp. 23–44.

5. "Towards a Definition of American Modernism," *American Quarterly* 39 (1987), pp. 7–8. Subsequent citations will be indicated in the text.

6. Michael Bell identifies a "pervasive concern with the construction of meaning" as a key feature of modernism in his useful essay, "The Metaphysics of Modernism," in Michael Levenson, ed., *The Cambridge Companion to Modernism* (Cambridge: Cambridge University Press, 1999), p. 16.

7. Singal identifies the new anthropology as "perhaps the most influential" of the cultural manifestations of modernism (p. 18). The historical account of the emergence of cultural relativism I offer here is derived from Singal's essay, from Lewis Perry, *Intellectual Life in America: A History* (New York: Franklin Watts, 1984), and from George W. Stocking, *Race, Culture, and Evolution: Essays in the History of Anthropology* (New York: Free Press, 1968). James Clifford offers an important account of this history, chastened by a sense of the tendency of such intercultural exchanges to leave hierarchies mutedly intact, in *The Predicament of Culture: Twentieth-Century Ethnography, Literature, and Art* (Cambridge, MA: Harvard University Press, 1988), pp. 230–6. For a fuller version of this discussion, see Millington, "Where is Cather's Quebec?" pp. 24–7. Edward Sapir's essay, "Civilization and Culture," may be found in *The Dial* (20 September 1919), pp. 233–6.

8. On the dissemination of Boas's ideas see Perry, *Intellectual Life in America*, pp. 322–3. The *McClure's* article on Boas is Burton J. Hendrick, "The Skulls of Our Immigrants," *McClure's Magazine* 35 (May 1910), pp. 36–50. Cather's essay "Nebraska: The End of the First Cycle" appeared in *The Nation*, September 5, 1923, pp. 236–8. For a much more skeptical view of the effect of the "culture concept," as disseminated in fiction, on twentieth-century American society and politics (especially its conceptualization of race) and for a valuably complex account of Cather's relation to this idea of culture, see Walter Benn Michaels, "The Vanishing American," *American Literary History* 2 (1990): pp. 220–41.

9. *Willa Cather on Writing: Critical Studies on Writing as an Art* (1949; Lincoln, NE: University of Nebraska Press, 1988), pp. 91–4.

10. "On *Shadows on the Rock*," in *Willa Cather on Writing*, p. 16.

11. Bell, "The Metaphysics of Modernism," p. 27.

12. Willa Cather, *Shadows on the Rock* (1931; New York: Vintage, 1971), pp. 197–8.

13. Willa Cather, "Old Mrs. Harris," in *Obscure Destinies* (1932; New York: Vintage, 1971), pp. 136–7.

4

LISA MARCUS

Willa Cather and the geography of Jewishness

Willa Cather and the criticism of politics

In 1996, Elizabeth Ammons confidently asserted that "the new canon in American literature – the one . . . that it is imperative to think about Willa Cather within – is multiculturalism."[1] Undoubtedly, multiculturalism – including feminist, queer, and ethnic studies – has brought an enormous vitality to Cather criticism. Yet the composite of Cather constructed by such approaches – queer opera diva, rugged cowgirl, and Greenwich Village cosmopolitan[2] – has barely dented the image of Cather that persists in the public imagination. When Laura Bush recently proclaimed, after hosting a literary salon celebrating the writing of Cather, Edna Ferber, and Laura Ingalls Wilder, that "there is nothing political about American literature," it was clear that the Cather she had invited to the White House was safely apolitical, the author of slightly more grown-up, highbrow versions of *Little House on the Prairie*.[3] The First Lady's appropriation of a bland, antiseptic Cather follows close on the heels of Joan Acocella's reactionary crusade to cleanse Cather criticism of ideology – recuperating Cather from an academic trend towards what Acocella terms "spun-from-nothing hypotheses" about race, sex, and politics.[4] Multicultural critics, in Acocella's view, anachronistically impose on Cather the politics of our contemporary moment, interrogating Cather "as to whether her views were sufficiently antipatriarchal, anticolonial, antihegemonic," resulting in a self-righteous criticism that is "all excoriation, all easy triumphs" (pp. 67–8).

Acocella's project, despite her protestations against sullying art with politics, clearly serves its own political agenda. To employ the familiar and ultimately transparent gesture of dismissing others' views as "political" is to elevate oneself above the crass motives of politics and to mask as politically neutral the literary and political status quo. The White House's eager embrace of a homogenized Cather perfectly illustrates the political use to which an apolitical celebration of "Art" can be put. If any critical approach is anachronistic, surely it is Acocella's. Her Cather, the familiar poetess of the great prairie, mainstay of high-school reading-lists, is a whitewashed Cather, detached from the cultural politics of early twentieth-century America. A multicultural approach to Cather does not impose our politics on her, so much as it seeks to understand the political anxieties that infuse her fiction. As Ammons argues, Cather too often is "idealized in order to satisfy a reassuring, made-up, version of U.S. history and literary production as only incidentally racially influenced. Yet, in fact, her work is not separate from and somehow above the culture in which she lived and wrote" (p. 265). To focus on racial and sexual politics is hardly to impose contemporary concerns on the literature of the past. What kind of nation America is on the way to becoming, what it means to be an American, and *who* can be an American – these have been central concerns (if not obsessions) of American literature since its inception. For Cather and other writers of her generation, these abiding cultural anxieties became inflected, during the late 1910s and early 1920s, by the growing chorus of nativist concern over the waves of immigrants from eastern and southern Europe – perhaps most notably Jews.[5]

In order to understand fully the scope of Cather's cultural and artistic vision, it is necessary to situate her in this historical context. Indeed, the famous fictions of the great prairie, such as *O Pioneers!* (1913), *The Song of the Lark* (1915), and *My Ántonia* (1918), which have forever linked Cather to the heroic images of white European immigrants settling the American West (that image that the Bush White House could so comfortably celebrate), are not the whole story. Indeed, many of these works were written while Cather was living in cosmopolitan New York City (Cather moved to New York in 1906, and it was her main residence until her death in 1947), during and following her literary apprenticeship as an editor at *McClure's* magazine.[6] This tenure at *McClure's* gave her an intimate exposure to the culture wars of her day, specifically to nativist salvos about the threat immigrants posed to American culture. Thus, while Cather was casting her gaze westward, back to the Great Plains, she was also training her fictional eye on a far different landscape: the ethnic cityscape of the great American metropolis, teeming with newly arrived immigrants.

The recent collection of essays on *Willa Cather's New York* has done much to call our attention to this relatively neglected Cather.[7] And yet the pieces in that collection celebrate Cather's artistic engagement with the high culture of the bustling city, paying scant attention to the ethnic fabric of Cather's New York. It is to this ethnic geography, and specifically to Cather's fictional portrayals of Jews, that I want to turn my attention. Cather's depictions of Jews express a marked ambivalence that is manifested in two divergent types of characters: on the one hand, a grasping, ambitious Jewish figure, linked to New York City, who threatens to infect American culture with a crass commercialism and to taint the purity of the American family through miscegenation; and, on the other hand, a much less frequent figure in Cather's fiction – "the finest kind of Jews," as she wrote in *The Song of the Lark* – admirably cultured intellectuals, often second-generation German Jews, living in the Midwest, who, crucially, pose no threat of inter-marrying with Anglo-Americans. Two stories dating from the years 1912–16,[8] "Behind the Singer Tower" and "Scandal," dramatically illustrate how the first of these two figures – the threatening Jew – had entered the fictional landscape of Cather's America.

The invasion of Potash and Perlmutter: *McClure's*, Cather, and the Jews

Before turning to Cather's fictions of Jewishness, I want to situate them in the context of the nativist discourse Cather encountered in her *McClure's* years. Burton Hendrick, writing for *McClure's* in 1907, alerted readers to what he termed "the great Jewish invasion" of New York. The article, which appeared during Cather's tenure as an editor of the magazine, catalogues with some anxiety New York's increasingly Jewish visage. Writing that "our greatest city is already, as far as numbers are concerned, largely Semitic,"[9] Hendrick goes on to describe New York as a veritable Jewish "colony," a "modern Zion," and concludes:

> Unquestionably, we are thus face to face with one of the most remarkable phenomena of the time. New York, the headquarters of American wealth, intelligence, and enterprise – the most complete physical expression, we have been told, of the American idea – seems destined to become overwhelmingly a Jewish town.
> (p. 310)

A largely favorable treatment of Jewish immigration and industry, the article nevertheless expresses a certain trepidation about the Jewish infiltration of New York. While Hendrick seems to admire Jewish enterprise, he describes the streets of New York as "impassably clogged with Jewish pushcarts," noting that "the New Yorker constantly rubs elbows with Israel" (p. 309). In an odd mixture of lament and admiration Hendrick advises: "take a walk up Broadway or the business sections of Fifth Avenue – the names on the signs are almost invariably Jewish . . . Drop in at the Opera or the theater – the bediamonded audience, and even the performers, are frequently members of this race" (p. 309).

The kind of anxious admiration that Hendrick expresses about Jewish industry and enterprise shows up in Cather's own journalistic reflection

From Fourteenth to Twenty-third Street, Fifth Avenue, the former homes of the Knickerbocker aristocracy have been replaced by Jewish business blocks. In the building at the corner of Twenty-first Street and Fifth Avenue every floor bears a Jewish sign

Figure 1: Fifth Avenue signs, from Burton J. Hendrick, "The Great Jewish Invasion," *McClure's Magazine*, 28 (January 1907), pp. 307–21 (316).

about New York Jews. In a 1914 *McClure's* essay on New York character acting, specifically in its review of the successful and long-running play
Potash and Perlmutter,[10] one can see Cather embracing ethnic caricature of
the sort she employed in her own fiction of this period. Praising the play's
verisimilitude in portraying New York life, Cather accepts Potash and Perlmutter not as mere character types, but as representative Jews. Describing
the play's depiction of New York, she writes:

> This is not the New York of Babylonian towers and sky-effects which the
> settlement house school of poets write about, but it is the city with which the
> humble resident of Manhattan island has to reckon and to which he has to
> adapt himself. The apartment houses are built for – and usually owned by –
> Potash or Perlmutter; the restaurants are run for them; the shops are governed
> by the tastes of Mrs. Potash and Mrs. Perlmutter; and, whether one likes it or
> not, one has to buy garments fundamentally designed to enhance the charms
> of those ladies.   (p. 46)

Whether one likes it or not, we hear Cather saying here, one must acclima-
tize to the Perlmutters – to a New York increasingly run by and for Jews.
Like Hendrick's depiction of a New York "impassably" crowded with Jews,
Cather's claim that one cannot escape Jewish influence reflects a paranoid
over-inflation of Jewish affluence. But again like Hendrick, Cather's portrait
is ambivalent, her anxiety infused with admiration. Jews are highly successful, woven into (and weaving) the fabric of the nation, but at the same time,
they are pushy, gaudy, and imposing – unwanted, obtrusive outsiders.

Potash and Perlmutter's imaginary New York resonated with Cather's own
vision of the city:

> In this play you have a group of people who make the external city, who are
> weaving the visible garment of New York, creating the color, the language, the
> "style," the noise, the sharp contrasts which, to the inlander, mean the great
> metropolis. People who are on their way to something are always more con-
> spicuous and more potent than people who have got what they want and are
> where they belong. The city roars and rumbles and hoots and jangles because
> Potash and Perlmutter are on their way somewhere.   (p. 46)

Here as elsewhere, Cather registers an ambivalent response to an increasingly
Jewish New York. For Cather, Jews at once provide glitter and excitement
while also being conspicuous and crass, offering up ethnic local color that
represents the "great metropolis" to an "inlander" like Cather. Jews are thoroughly American – as "people on their way to something" they embody the
vitality and energy of American commerce. But their very conspicuousness
and potency evokes in Cather a nagging discomfort at the fact that, "like

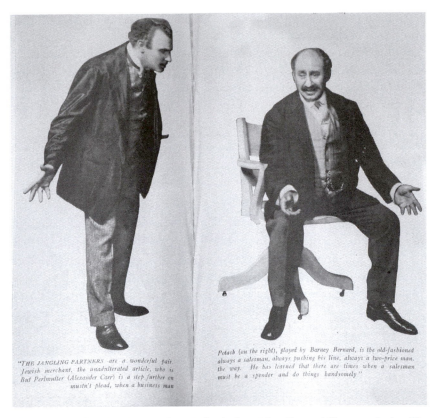

"THE JANGLING PARTNERS are a wonderful pair Jewish merchant, the unadulterated article, who is But Perlmutter (Alexander Carr) is a step further on mustn't plead, when a business man

Potash (on the right), played by Barney Bernard, is the old-fashioned always a salesman, always pushing his line, always a two-price man, the way. He has learned that there are times when a salesman must be a spender and do things handsomely"

Figure 2: Potash and Perlmutter, from Willa Cather, "New Types of Character Acting: The Character Actor Displaces the Star," *McClure's Magazine* (February 1914), pp. 41–51 (46–7).

it or not," Jews have knitted themselves into the cultural tapestry of New York.

The ambivalence about New York's Jews that we see registered in both Hendrick's and Cather's essays for *McClure's* increasingly gave way, in the America of the late 1910s, to a more virulent anti-Semitism. Madison Grant, New York patrician and racial nativist, did not take kindly to the suggestion that New York was being "invaded" by Jews. In his 1916 treatise *The Passing of the Great Race* he cautioned:

The man of the old stock is being crowded out of many country districts by these foreigners just as he is to-day being literally driven off the streets of New York City by the swarms of Polish Jews. These immigrants adopt the language of the native American, they wear his clothes, they steal his name and they are beginning to take his women, but they seldom adopt his religion or understand his ideals.[11]

For Grant this was cause for the United States to close its borders to immigrants from undesirable quarters of the globe, and he was instrumental in promoting the passage of the anti-immigrant legislation that burgeoned after World War I. While Grant's nativist animus extended to all non-Nordic peoples, his most venomous attacks targeted Jews and were fueled by an anxiety over the future of his native city, New York:

> Large cities from the days of Rome, Alexandria, and Byzantium have always been gathering points of diverse races, but New York is becoming a *cloaca gentium* which will produce many amazing racial hybrids and some ethnic horrors that will go beyond the powers of future anthropologists to unravel.
>
> (p. 92)

Grant's disturbing metaphor of the *"cloaca gentium"* – though cloaked in scholarly Latin, this scatological term translates as a "sewer of the nation" or a "drainage ditch of the races" – evinces a visceral disgust for those immigrants who threaten America's racial purity.

While Cather never approached Grant's virulent anti-Semitism, Burton Hendrick did. In 1923 he published *The Jews in America*, which painted an unflattering portrait of Jews from eastern Europe and encouraged immigration laws calling for their exclusion (in 1924 such laws were enacted as part of the Johnson-Reed Immigration Act).[12] Hendrick's shift from anxious admiration to anti-Semitic nativism between 1907 and 1923 captures the change in attitudes towards Jewish immigration and assimilation that are reflected in Cather's fictions of Jewishness.[13] This cultural framework of shifting attitudes towards New York Jews is symbolized in the ethnic cityscape of Cather's "Behind the Singer Tower," in which the growing Jewish presence is literally embodied in the archictecture of the New York skyline.

Architectures of ethnicity

"Behind the Singer Tower" has been read as a muckraking expose, a Flaubertian exercise, a veritable American "heart of darkness."[14] Of Cather's recent critics, only Loretta Wasserman details what she calls Cather's "Semitism" in "Behind the Singer Tower," and it is her lead that I wish to follow here.[15] Wasserman's important study chronicles Cather's Jewish figurations in an attempt to reconcile them with her reputation for celebrating other immigrants, particularly Scandinavians and Bohemians. Like Wasserman, I am not interested here in condemning Cather as an anti-Semite, but rather in culturally situating her "Semitism." Though, as Wasserman reminds us, "some of [Cather's] best friends were Jews" (p. 3), one can hear in Cather's symbolic figurations of Jewish New York echoes of the "ethnic horror" registered by nativists such as Madison Grant.

In the opening pages of Cather's story, the Singer Tower and the Statue of Liberty are posed as oppositional symbols of New York's ethnic architecture dueling for the city's soul. One character, with the solidly Anglo-American name of Johnson, muses aloud, reading the New York skyline from a launch on the Hudson river: "Did you ever notice . . . what a Jewy-looking thing the Singer Tower is when it's lit up? The fellow who placed those incandescents must have had a sense of humor. It's exactly like the Jewish high priest in the old Bible dictionaries."[16] Zablowski, a Jewish doctor with "sad" and "thoughtful eyes," shakes his head and responds: "No, it's not Semitic, Johnson, that high-peaked turban is more apt to be Persian. He's a Magi or a fire-worshiper of some sort, your high priest. When you get nearer he looks like a Buddha, with two bright rings in his ears" (p. 46). Gazing at the great cityscape of Manhattan, Zablowski deflects the Anglo-American gaze that equates materialistic excess with Jewishness, replacing it with his own orientalizing vision: he sees a turbaned "Magi" or a Buddha atop the noted building rather than a praying Jewish patriarch. Yet despite Zablowski's dissenting reading, Cather's story persists in portraying the New York skyline as an ethnic landscape over which a threatening Jewishness looms:

> Zablowski pointed with his cigar towards the blurred Babylonian heights crowding each other on the narrow tip of the island. Among them rose the colossal figure of the Singer Tower, watching over the city and the harbor like a presiding Genius. He had come out of Asia quietly in the night, no one knew just when or how, and the Statue of Liberty, holding her feeble taper in the gloom off to our left, was but an archeological survival. (p. 46)

This account – of masculine genius and potency dominating the feeble relic of femininity – suggests the rise of vulgar capitalism over and against the more progressive forces of democratization embodied in the weakened and dimly visible Statue of Liberty. But this reading of the New York skyline tells us something more, I think, about the landscape of ethnicity – what I am calling Cather's architecture of ethnicity. The somewhat indeterminate ethnic markers here – the "Babylonian" genius that has slipped in from "Asia" – become conflated in the story, despite Zablowski's efforts, with Jewishness. New York is rendered legible in this scenario, indeed it is personified, as a giant Jewish body threateningly imposing its "New York idea" on the nation. That Johnson personifies the Singer Tower as a Jewish Gulliver whose "presiding genius" outshines Lady Liberty's indicates some measure of the paranoia that many Americans felt about Jewish infiltration and, as Hendrick put it, "invasion."

Hallet, another member of the boating party and a central voice in the story, points to the irony of Lady Liberty's enfeebled position in relation to the eastern giant:

> "Who could have foreseen that she, in her high-mindedness, would ever spawn a great heathen idol like that?" Hallet exclaimed. "But that's what idealism comes to in the end, Zablowski."
>
> Zablowski laughed mournfully. "What did you expect, Hallet? You've used us for your ends – waste for your machine, and now you talk about infection. Of course we brought germs from over there," he nodded to the northeast.
>
> (p. 46)

Zablowski cannily points to the ambivalence expressed in Hallet's reading of the skyline. On one hand, New York represents the idealistic view of America as a nation of immigrants, welcomed through the skirts of Liberty's gate. But on the other hand, these same immigrants, Liberty's "spawn," have the potential to turn on their mother, polluting the nation with germs of their difference. While Hallet sees the "Jewy-looking" Singer Tower as embodying threat and disease, impurity and infection, Zablowski calls him on it: he critiques the hypocrisy of Hallet's "ideal," which chews up immigrants, and suggests that these newcomers who serve as "waste" for the American "machine" have in fact embraced and epitomized the most American of ideals in aspiring to Liberty's dream.

If Cather's ambivalent attitude towards Jews is figured in the opposition of the Singer Tower and the Statue of Liberty, the heart of her story centers around a third symbol of New York's ethnic architecture, the fictional Mont Blanc Hotel. In the story's frame tale, Cather's characters view the New York skyline on the eve after the hotel has been ravaged by a terrible fire, killing hundreds. This fire seems to symbolize a rottenness at the core of what the story calls the "New York idea." Indeed, the story seems to function as a kind of cautionary tale about dangerous industrial zeal and unchecked greed, hence its reputation as Cather's one attempt at social protest fiction. Thus Cather uses Jews as both the perfect embodiment of American industry and a destructive or excessive perversion of that American ideal. The narrator observes:

> We realized that, after the burning of the Mont Blanc, the New York idea would be called to account by every state in the Union, by all the great capitals of the world . . . [It] would bring our particular type of building into unpleasant prominence, as the cholera used to make Naples and conditions of life there too much a matter of discussion . . . For once we were actually afraid of being too much in the public eye, of being overadvertised.　(pp. 45–6)

Significantly, the rottenness contaminating the "New York idea" is linked to a Jew – Stanley Merryweather, the builder of the Mont Blanc. The story within Cather's story, narrated by Hallet, himself an engineer, recounts his experience working under Merryweather on the foundation of the Mont Blanc, and his affection for a young Italian immigrant brutally sacrificed to Merryweather's unethical and stingy eagerness to cut corners despite risking his workers' lives.

Hallet's story offers us two versions of the American immigrant; Italians, though constantly referred to as "dagos" by Hallet, figure as desirable immigrants in this narrative. As the story opens, the men in the launch are passed by a boat filled with immigrants, called the *Re di Napoli*, and the regal title of the ship is mirrored by the succeeding images of Italians in the story, which stress the noble western traditions of Italian culture.[17] Even the humble worker who captures Hallet's affection, Caesarino, is a diminutive Caesar, recalling the glory of Rome. Although he hails from a "goat track" and is portrayed as an idyllic, romanticized peasant, his pastoral virtues also makes him the ideal immigrant: he is hardworking, respects his boss Hallet, loves his mother, and most significantly, is a temporary pilgrim who desires to return to his native Italy once he has earned a sufficient sum of money. Hallet's rather maudlin affection for Caesarino seems dependent on Caesarino's dog-like humility and loyalty. The story's other noble Italian, an opera singer, is also a transient in New York, bringing his European high culture to the United States, with the promise that he will always return to his country estate in Naples at the end of the opera season. Both of these Italians are killed by the Mont Blanc: Caesarino is crushed beneath falling equipment when a faulty cable about which Hallet warned Merryweather snaps, and the tenor dies leaping dramatically from the flaming building. The opera singer's death is described in particularly grisly detail – his severed hand, left hanging off a window ledge, seems an especially gruesome pound of flesh exacted by the Jewish industrialist as a sacrifice to his American dream.

While the Mont Blanc consumes the noble Italians, the story's other immigrants, Jews, not only survive the horror, but lie at the heart of this "New York idea" gone wrong. The Mont Blanc is, after all, Stanley Merryweather's hotel: the fire, the story tells us, is his fault. Merryweather is a curious character who fortuitously inherits his wealth and his legitimacy from a rich Scotch Presbyterian uncle who funds the Mont Blanc project. But even though Merryweather is only half Jewish, his "racial characteristics" are readily apparent to characters like Hallet. As Madison Grant insisted, "the cross between any of the three European races and a Jew is a Jew" (p. 18). Confirming his racial identity, Merryweather marries a "burgeoning Jewish beauty" named Fanny Reizenstein, whom he bedecks with "the jewels of the East until she looked like the Song of Solomon done into motion pictures" (p. 48). Merryweather is depicted in what Loretta Wasserman calls "venomous" terms: the story describes him as "glitteringly frank" and "insultingly cordial"; he would "blossom out" in clothes of "some unusual weave and haunting color" – in short, he is the gaudy and stock caricatured Jew of the Perlmutter variety. Like Perlmutter, Merryweather earns a kind of grudging respect for his brash American initiative: "I'm not underestimating the value of dash and intrepidity," Hallet remarks, "he made the wheels go round" (p. 51).

Although he functions as a double for Merryweather in the story, Zablowski is a different kind of Jew. While Merryweather's name registers assimilation and aspiration, Zablowski seems a newer comer – he has not taken an anglicized name – and is thus more containable because more recognizable. While he is an invited member of the boating party, Zablowski is the butt of Hallet's teasing throughout the story, and the final jab comes when Johnson claims that whatever happens to New York, the city is none the less "ours" – meaning American. Hallet jumps in to say, in the final lines of the story: "Don't call anything ours, Johnson, while Zablowski is around" (p. 54). This closing reference to Jewish acquisitiveness offers a climax to the story's homily about Jewish infiltration. Hallet's uneasy laughter provokes the reader to believe that the Jew might indeed take what is proclaimed by the story as "ours." Zablowski, we note, is not one of "us."

The story concludes its "reading" of the ethnic future of America by musing again on the "Jewy-looking thing" that pollutes Cather's New York skyline. After Hallet finishes his tale of the unfortunate Caesarino, he wonders aloud, "There must be something wonderful coming. When the frenzy is over, when the furnace has cooled, what marvel will be left on Manhattan Island?" Zablowski, dipping back into a kind of eastern relativism, sighs "dreamily," "What has been left often enough before . . . What was left in India, only not half so much" (p. 54). Zablowski implies that the Empire State is fated to be like other empires: the monuments it builds, at tremendous human sacrifice, will endure as vestigial relics of the glory and costs of empire-building. But the text tells us that Hallet "disregarded him," offering this vision instead:

> What it will be is a new idea of some sort. That's all that ever comes, really. That's what we are all the slaves of, though we don't know it. It's the whip that cracks over us till we drop. Even Merryweather – and that's where the gods have the laugh on him – every firm he crushes to the wall, every deal he puts through, every cocktail he pours down his throat, he does it in the service

of this unborn Idea, that he will never know anything about. Some day it will dawn, serene and clear, and your Moloch on the Singer Tower over there will get down and do it Asian obeisance.   (p. 54)

Hallet's startling reference to the terrible biblical Moloch completes the story's vision of ethnic horror. Whereas in the story's first personification of the Singer Tower Johnson saw a praying Jewish patriarch, Hallet now overlays that image with the figure of Moloch – a heathen idol who requires propitiatory sacrifice to fuel his furnace – collapsing the two figures together and thus conflating them. The story seems to suggest that the destructive, consuming materialism of New York is the false god of Jews such as Merry-weather. The dawning of a new age – the "unborn Idea" that Hallet proph-esies – will cause this false idol to kneel in obedience to a higher power. Of course, the Singer Tower did not long remain the tallest building in New York, and increasing nativist sentiment against Jews, and other immigrant groups, led to severe immigration restrictions in the 1920s. Cather's story leaves us with two opposed readings of New York's ethnic architecture: Hallet's prophecy of a transcendent and ethnically cleansed ideal emerg-ing from New York's conflagration, and Zablowski's quiet, and ultimately silenced, dissenting voice that counters Hallet's ethnocentrism.

Critics of "Behind the Singer Tower" have cautioned against aligning Cather with Hallet's anti-Semitism, and some have even suggested that, by making Hallet so vicious, her story offers a critique of anti-Semitism. Cather's own retrospective reflections on her *McClure's* years seem to disown any such clearly political motive in her fiction:

> When I first lived in New York and was working on the editorial staff of a magazine, I became disillusioned about social workers and reformers. So many of them, when they brought in an article on fire-trap tenements or sweat-shop labour, apologetically explained that they were making these investigations "to collect material for fiction." I couldn't believe that any honest welfare worker, or any honest novelist, went to work in this way. The man who wants to get reforms put through does his investigating in a very different spirit, and the man who has a true vocation for imaginative writing doesn't have to go hunting among the ash cans on Sullivan Street for his material.[18]

Between the literary ambiguities of Cather's fiction and her disavowals of politics, it becomes very difficult, and perhaps fruitless, to try to pin down her own ethnic politics and prejudices. Yet despite her professed disdain for fiction that rummaged among fire-trap tenements and ash cans, "Behind the Singer Tower" is, whether one likes it or not, "fire-trap" fiction. Moreover, if the muckraking flavor of "Behind the Singer Tower" is a departure for

Cather, the figure of a Jew who infiltrates the ethnic architecture of American society is one that recurs in her fiction.[19] One striking example is the 1916 story "Scandal." Long ignored by Cather scholars as an artistic and political embarrassment, "Scandal" takes place far from the "ash cans of Sullivan Street," on Fifth Avenue's realm of high culture, where Cather again projects a lurking Jewish interloper.

Stein and circumstance

If "Behind the Singer Tower" is about commercial capital, "Scandal" is about cultural capital. The Jew in "Behind the Singer Tower" penetrates the financial world and his presence is symbolically figured in a changing architectural landscape; in "Scandal" the Jew infiltrates the gentile world financially, but also, significantly, he penetrates the elite world of upper-class art and society. "Scandal," written in 1916 while Cather was on a trip west, took years for her agent to place. When it finally appeared in *Century* in 1919, it had been rejected fifteen times. Despite being a favorite of F. Scott Fitzgerald's, this story, with its embarrassing publishing history and its explicit anti-Semitism, has received only limited attention from critics and biographers.[20] In my view, "Scandal" reads as an absorbing companion text to "Behind the Singer Tower," as it turns away from the architecture of ethnicity and towards the more intimate and (seemingly) less permeable realms of culture and the family.

"Scandal" opens with opera diva Kitty Ayrshire cloistered in her sunny, many-windowed Upper West Side apartment and rendered voiceless under the spell of a nasty cold and a "nervous condition" that hinders her recovery.[21] Cather invites readers to situate her heroine in any one of several intersecting discourses: Kitty's "condition" is simultaneously legible in economic, sexual, and ethnic terms. From an economic perspective, her incapacitating cold is symptomatic of her tenuous status as an object of cultural capital: as both an artist and a woman she functions as a luxurious commodity, a performance that exacts a high cost from her. Kitty imagines her performative role in strikingly pecuniary terms, refusing to "hoard her vitality," or to be "systematically prudent and parsimonious" (p. 99). Indeed, her value in the public imagination depends on her expensiveness: she needs "to believe that everything for sale in Vanity Fair was worth the advertised price," for it is this lure of cultural luxury that draws her fans, without which belief "her pulling power would decline and she would go to pieces" (p. 99). Kitty draws sustenance from the "oscillating tail" of the box-office line, a public that she imagines as markedly foreign and ethnic, composed of "little fellows in thin coats, Italians, Frenchmen, South-Americans, Japanese" (p. 99). What Kitty sells to this audience is an image of American culture that is clearly aligned with Europe: her apartment is adorned with a painting that depicts Kitty, in a Parisian salon, surrounded by European intellectuals, and a rumor circulating among her public links her romantically to a Russian duke. She embodies New York as the height of American culture – functioning like a member of a "royal family" (p. 103) in the popular imagination.

Even as Kitty is imaged here as "the sort of person who makes myths" (p. 103), her lost voice at the story's opening cannot be overlooked. A friend describes Kitty's penchant for generating rumors as her "singular good luck" – better than a "whole staff of publicity men" (p. 103) – but the story's emphasis on her muteness suggests a more sinister effect. Being a celebrity who requires gossip and publicity to maintain her currency in the public imagination threatens to render her a passive and voiceless projection of her public's desires, as is symbolized by the mockingbird in a "big gilt cage," who sings improvizations with a vigor unavailable to his "disconsolate mistress" (p. 101). Into the void left by Kitty's imposed silence, rumors spring forth to account for her absence from the stage – rumors that she has "lost her discretion," lost her voice, had a son by the Russian Grand Duke (pp. 98, 103–4). Cather's story ultimately centers on one particularly scandalous rumor that Kitty learns of during the visit of the "interesting, but not too interesting, Pierce Tevis" (p. 100). The scene of Tevis's visit is artfully arranged, and offers a strong critique of how femininity is constructed within a patriarchal economy. Kitty displays herself for Tevis as part of an ingenious tableau of art and femininity. Sitting below the painting that links her to Parisian culture, her ephemeral white femininity is revealed as an artificial composition:

> Her costume was folds upon folds of diaphanous white over equally diaphanous rose, with a line of white fur about her neck. Her beautiful arms were bare. Her tiny Chinese slippers were embroidered so richly that they resembled the painted porcelain of old vases. She looked like a sultan's youngest, newest bride; a beautiful little toy-woman, sitting at the end of the long room which composed about her, – which, in the soft light, seemed happily arranged for her. (p. 102)

While Kitty eagerly presents herself as a "toy-woman" for her admirer, the artificiality of the scene calls our attention both to Kitty's shrewd participation in her own objectification, and to the exhausting performance of femininity that threatens to freeze her within the frame of someone else's composition (as the picture has done).

While Kitty is orientalized in this composition, her diaphanous costume reminds readers that the image of femininity she wishes to project is fastened to an almost exoticized whiteness. Kitty's bare flesh, framed in white fur, may be decorated by Chinese slippers, but they serve only to accessorize and highlight her white skin. Kitty's currency as cultural capital is dependent on her role as a symbol of a refined, genteel Americanness. When she sighs to Tevis, "I'm getting almost as tired of the person I'm supposed to be as of the person I really am. I wish you would invent a new Kitty Ayrshire for me" (p. 103), she exposes the limits of such objectified glamour and opens the path for Tevis's gripping story about how easy Kitty is to copy: his story about the counterfeiting of Kitty Ayrshire forms the crux of Cather's tale. It is into this nexus of Kitty's vulnerability – as an artistically constructed commodity of femininity and whiteness – that the story's Jew figure enters. By aligning American culture with a vulnerable heroine, Cather creates an image of America that is subject to the predations of the threatening Jewish interloper, Sigmund Stein.

Like Merryweather of "Behind the Singer Tower," Stein is rendered in a vicious ethnic caricature that marks him as a repugnant outsider. Tevis describes him as having

> one of those rigid, horse-like faces that never tell anything; a long nose, flattened as if it had been tied down; a scornful chin; long, white teeth; flat cheeks, yellow as a Mongolian's; tiny, black eyes, with puffy lids and no lashes; dingy, dead-looking hair – looks as if it were glued on. (pp. 107–8)

This distasteful immigrant, Tevis reports, has enjoyed a meteoric rise from a "hideous, underfed little whippersnapper" toiling in a garment-district sweatshop to "a mysterious Jew who had the secret of gold" (p. 108). What sets Stein apart, however, from the Potashes and Perlmutters, and what ultimately makes him more threatening, is his shrewd recognition that financial success alone will not gain him entrée to polite society, and his subsequent pursuit of cultural capital: he "haunted the old Astor Library and the Metropolitan Museum, learned something about pictures and porcelains, took singing lessons, though he had a voice like a crow's" (p. 108). Stein becomes "a collector" not only of porcelain, but of people, assembling a retinue of "the unknown great; poets, actors, musicians," and earning a reputation as "a man of taste and culture, a patron of the arts" (pp. 108–9). The culmination of this rapacious campaign of acquisition is Stein's brazen counterfeiting of Kitty Ayrshire. Pygmalion-like, Stein constructs his false Kitty out of an immigrant girl, Ruby Mohr, whom Stein initially plucks from the factory to work as a "living model" in his department store, but whose "likeness to the newly arrived prima donna suggested to Stein another act in the play he was always putting on" (p. 109). Stein remakes Ruby into a living model of Kitty, conspicuously escorting her to his theater box on evenings when Kitty is not performing. This bold masquerade gives rise to scandalous

An East-Side Jew of the thriving proprietor class. "The East Side is possessed with an unending earth-hunger. Wherever you see a Russian Jew, however insignificant his station, you see a prospective land-lord"

Figure 3: An East-Side Jew, from Burton J. Hendrick, "The Great Jewish Invasion," *McClure's Magazine*, 28 (January 1907), pp. 307–21 (309).

rumors, both within the smart set in which Tevis travels, and among the "New York factory sports" and clothiers from "Sioux City" to "Council Bluffs" (p. 110).

Loretta Wasserman has argued that "the stereotype of the social climbing Jew" provided Cather with a convenient if cartoonish image for her larger theme in "Scandal," the "dangers of human commodification," the threat that "living by publicity" poses to "the integrity of the self" (p. 13). Yet Stein's Jewishness is not just incidental, for his elaborate charade above all else functions as a dramatization of the anxieties surrounding immigration, assimilation, and Americanness. Stein's skillful parading of Ruby Mohr epitomizes the masquerade that assimilating Jews enact to remake themselves as counterfeit Americans. Further, when he poses with a faux Kitty on his arm, Stein is not just infiltrating the world of high culture, but, by linking himself romantically with an icon of white femininity, he raises the specter of miscegenation that so worried nativists such as Madison Grant. What is so scandalous about Stein's trespass is that whiteness is so easily counterfeited, that culture and class are so permeable, and that white femininity, in particular, is so vulnerable to predation.

Stein's counterfeiting does not end, as it does in Tevis's account, with Stein "discontinu[ing] his pantomime at the right moment" (p. 110), as we learn when Kitty herself furnishes the "sequel" to Tevis's scandalous tale. Stein, it turns out, has choreographed a magnificent finale to his play, in which Kitty unwittingly replaces (and thus validates) her own counterfeit by agreeing to sing at a house-warming for Stein and his new bride, the former Miss Mandelbaum. Having purchased "a great house on Fifth Avenue that used to belong to people of a very different sort" (p. 111), Stein is the envy of his guests, whom Kitty disparagingly (and in an odd mix of mismatched religious iconography) describes as "Old Testament characters," "blooming like the hanging gardens of Babylon" and "glitter[ing] like Christmas-trees" (pp. 113, 112). At the party Kitty unknowingly appears in the role of jilted lover, graciously serenading her successful rival, granting her blessing and her cultural cachet to the new couple. When an artfully composed society-column photo of Stein, with his wife on one arm and Kitty on the other, appears in *The American Gentleman*, Stein's triumph is sealed – he has arrived, an American and a gentleman.

Cather's story ends with Kitty's musings upon this revelation that Stein has scandalously used her, and that she has unwittingly legitimated his counterfeit. If Stein has ascended through this association, Kitty, it is intimated, has suffered: her loss of voice, in retrospect, appears as coincident with her performance at the Stein house-warming; and, with her reputation compromised, her tenuous position as a cultural icon is in jeopardy. Kitty likens her predicament to that of Ruby Mohr, whom, cast off by Stein, Tevis has seen "going into a saloon with a tough-looking young fellow," looking "shabby" but still "amazingly, convincingly, like a battered, hardened, Kitty Ayrshire" (p. 110). Kitty complains, in the story's concluding lines, that, like Ruby, she has been Stein's puppet: "If the Steins want to adopt you into their family circle, they'll get you in the end. That's why I don't feel compassionate about your Ruby. She and I are in the same boat. We are both the victims of circumstance, and in New York so many of the circumstances are Steins" (p. 115). Kitty's naive alignment of herself with Ruby overlooks in a manner perhaps typical to the privileged the fact that her own vulnerability pales in comparison to Ruby's. She, when last seen by Tevis, was sinking into destitution and perhaps prostitution. While Kitty's comparison is excessive, it is also instructive, symptomatic of the elite's anxiety about the precariousness of their own status. If, in "Behind the Singer Tower," the enterprising Jew has corrupted the city skyline and business practices, "Scandal"'s Jew threatens the domains of culture, art, and the family. The dismayed and bitter resignation that marks the conclusion of Cather's story – Kitty's plaint that the Steins of the world "will get you in the end" – echoes, in a more sinister register, Cather's grudging acknowledgment that, "like it or not," New Yorkers must increasingly accommodate themselves to a city run by and for Potashes and Perlmutters. The New York idea is, in Cather's vision, a victim of circumstances, and those circumstances are, she seems to say repeatedly, Steins.

The figure of the Jew who infiltrates the ethnic and social architecture of American society is no mere aberration limited to early and obscure stories of Cather's, but a figure that reappears prominently in her 1925 novel *The Professor's House*, in the person of the gaudy, magnificent Louie Marsellus, who weds and impregnates the daughter of that bastion of Anglo gentility, Godfrey St. Peter, and sets up housekeeping in a reconstructed Norwegian manor house. Like the stories discussed above, *The Professor's House* seems to express both a grudging admiration for the brazen assimilationist and, simultaneously, a fearful chagrin at his bold incursions. There are a few instances in Cather's fiction, as some critics are wont to point out, of a different type of Jew, a kind of counter-figure to the ones I have explored here. These characters, labeled the "finest kind of Jews"[22] in *The Song of the Lark*, do indeed offer a stark contrast to New York Jews such as Stein and Merryweather. Both *The Song of the Lark* and the story "Old Mrs. Harris" contain characters apparently modeled on Jewish neighbors of Cather's from Red Cloud, Nebraska, of whom she was quite fond.[23] These figures are depicted as highly cultured patrons of the arts; isolated Jews living not in the East Coast, immigrant cosmopolis but in Chicago and Colorado; and both are elderly couples who pose no threat of intermarriage or even reproduction. Thus, far from being inconsistent with the more threatening figures like Stein, Merryweather, and Marsellus, these "finest kind of Jews" are the exceptions that prove the rule – the negative mirror image of the threatening Jews that haunt Cather's ethnic geography. To celebrate the multicultural prairie of Swedes and Bohemians that has rightly earned Cather a reputation for championing the immigrant, without at the same time acknowledging the fictions of Jewish New York that offer a far more insidious view of immigrants' impact on the fabric of America, is to offer a watered-down, simplified version of Cather with all her rough edges smoothed away for popular consumption.

NOTES

1. See Elizabeth Ammons, "Cather and the New Canon: 'The Old Beauty' and the Issue of Empire," in Susan J. Rosowski, ed., *Cather Studies* III (Lincoln, NE, and London: University of Nebraska Press, 1996), p. 256. Further references will be made parenthetically.
2. See Jonathan Goldberg, *Willa Cather and Others* (Durham, NC, and London: Duke University Press, 2001); Marilee Lindemann, *Willa Cather: Queering America* (New York: Columbia University Press, 1999); and Merrill Maguire Skaggs, ed., *Willa Cather's New York: New Essays on Cather and the City* (Madison, NJ: Fairleigh Dickinson University Press, 2000).
3. See Elizabeth Bumiller, "The First Lady Builds a Literary Room of Her Own," *New York Times*, October 7, 2002, p. A1.
4. See Joan Acocella, *Willa Cather and the Politics of Criticism* (Lincoln, NE, and London: University of Nebraska Press, 2000), p. 75. Further references will be made parenthetically.
5. In registering or reflecting the nativist anxieties and prejudices of her day, Cather is no different from her modernist peers, such as Hemingway and Fitzgerald. For a cogent overview of the intersections of modernism, and nativism in the USA, see Walter Benn Michaels, *Our America: Nativism, Modernism, and Pluralism* (Durham, NC: Duke University Press, 1995).
6. Cather joined *McClure's* in 1906 and was an editor from 1908 to 1912. See John March, *A Reader's Companion to the Fiction of Willa Cather* (Westport, CT: Greenwood Press, 1993), p. 450.
7. See note 2 above.
8. "Behind the Singer Tower" was published in 1912; "Scandal" was written in 1916, but not published until 1919. See note 20 below.
9. See Burton J. Hendrick, "The Great Jewish Invasion," *McClure's Magazine* (January 1907), pp. 307–21, quotation from p. 307. Further references will be made parenthetically.
10. For Cather's review, see Willa Cather, "New Types of Character Acting: The Character Actor Displaces the Star," *McClure's Magazine* (February 1914), pp. 41–51. Further references will be made parenthetically. *Potash and Perlmutter*, a play adapted from short stories by Montague Marsden Glass originally published in *The Saturday Evening Post*, opened at the Cohan Theatre on August 16, 1913. See Montague Glass, *Potash and Perlmutter* (1913; New York: Samuel French, 1935). A *New York Times* article announcing the play's debut editorialized that the play "proves to be an indescribably enjoyable entertainment." See "A Play to Cheer All New York," *New York Times*, August 17, 1913, sec. II, p. 9. The play was so popular for its mixture of ethnic comedy and sentiment that it ran for 441 performances and later opened in London. In 1923 Hollywood brought it to the screen.

11. See Madison Grant, *The Passing of the Great Race* (1916; New York: Arno Press, 1970), p. 91. Further references will be made parenthetically.
12. See Burton J. Hendrick, *The Jews in America* (1923; New York: Ayer, 1977).
13. For a more thorough examination of anti-Semitism during this period, see John Higham, *Send These to Me: Immigrants in Urban America* (1975; Baltimore: Johns Hopkins University Press, 1984); Carey McWilliams, *A Mask for Privilege: Anti-Semitism in America* (Boston, MA: Little, Brown & Co., 1948); and Gerald Sorin, *A Time for Building: The Third Migration, 1880–1920* (Baltimore: Johns Hopkins University Press, 1992; vol. 3 of *The Jewish People in America*, ed. Henry Feingold. 5 vols.).
14. For the Conrad allusion, see Joan Wylie Hall, "Cather's 'Deep Foundation Work': Reconstructing 'Behind the Singer Tower,'" *Studies in Short Fiction* 26.1 (Winter 1989), pp. 81–6. For a discussion of Flaubert's influence, see Evelyn Haller, "'Behind the Singer Tower': Willa Cather and Flaubert," 36.1 (Spring 1990), pp. 39–55. Haller's piece, beautifully illustrated with images of the Singer Tower, offers a particularly insightful history to the Singer building and to Cather's *McClure's* years.
15. See Loretta Wasserman, "Cather's Semitism," in Susan J. Rosowski, ed., *Cather Studies* 11 (1993): pp. 1–22. Further references will be made parenthetically.
16. Willa Cather, "Behind the Singer Tower," *Willa Cather's Collected Short Fiction, 1892–1912*, ed. Virginia Faulkner (Lincoln, NE: University of Nebraska Press, revised edition, 1970), p. 46. Further references will be made parenthetically.
17. For a dissenting reading of these Italian figures in the story, see Robert K. Miller, "'Behind the Singer Tower': A Transatlantic Tale," in Skaggs, ed., *Willa Cather's New York*, pp. 75–89.
18. See Willa Cather, "Escapism," in *On Writing: Critical Studies on Writing as an Art* (Lincoln, NE: University of Nebraska Press, 1988), p. 24.
19. For a more comprehensive account of Cather's fictional Jews, see Wasserman, "Cather's Semitism."
20. For a discussion of "Scandal"'s publishing history, see James Woodress, *Willa Cather: A Literary Life* (Lincoln, NE, and London: University of Nebraska Press, 1987), p. 282.
21. Willa Cather, "Scandal," in *Coming, Aphrodite! and Other Stories* (New York: Penguin, 1999), p. 98. Further references will be made parenthetically.
22. Willa Cather, *The Song of the Lark* (Boston, MA, and New York: Houghton Mifflin, 1915), p. 274.
23. According to March, *A Reader's Companion*, pp. 638–9, the Rosens of "Old Mrs. Harris" are modeled on the Weiners, Jewish neighbors of Cather's in Red Cloud. The Nathanmeyers of *The Song of the Lark* probably have the same origin.

5

JONATHAN GOLDBERG

Willa Cather and sexuality

The study of the significance of Cather's sexuality for her writing was decisively launched by Sharon O'Brien in a 1984 essay; subsequent work in this area takes O'Brien's 1987 biography of Cather as a benchmark, a necessary point of departure.[1] In "'The Thing Not Named': Willa Cather as a Lesbian Writer," O'Brien linked the topics I address here – the question of Cather's artistic practices; the question of her sexuality – in the phrase she highlights from Cather's programmatic 1922 essay, "The Novel Démeublé." "The thing not named" names the love that dare not speak its name, the crime not to be named among Christians. For O'Brien, Cather's self-recognition as a lesbian was inscribed under this prohibition (O'Brien found evidence for this self-understanding in an 1892 letter of Cather's to Louise Pound). "Cather did not fully or uncritically internalize the emotionally crippling definition of lesbianism as 'sick' or 'perverse' and challenged the social construction of female friendship as unnatural. And yet simultaneously she could not help accepting it" (p. 81). Out of this ambivalence, O'Brien argued, Cather fashioned gender-ambivalent characters (as she had early named herself William Cather, MD; she signed the letter to Pound "William"), displaced samesex desire into luscious descriptions of feminized landscapes, and eventually molded strong women characters who, however, never were coupled with other women. By *O Pioneers!*, where O'Brien's biography ends, and Cather's career as a novelist effectively began, Cather had consolidated an identity as a woman and as a lesbian, and had found her voice in depicting Alexandra Bergson.

In *Willa Cather: Queering America*, Marilee Lindemann notes the thesis of consolidation in O'Brien's biography – "as the subject of biography, O'Brien's 'Cather' is necessarily unified and coherent, and her shift from male to female identification is decisive and, one assumes, permanent" – in order to point to a different agenda in her own book, one not tied to the consolidations of the life of the author but to the conflicted terrains of national identity.[2] Lindemann's analysis can be situated through feminist inquiry that does not depend upon solidifications of the category of "woman." In that respect it might be compared to the decisive work of Judith Butler in *Gender Trouble*, or, more to the point here, to the starting point in Butler's chapter on Cather's "masculine names" in *Bodies That Matter*.³ Whereas O'Brien had found Cather's ambivalence with respect to her gender and sexuality resolved in "a putative identificatory bond with her mother," Butler writes, and had read Cather's characters as "mimetic reflections of these identifications" (p. 143), Butler insists that identification cannot be severed from "unresolved aggression or, minimally, ambivalence" (p. 144). For Butler, naming – as an act of self-identity – remains in question, in part because, sociologically, women are named by way of the father or husband; because, psychically, women are placed by the Law of the Father. Cather never gave up what O'Brien terms male identification, but, for Butler, gender identity cannot be understood in an essentialized fashion: Cather's masculine names do not necessarily carry masculine identity. Butler refuses mimetism as Cather's artistic principle in part to identify a deep psychic level, rather than a psychology, where resistance to the paternal law could be registered.

Butler shares with O'Brien before her, or Lindemann after, a feminist analysis of the prohibitions under which "woman" or "lesbian" is inscribed, what Lindemann refers to as, and reads Cather's texts as furthering, "networks of surveillance and prohibition" (p. 9). But in Foucauldian fashion, Butler breaks with these repressive hypotheses in order also to argue for the productive nature of prohibition. Because Cather did not, could not, name what cannot be named, she offers "lesbian sexuality *as* a specific practice of dissimulation produced through the very historical vocabularies that seek to effect its erasure" (p. 145). Lesbianism does not emerge *as itself*; it is never "radically distinct from heterosexuality" (p. 145):

> The love that dare not speak its name becomes for Cather a love that proliferates names at the site of that nonspeaking, establishing a possibility for fiction as this displacement, reiterating that prohibition and at the same time *working, indeed, exploiting that prohibition for the possibilities of its repetition and subversion.* The name thus functions as a kind of prohibition, but also as an enabling occasion.   (p. 152, italics original)

What is produced in the name is the unnameable. Although Butler does not cite "The Novel Démeublé," her formulation reads as a gloss on what Cather says her fiction *does*, what she does as a writer:

> Whatever is felt upon the page without being specifically named there – that, one might say, is created. It is the inexplicable presence of the thing not named, of the overtone divined by the ear but not heard by it, the verbal mood, the

emotional aura of the fact or the thing or the deed, that gives high quality to
the novel or the drama, as well as to poetry itself.[4]

Butler begins her essay engaging O'Brien, but her main interlocutor is Eve
Kosofsky Sedgwick.[5] As Christopher Nealon parses her response in an essay
on Cather published in *American Literature* in 1997 and incorporated into
his *Foundlings*, "Butler is playing the feminist to Sedgwick's queer theorist."[6]
Butler worries about Sedgwick's ease at accounting for Cather's movements
of identification across gender and sexuality (for, *pace* O'Brien, Cather's
depictions of Alexandra Bergson, Thea Kronborg, or Ántonia Shimerda are
not an endpoint: Claude Wheeler, Professor St. Peter, Archbishop Latour,
among others, lie ahead): "What becomes visible in this double refraction
are the shadows of the brutal suppressions by which a lesbian love did not
in Willa Cather's time and culture freely become visible as itself," Sedgwick
writes (p. 69). Butler disputes the "as itself" now and then, and thus demurs
as well from the translations Sedgwick makes when, for instance, she reads
"Paul's Case" as a "coming out" story (p. 65) in which the narrator/author
effects an identification between two gender-liminal characters – the mannish lesbian author, the sissy boy hero – a shared minoritizing identity that
is the basis for modern gay identity and identity politics. Although Sedgwick is aware that Cather's choices are "brutal," "expensive and wasteful"
(p. 69) in so far as she could not make lesbianism valuable or representable
as such, Butler hammers at the "cost" (p. 144). For her, one cannot achieve
what Sedgwick seems to assume possible – identity and identification. While
Sedgwick believes it would be possible someday, and perhaps is now, to
affirm "lesbian truths" (p. 69), Butler counters, "what cannot be named or
named with satisfaction exceeds every apparently satisfying act of nomination" (pp. 149–50). In that excess, which is never capable of self-identity,
also lies possibility, but the possibility will necessarily preclude identification or total translation (for example, the transportation of the mannish lesbian into the effeminate gay boy); it will block crossing, rendering it always
incomplete and inexact. Following the opening paragraph of "Paul's Case,"
Butler calls this "the ban of suspension." Nealon summarizes the differences
between Sedgwick and Butler towards a point of meeting, acutely locating
in both "the passion involved in clumsy, difficult cross-identifications"; he
epitomizes what they share and how they differ by contrasting Sedgwick's
nomination of Cather as a "passionate young lesbian" with Butler's fasten-
ing instead on the figure for the author in her texts, the narrator as a site for
"the passion of that nameless 'I'" (Nealon, p. 33).

To illustrate and clarify this argument, it is worth pausing over "Paul's
Case," the one text by Cather that both Sedgwick and Butler read. Butler

comes to the 1905 story by way of "Tommy the Unsentimental" and *My Ántonia*, providing readings attentive to the ways "Tommy" provides a model masculine name, the ways Cather inscribes and displaces herself as Jim Burden and as a "W" snaking its way across the text of *My Ántonia*. Sedgwick reads "Paul's Case" en route to *The Professor's House* and its "gorgeous homosocial romance" (Sedgwick, p. 68), which serves as a counterpoint to, and yet is the story hidden in and framing, the unpleasant family scene of the novel. Through the crossing in "Paul's Case," Sedgwick wrests possibilities from a plot that otherwise abjects and ultimately destroys the boy. For Butler, on the other hand, Paul never consolidates an identity – not even as a boy, let alone as proto-gay; he is as an amalgam of ill-fitting body parts, flying off in differently gendered directions, and existing at different levels of representation, a willful and yet will-less being, smirking and twitching.

For Sedgwick, the brutality of the story, the malice generated against Paul, is momentarily but breathtakingly rescinded when Paul looks at himself in the mirror in his room at the Waldorf. Having fled from Pittsburgh to New York with stolen money, he has taken a posh room and bought handsome clothes and gazes at himself in satisfaction: "he was exactly the kind of boy he had always wanted to be."[7] Sedgwick reads Paul's "kind" as "a gender-liminal (and very specifically classed) artifice that represents at once a particular subculture and culture itself" (p. 65). Paul has become "the seeing consciousness of the story" (p. 65), a consciousness that could be called gay. Butler, instead, refuses to read this scene of seeing as liberatory: "That Paul now assumes the place of the one who *watches* himself constitutes a displacement of the persecutorial 'watchers' who hounded him in and from Pittsburgh" (p. 166). Moreover, the mirror scene necessarily divides Paul into the watcher and the watched, reconstituting in him – in this doubling and self-division – the dynamic earlier in the story enacted between Paul and the world from which he sought to escape. Paul does escape, Butler argues, but only in so far as the suicide that ends the story is the terminus of this doubling and displacement of identity. To the degree that it is, Butler can ask, "is this death or his erotic release?" (p. 166) of the moment when Paul loses consciousness at the end of the story and drops "back into the immense design of things" (p. 488). The way out is still within, just as Paul's fantasy of escape from the dreary routines of lives lived under the shadow of capital is an arrival in a world where he has money. This is the explicit register of belongingness for Paul, the "kind" he acknowledges as his.

"The immense design of things" would seem, however, to exceed this fantasy of instantaneous, effortless class mobility (a fantasy Cather may well have shared, living in Judge McClung's house, and, like Paul, haunting the backstages of theaters – it was there she had met Isabelle McClung). The final phrase of "Paul's Case" suggests something Cather stresses throughout her career, that there is a life beyond consciousness, certainly beyond its manifestations in individuals, that houses enormous energies. It is often a life that effaces what is ordinarily termed life, as when Jim Burden, arriving on the prairie, first feels himself annihilated, erased, blotted out, "nothing" in the face of its immensity, almost immediately to discover happiness in erasure, as he sits in the garden and listens: "Nothing happened," and he becomes "something that lay under the sun and felt it." "Perhaps we feel like that when we die and become a part of something entire," he muses; ". . . that is happiness; to be dissolved into something complete and great."[8] Jim's final sentence is inscribed on Cather's gravestone.

This "design of things" has all the feel of being transcendent and transcendental, yet it is, at the moment of Paul's shattering, still a truth lodged in things; it is, for Jim, both a discovery of life and of death. Cather does not exactly say what this "something," this "design of things" is, yet it seems fair to associate it with a principle of life (even of life beyond life) and as a principle of art (whose life obviously is not limited to anyone's lifespan): it is the principle of "the thing not named." Following Butler, we might call it the death drive or it might be eros. But whatever it is, it also resonates with the scene of watching from "Paul's Case" that Sedgwick summons around Paul's mirror announcement. It echoes "the dark place into which he dared not look," the place where "something" unnameable – it is called "it" – "behind him, or before, or on either side . . . seemed always to be watching him" (p. 481). Cather never says what this figure might be, just as she never says what the immensity into which Paul is gathered is called. "It was always there" (p. 481).

If we see in this dark place of "seeing/being seen" the irremediable condition of an inescapable and not necessarily very welcome alterity or of the equally unpleasant exactions and deformations that the world necessitates as the condition of lived difference ("Paul had done things that were not pretty to watch, he knew" [p. 481]), we might also recognize that this alterity is not finally a difference apart: it structures the "design of things." As Sedgwick says, the specifics of a subculture are tantamount to culture; the impossibility of self-identical identity, in Butler's reading, reveals a life that exceeds the law.

The divide in these readings – and in Cather – can be illuminated by Cather's 1925 essay on Katherine Mansfield. There, she speaks of the "double life" all individuals endure: the group life of family and community and "underneath, another – secret and passionate and intense," which drives one away from the group.[9] These two spheres plot "Paul's Case," his flight from the dreary sameness of Cordelia Street; in its prairie translation this is the story of Thea, Claude, and others. The plot, however, has a complication; the secret drive inward and away also propels one towards others, to those Cather names in the Mansfield essay as "friends"; what one hears or sees in them is "the real life that stamps the faces and gives character to the voices of our friends." Hence, "human relationships are the tragic necessity of human life." One yearns to be oneself, to embrace one's own unique, secret source of being. But one also is located in circumstances, the given of the family in which one is born, and the affective world one has made – a secret society of sought-for sameness and identification. When Paul says he is "the kind of boy he wished to be," he imagines himself as someone else, as related to others who are like him. He sees himself as some "kind." But, as Cather's essay on Mansfield suggests, that is everyone's condition. And, as she does not quite suggest there, but does in novel after novel (Nealon demonstrates this), there is almost no chance that the family in which one is born – or by extension, the world ruled by the Law of the Father (menacingly represented in "Paul's Case" by the hairy-legged man at the top of the stairs) – will be most accommodating to energies that exceed conformist compulsion. Cather suggests that in everyone there is this other force, that one gropes towards like-minded others in the hope of discovery of sameness; that one never in fact finds that mirroring other. On the one hand, that the family is not where these ties will be made is one indication that this fact about everyone exceeds the ways in which lives are ordinarily ordered socially. But it suggests, on the other hand, an immense design of things in which these "other" desires have their place. It is the task of Cather's fiction to represent these alterities.

In theoretical terms, this means that Cather's fiction is riven between incipient moments of minoritizing identity (the few who know their difference and the impossibility of living it) and universalizing identifications (what few realize everyone potentially has), to use Sedgwick's terms; between ethnic and cross-gender models, in Nealon's terminology. Butler radicalizes these claims in so far as she suggests that Cather cannot be read as some kind of realist writer aiming at mimesis, that therefore her texts deliver the site of the impossibility of mediation of the kinds of oppositions and ambivalences that other readers mobilize towards legibility. Butler's Cather challenges legibility: "lesbian sexuality within the text is produced as a perpetual challenge to legibility" (p. 145). "Lesbianism" thus will never translate and name what cannot be named. Rather, Cather keeps nomination at the level of the unnameable "something" where meaning lies. "Lesbianism" is the "name" of the erasure, the "immense design" lodged in "it" and "something."

In The Song of the Lark, Thea is soon aware of her difference in just these terms: "She knew, of course, that there was something about her that was different."[10] That "something" she likens to a "friendly spirit," not as a part of herself: "She brought everything to it, and it answered her; happiness consisted of the backward and forward movement of herself. The something came and went, she never knew how" (p. 72). Later, the "something," the "it," manifests itself as her voice, or, rather, is manifest as a voice in her. Harsanyi feels it vibrating – it's not quite something he ever hears, not quite something ever to be located in her although that is where he feels it: "no one knew that it had come, or even that it existed; least of all the strange, crude girl in whose throat it beat its passionate wings" (p. 171). Thea comes to be possessed by this spirit, which grows less friendly and more demanding as she begins her flight to success. "There had always been something," she recalls herself saying and thinking, a secret part of herself that she needed to keep "from being caught up in the meshes of common things. She took it for granted that some day, when she was older, she would know a great deal more about it. It was as if she had an appointment to meet the rest of herself sometime, somewhere. It was moving to meet her and she was moving to meet it" (p. 196). When Thea arrives, she keeps this assignation with "the other woman down at the opera house, who had used her hardly" (p. 362). That other woman is herself; Thea's internalization and her externalization – her vocalization – is the uncanny place of meeting of a driving force that is her unnameable devouring secret. Her self-identity is an unnameable alterity within her, manifest in a voice that she produces and that exceeds her production.

Thea's self-realization is thus of something not herself, something that drives her – away from all conventional relationships, into the passionate dyad of an impossible self-meeting realized only in the opulent bestowal of a voice that is not exactly hers to bestow. In light of this dynamic, it might finally be possible for critics to stop lambasting Paul as someone who merely (effeminately) absorbs art. These punishing dynamics of possession and dispossession can be linked to those that Butler identifies through the name, or that Nealon tallies in the repeated abuses heaped upon cherished impossibilities of relationship (a lacerating dynamic that applies as well to "Paul's Case").

Thus, in *One of Ours*, Claude's self-understanding of his shameful difference comes from his imagining a kind, a "race," to which he belongs, children of the moon, misfits and outcasts, old maids and effeminate men, people who read literature rather than law books, dreamers.[11] Misfits, they are like Butler's reading of the suspended parts of Paul's body; and indeed Paul's case anticipates Claude's, who also is manhandled by his father, sent into war to be shattered but also there to find a camaraderie not possible to him in family or married life (his wife refuses sex on their wedding night).

Nealon has written especially movingly about Cather's treatment of Claude, the bruising to which she subjects him, the loving sadism of her stance. It could be related to the exactions Butler traces, the cost to Cather of a writing in the masculine, which also is necessarily a wounding of the very position supposedly denied her and assumed by men. It is related as well to the impossible reach of cross-identification in Sedgwick's arguments, the imperfect translation of female–female desire into male–male romance.

As Lindemann suggests, these possibilities are best realized in *Death Comes for the Archbishop*, not, she cautions, that one should read through Latour and Vaillant to find a lesbian couple beneath their male masquerade; nor should one read them as a homosexual couple, for to do either is "to miss how far the text goes to destabilize the connection between sex and gender through a complex process of mingling, switching, and redistributing of attributes and energies that achieve a particular intensity within the unit of the couple" (p. 123). Lindemann urges, then, a reading of what is there. A key is offered as the first part of the novel closes. Father Vaillant responds to the miraculous story of the Virgin of Guadeloupe, the apparition of her image in the folds of a poor mantle. Latour does not really believe that miracles go beyond the designs of nature. They are rather for him a secret in nature, in perception; "it was just this in his friend that was dear to him":

> "Where there is great love there are always miracles," he said at length. "One might almost say that an apparition is human vision corrected by divine love. I do not see you as you really are, Joseph; I see you through my affection for you. The Miracles of the Church seem to me to rest not so much upon faces or voices or healing power coming suddenly near to us from afar off, but upon our perception being made finer, so that for a moment our eyes can see and our ears can hear what is there about us always."[12]

Here, as in the essay on Katherine Mansfield, Cather stresses the working of affect, the reaching out in friendship to another. Miracles do not come from elsewhere, but from within; from within perception and from within the world. They are to be seen and heard, but, as in "The Novel Démeublé," they exceed ordinary hearing and seeing. In the relationship of Jean Latour and Joseph Vaillant, Cather plots an alternative to family, the "affect-genealogy" that Nealon explores, in their pained joining – as Latour takes Joseph away from his family, draws him to him ("*L'invitation du voyage!*" [p. 285]), only, again and again, to exact separations, only, again and again, to feel the need to bring Joseph back to him. Finally, as he approaches his own death, he approaches his friend in death. There what is impossible to sustain will be impossibly sustained, the back and forth between the drive deep within to an unnameable site, the drive outward to its fulfillment will perhaps be met. Cather summons all the force of Christian belief in order to glimpse something that lies beyond it, an immense design in things – in material existence – conveyed in ranges of feeling that exceed all conventional designs: the image of the Virgin in the threads of an ordinary mantle.

Cather's novels, so recalcitrant to analysis, so insistent upon levels of inarticulateness, are devoted to the unnameable found in the relationship to an alterity that she plots: at times, as a division within the self, never quite to be breached; at other times, in the yearning for relationships with others, never quite to be cemented, and in all the recoils within these relationships that signal the impossibility of the realization of a desire that is there to be had at any moment, were we only to see or hear it. In her laconic texts, as Sedgwick says, there spring suddenly and unexpectedly miraculous moments of the realization of the all-but-unrealizable and the all-but-unnameable, "unrecognized pockets of value and vitality that can hit out in unpredictable directions" (p. 70).

In the pages above, it has been my aim to suggest how Cather's aesthetic principles and artistic practices can be understood through the lens that sexuality provides, and I have drawn upon the criticism that I think helps best to further this area of study. Inevitably, I write under the shadow cast on such inquiry by Joan Acocella in an article that appeared in *The New Yorker* in 1995 and was expanded as *Willa Cather and the Politics of Criticism*.[13] Those who know her argument may notice that some of the features of Cather's writing emphasized above, especially the sense of an enormous "design" in which humans are caught, are also features that Acocella values in her work: "all the while that Cather is describing life's terrors, she never stops asserting its beauties: the dome of heaven, the flaming sun. The dream is still there; we just can't have it" (p. 6). This is well said if a bit vague and evasive. What terrors? What beauties? What dream does life open and refuse? Acocella charges that to ask further is to politicize Cather. Yet, in the simplest meaning of the term, Acocella's venture is political, for she sounds like no one more than William Bennett as she deplores the excesses of the academy, the harm done to innocent children by educators: "Why should all this wild-eyed academic writing concern anyone but academics? Because it filters down quickly to the public. Academics, after all, are the people who teach students" (p. 60). If her logic were followed to its conclusion, Acocella would seem to be advocating the closure of the academy. Her politics are reactionary.

Acocella does see some things about Cather worth seeing; she even scores some points about critical practice that could be worth making, were they made responsibly. She starts well, for instance, by noting that breathtaking sentence Thea utters to Fred late in *The Song of the Lark*, "Who marries who is a small matter, after all" (p. 401), and its stunning applicability both to Cather and to her writing project, which summarily dispenses with the marriage plot as female destiny: "Thea takes for herself the privilege of a man: to have a sex, indeed to have sex . . . and yet not to make these facts and their ramifications – marriage, family – the boundary of her imagination. The reason she is able to do so is that this, basically, is what her creator did" (p. 2). If so, how can Acocella then assert that "Cather was homosexual in her feelings and celibate in her actions" (p. 48)? "For thirty-nine years . . . Cather lived with Edith Lewis, who, whatever other role she filled in Cather's life, took care of all the practical details of their household, freeing Cather to work. Lewis fended off the callers; she helped correct the galleys. She did everything that 'literary wives' used to do" (p. 46). The evidence Acocella presents about the relationship is compelling, but it does not support her claim that Cather's life was sexless. Rather, Acocella presents Cather as conventionally married – but to another woman, and not at all reticent about it. Because she treats Cather so conventionally, she can't understand the lifelong passion for Isabelle McClung that the relationship with Lewis allowed. Moreover, in Acocella's version of the letter to Louise Pound upon which O'Brien founded her sense of Cather's ambivalence about lesbian relations, Cather writes that erotic relations between women should not be thought of as "unnatural" (p. 50).[14] Because Cather seems unconflicted, Acocella assumes she could not have been lesbian, since lesbianism is one of those "ugly allegations" (p. 49) that ought not be made about anyone.

What Cather finds unnatural and largely unfulfilling, however, is marriage, as Acocella all but says in summarizing the plot of *The Professor's House* as a story "in which a man, in the *normal* course of things, loses everything he lived for, almost succeeds in killing himself, and then decides that he will simply live with nothing to live for" (p. 21). Fair enough (if one ignores the point stressed by Sedgwick, that the Professor has lived off his family – his wife and daughters – and that a large dose of straight male self-pity creates the pathos to which Acocella responds): but if marriage – normal life, Acocella stresses – has been such a disappointment, what was it that St. Peter desired? What drives him to despair? Not just his family's commercialism, its material success, but the loss of Tom Outland, which is surely the source of his sadness, but whose memory gives him hope to go on living. He can never recover the dead young man, or his own former self, the boyhood he lost when he gave himself over to marriage: "His career, his wife, his family, were not his life at all, but a chain of events that had happened to him. All these things had nothing to do with the person he was in the beginning."[15] At the center of Cather's novel stands Tom's story; at the heart of St. Peter's life alone – his family off in Europe on a holiday he cannot bear to take, since he had planned to take it with Tom – he reads Tom's diary as he prepares an edition of it. We are never given that text, but we know the Professor's response to its "plain account":

> To St. Peter this plain account was almost beautiful, because of the stupidities it avoided and the things it did not say . . . The adjectives were purely descriptive, relating to form and colour, and were used to present the objects under consideration, not the young explorer's emotions. Yet through this austerity one felt the kindling imagination, the ardour and excitement of the boy, like the vibration in a voice when the speaker strives to conceal his emotion by using only conventional phrases. (p. 238)

Tom's diary sounds, of course, like the description of her own writing that Cather provided in "The Novel Démeublé," stripped down and vibrating all the while, if we have ears to hear. It suggests that the infinite sadness of the Professor, to which Acocella responds, and which she sees written over Cather's work, is caused by the loss of a love object, by denial of his best impulses. It is a loss connected to vast impersonal and universal energies, as Cather suggests by linking Tom to the extinct Anasazi and the treasures of their civilization. It is a loss compounded by the unnatural exactions of family and marriage.

In her partial and unfair way, Acocella summarizes the work of gay criticism around *The Professor's House* as a game of finding the homosexual in the text (a game to which she actually also contributes). Readings framed by identity politics are reductive. But that is not the task in all the criticism that Acocella cites. Cather's sense of a "secret" most people refuse to acknowledge about themselves, often to their own destruction, is less a statement about identity than, to use Sedgwick's word, one about "tendencies" more widely available. Part of the virulent defense against homoerotic meaning in Cather must lie in homosexual panic. How terrible to discover that what one has been responding to, reading her work, has been *that*.

Acocella claims to sponsor close, attentive reading, yet she lights on the last moment in Sedgwick's essay (she ignores everything else in it), an elaborate unravelling of possible phrases buried in the name of the ship, the *Berengaria*, returning the Professor's family home from France. "This list of anagrams, which must have taken a while to work out," Acocella sneers, is beside the point; *Berengaria* "was the name of a real ship" (p. 56), as Cather knew, and as Acocella presumes Sedgwick does not. How is this a practice of reading? How an answer to the question, why did Cather choose this name from those of the many other ships crossing the Atlantic in the 1920s? How does the "real" enter into literature? Is a novel a reference book? Do authors not care about words? Cather names the hero of *One of Ours* Claude Wheeler: as it happens her name and his are almost perfectly anagrammatic.[16] Perhaps what Sedgwick heard in the word Cather did too, whether consciously planning the anagrammatic possibility or not. As Butler suggests, Cather is not a mimetic writer, and her work offers "figuration that enables precisely the sexuality it thematically forecloses" (p. 161). The "life" that exceeds the surface of Cather's texts, and that a reading such as Sedgwick's attempts to plumb, lies precisely in the fact that these texts are texts.

As Acocella sidles up to produce a one-liner on Butler, she offers a page-long citation from *My Ántonia* and a paragraph of analysis as exemplary reading practice (pp. 70–1). Such full citation is Acocella's equivalent of a certain old-fashioned form of pedagogy, reading aloud, as if just hearing the beauties of the language automatically conveys the meaning. Acocella chooses an early scene between Jim and Ántonia, a language lesson, a lesson in names. For her, the scene is powerful because it is proleptic. The wind blows up Ántonia's skirt: "Her illegitimate pregnancy is prefigured here" (p. 71). Jim refuses a ring that Ántonia offers: "the two won't marry" (p. 71). "The whole book is there" (p. 71). The whole book? What kind of reading is this? Again, high school comes to mind, guessing ahead through symbolic meaning to how the novel ends (as if plot were a major value in Cather's writing). Suppose for a moment that the scene were proleptic this way: in what marriage ceremony does the bride alone offer the groom a ring? If it is a marriage, Cather has got it backwards. If there were to be a marriage between these characters, it would be like the one that ends *O Pioneers!*, where an assertive woman marries a shrinking man, where something like the crossing plot that Sedgwick identifies is effected, a marriage between friends that is only nominally heterosexual and certainly not the endpoint of a romance plot (that has been shattered in the murder of the lovers Emil and Marie). Acocella reads the page from *My Ántonia* wondering whether Jim and Ántonia will marry; were she true to her insight about *The Song of the Lark*, she might consider that such a question could not interest Cather less.

This scene in *My Ántonia* is important for Butler – it is where the question of naming arises. Ántonia attempts a connection between the blue of Jim's eyes and the blue of the sky. If the word "blue" serves as a sign for larger connections, it is because, as Butler argues, words are not merely referential, and they point beyond themselves to meanings about kinds of connections otherwise inarticulable, as St. Peter discovered reading Tom's diary. Why cannot Jim and Ántonia be a romance couple? Surely not because his eyes are blue and hers are brown, or because she is impulsive and he is reflective, as Acocella implies. Those surely are not barriers to marriage. The terms that *My Ántonia* suggests for the impossibility – class and proto-racial difference, as I argue in *Willa Cather and Others*, also seem inadequate. The unsaid here is the locus of difficult cross-identifications.

During the 1950s and 1960s, when she had fallen out of critical fashion, Cather was preserved by a hardcore group of believers who found her work the repository of deep spiritual meaning. This is Acocella's Cather as well, a Platonist and a Christian, she tells us over and again in the closing pages of her book, but also, she says, a believer in Nature, source of life and its cruelty. (As usual, Acocella speaks only in generalized, abstracted categories, failing to register the discrepancies between these concepts, acting as if some potted Great Books curriculum constituted the limits of Cather's knowledge, which was, in fact, wider and more complex – Bergson, for example, interested her.) "Nature showed her that the world might be beautiful, and loud with life, yet wholly indifferent to the happiness of its creatures" (p. 89). Once again, Cather is made fit for a high-school lesson plan, slotted under the supposedly timeless rubric of "Man vs. Nature." (To the extent that her observation has validity, Acocella's terms can be brought within the orbit of a central question for Cather – how the crime against nature was none the less natural.) The 1950s and 1960s were, Acocella says, a time for symbol-hunters, small-minded critics who turned Cather into prepackaged themes and mythic designs. These descriptions of a criticism that Acocella admits to have been political in its very refusal of politics, "Cold War criticism" (p. 34), also describe Acocella's procedures.

In *Foundlings*, Nealon sums up the case:

> I suggest, then, that far from coldly manipulating Cather in the name of a purely political "lesbian agenda," as Joan Acocella might have it, contemporary queer theorists are struggling to use theoretical insights to bring them closer to what they love. This attempt at claiming, at bringing close, is also deeply political, of course: not everyone is going to want to hear that Cather's literary value is utterly related, at every level, to her being a lesbian. But the politics involved are not merely some kind of "special interest" politics. (p. 96)

For, Nealon continues, in the impossible desire that moves Cather to a "life" beyond what ordinarily seems possible, she offers a vision that "posterity most needs to know." Acocella would have critics repeat pieties, stop thinking, turn back the clock. It is a dim recipe for education, and it does Cather no service at all.

I began this chapter by pointing to the inspiring role of Sharon O'Brien, and O'Brien is the one critic to whom Acocella gives any time (although certainly never in a spirit of fairness, as Terry Castle points out in a review of Acocella's book[17]). For Acocella, O'Brien is the evil agent who began the "ugly allegations" about Cather (p. 40). If O'Brien is to be faulted, as Butler suggests, it is for overstating the resolution of the mother–daughter bond in Cather as a key to her lesbianism. This is most evident in relation to Cather's final novel, *Sapphira and the Slave Girl*, a book deformed by the breaking of the mother–daughter bond. This novel comes closest to representing female–female desire, but in the spirit of aggressivity that Butler underlines. Its plot, after all, involves a woman's attempts to engineer the rape of another woman.[18] This final scene in Cather's career as a novelist could be compared to one she wrote much earlier, where heterosexual rape is averted when the man who attempts it is foiled by a boy he finds where he expected a girl. The would-be rapist is named Wick Cutter. WC for short. "Name? What name?," Ántonia might ask.[19]

NOTES

1. I refer to Sharon O'Brien, "'The Thing Not Named': Willa Cather as a Lesbian Writer," *Signs* 9.4 (Summer 1984), pp. 576–99, and cite its reprint in Estelle B. Freedman, Barbara C. Gelpi, Susan L. Johnson and Kathleen M. Weston, eds., *The Lesbian Issue* (Chicago: University of Chicago Press, 1985); and to O'Brien, *Willa Cather: The Emerging Voice* (New York and Oxford: Oxford University Press, 1987), which incorporates and expands upon the earlier essay.
2. Marilee Lindemann, *Willa Cather: Queering America* (New York: Columbia University Press, 1999), p. 6. Further references will be made parenthetically.
3. See Judith Butler, *Gender Trouble: Feminism and the Subversion of Identity* (New York: Routledge, 1990), ch. 1; "'Dangerous Crossing': Willa Cather's Masculine Names," in *Bodies That Matter: On the Discursive Limits of "Sex"* (New York and London: Routledge, 1993), from which all citations, made parenthetically, are drawn.
4. "The Novel Démeublé," in Willa Cather, *Not Under Forty* (1936; Lincoln, NE: University of Nebraska Press, 1988), p. 50.
5. Butler responds to Eve Kosofsky Sedgwick, "Across Gender, Across Sexuality: Willa Cather and Others," *South Atlantic Quarterly* 88.1 (Winter 1989), pp. 53–72, from which I will be citing parenthetically in the text. The essay is reprinted in Ronald R. Butters, John M. Clum, and Michael Moon, eds., *Displacing Homophobia* (Durham, NC: Duke University Press, 1989); its theoretical overture is incorporated into *Epistemology of the Closet* (Berkeley: University of California Press, 1990), pp. 27–35, while the reading of Cather appears as "Willa Cather and Others" in *Tendencies* (Durham, NC: Duke University Press, 1993), pp. 167–76.
6. Christopher Nealon, "Affect-Genealogy: Feeling and Affiliation in Willa Cather," *American Literature* 69.1 (March 1997), pp. 5–37; I cite p. 32, and, unless otherwise noted, will be citing this version of the essay, which is recast and expanded as "Feeling and Affiliation in Willa Cather," in *Foundlings: Lesbian and Gay Historical Emotion Before Stonewall* (Durham, NC, and London: Duke University Press, 2001). The cited sentence does not appear in the book. My analysis of the exchange between Butler and Sedgwick is indebted to Nealon.

7. "Paul's Case," in Willa Cather, *Stories, Poems, and Other Writings*, ed. Sharon O'Brien (New York: Library of America, 1992), p. 482. Further references will be made parenthetically.

8. Willa Cather, *My Ántonia* (1918, rev. 1926; Boston, MA: Houghton Mifflin, 1988), pp. 7–8, 14.

9. "Katherine Mansfield," in Cather, *Not Under Forty*, p. 136. On this passage, see Nealon, "Affect-Genealogy," pp. 8–9, and Jonathan Goldberg, *Willa Cather and Others* (Durham, NC: Duke University Press, 2001), pp. 8–9, 13.

10. Willa Cather, *The Song of the Lark* (1915; Boston, MA: Houghton Mifflin, 1988), p. 72. Further references will be made parenthetically.

11. Willa Cather, *One of Ours* (1922; New York: Vintage, 1991), see, e.g., p. 171: "these children of the moon, with their unappeased longings and futile dreams, were a finer race than the children of the sun." Because Cather employs an "ethnic" model for Claude's "kind," discourses of sexuality in her novels are entangled with discourses of race.

12. Willa Cather, *Death Comes for the Archbishop* (1927; New York: Vintage, 1971), p. 50. Further references will be made parenthetically.

13. Joan Acocella, "Cather and the Academy," *The New Yorker*, November 27, 1995, pp. 56–71, enlarged as *Willa Cather and the Politics of Criticism* (Lincoln, NE, and London: University of Nebraska Press, 2000), from which all citations will be made parenthetically.

14. This is also Lindemann's reading (p. 20), as well as the summary in Janis P. Stout, ed., *A Calendar of the Letters of Willa Cather* (Lincoln, NE: University of Nebraska Press, 2002), p. 2.

15. Willa Cather, *The Professor's House* (New York: Vintage, 1990), p. 240. Further references will be made parenthetically.

16. On this, see Goldberg, *Willa Cather and Others*, p. 116.

17. Castle's review appeared in *The London Review of Books* 22.24 (December 14, 2000).

18. For an account of the relationship between cross-racial and lesbian desire in the novel, see Naomi Morgenstern, "'Love is Home-Sickness': Nostalgia and Lesbian Desire in *Sapphira and the Slave Girl*," *Novel* 29 (1995–6), pp. 184–205.

19. For more on these connections, see Goldberg, *Willa Cather and Others*, pp. 20–42.

6

JANIS P. STOUT

Willa Cather and the performing arts

Readers of Willa Cather's fiction are well aware that many of her most interesting and memorable characters are performing artists. Probably Thea Kronborg, of *The Song of the Lark*, comes most immediately to mind, but there are many others, some familiar and some not. Even well-informed readers of Cather's novels and stories may not realize, however, the extent of her own familiarity with the performing arts and how much her development of these performing-artist characters rests on direct experience. Cather was in fact intensely devoted to music and theatre throughout her life, and wrote numerous theatre reviews and critical columns about the performing arts during her twenty or more years as a journalist. After she became associated with the successful and influential magazine *McClure's*, she also wrote informative articles about performing artists, thereby adding to her expertise. The knowledge she accumulated, as well as her personal passion for the theatre and music, contributed importantly to the development of her artistic principles and goals, her conception of herself as an artist, and even her conception of gender – as well as to the success of her stories and novels that involve performers and performances.

Cather's interest in theatre traces back to her childhood and adolescence in Red Cloud, Nebraska. In those days, many small towns had performance halls, usually called opera houses. Red Cloud was such a town. Touring companies, lecturers, and musicians came to town to put on plays and concerts, and we know from her own reminiscences that the young Cather took keen delight in the bustle of excitement that preceded these events, as well as in the performances themselves. In a tribute to the magic of the old opera house written many years later, she recalled the enchantment of studying the advertising posters and the thrill of seeing the members of the company arrive at the railroad station. These "barnstorming companies," she wrote, "command[ed]" her "breathless, rapt attention and deep feeling" and "fired" her imagination.[1] Besides attending such professional productions, she also took part in amateur theatricals. The photographic record shows her as a child costumed as Hiawatha and as the top-hatted father in a version of *Beauty and the Beast.*[2]

When she went away to Lincoln in September 1890 to attend the University of Nebraska's Latin school for a year preparatory to her four years at the university, she had ample opportunity to expand this well-established interest in theatre. Professional theatre was Lincoln's "greatest cultural distinction," with several plays a week and perhaps a hundred companies a year making appearances.[3] During her student days there, from fall 1890 to June 1895, Cather attended plays and concerts avidly and wrote reviews. Her interest in music was greatly enriched, too, under the influence of her favorite professor, who served as music critic on a local paper. In the spring of her senior year, already a seasoned reviewer, she combined her interests in drama and in music in a trip to Chicago for five nights of opera.

At the university Cather also continued her amateur acting, taking roles in productions of classic Greek dramas. These were the last of her own performances – that is, on stage. But in a larger sense we can see that she had long been performing and would continue to perform on the stage of her own life. As an adolescent she had played the role of the masculine girl, with a closely cropped haircut and masculine-looking clothes. This self-costuming is sometimes interpreted as cross-dressing, an avowal of a lesbian self. And perhaps it was. But even though photographs show her appearance as startlingly boyish, her square-shouldered jackets and mannish hats were actually fashionable styles for women.[4] Perhaps, then, she was simply performing the role of the New Woman, in the simpler clothes, affording greater freedom of movement, that accompanied the widening of career opportunities for women, especially in journalism.

However we interpret her youthful persona, it is clear that Cather learned greater versatility in self-presentation by the time she graduated from college. Pictures in her graduation ball gown or her opera cloak show that she was choosing to project a more feminine image by then, perhaps in preparation for entering a career, when she would have to be keenly aware of the impression she was making. In later years, as well, she demonstrated enormous versatility in the images she projected. Always, of course, she was constructing herself as a literary artist, but her emphasis varied from the bold and jaunty New Woman she presented when she first went to Pittsburgh to work as a journalist, to the urbane professional image she cultivated when she joined *McClure's Magazine* in 1906 in New York, to the hearty westerner she portrayed when she "hit the home pasture" (as she put it in a letter to Carrie Miner Sherwood)[5] in her novels set on the plains and in the Southwest. As her theatre reviews show, she was keenly aware of such factors as costume and bodily carriage in the projection of character. We have to believe that these observations of performance contributed to her virtuosity in performing a personal identity.[6] She gave fascinated attention to the ways in which actresses performed gender – that is, how, through costume and walk, voice and posture, they conveyed various ways in which to be female. Cather, too, maintained, through a certain theatricality in dress, a performative repertoire of ways to be a woman.

Cather became a journalist at a strikingly early age. By the fall of her sophomore year she was an editor on the campus literary paper, the *Hesperian*, and in the fall of her junior year, when she was not yet twenty, became a regular contributor to the *Nebraska State Journal*, a leading regional newspaper, primarily writing theatre reviews and critical columns. Her output was voluminous. In the single month of February 1894, she reviewed eight plays and published an additional three opinion columns on theatre. These early pieces were unsigned, but by May of that year she occasionally had a byline, though she would continue to publish unsigned reviews, too, for some years. By the age of twenty-one Cather was already respected for her seriousness and high standards as a theatre critic/reviewer and feared by members of traveling companies for her severity when her standards were not met. This surprisingly extensive experience in the theater, for one so young, taught her to recognize and value quality in performance. It also helped her develop a fairly cogent set of aesthetic theories that carried over into her writing. Thus, both in providing subject-matter for her fiction and in shaping the ideas that governed how she wrote, it was enormously important in shaping her literary career.

She was fortunate in being able to see some of the greatest performers of her time, both male and female, both actors and singers. Many of the newspaper columns and magazine articles she wrote about them would, in fact, make lively reading today if reprinted in a volume. Indeed, if she had carried through with one of her early ideas, we would have such a volume. In the late 1890s she approached publishers with a proposal or perhaps a complete manuscript for a book made up of open letters to famous actors. Although the idea of a full volume of such pieces (probably based on earlier reviews) came to nothing, three of the pieces were published as columns, including "letters" to two of her favorites, Nat Goodwin and Joseph Jefferson, the latter known for his performances as Rip Van Winkle, a role he played for over thirty years. Cather saw Jefferson as Rip at least twice, several years apart, and praised his warmth and engaging humanity in the role both times. Like many other writers of her time, however, she gave more attention to actresses than to males. Actresses were figures of great interest, not least for their unsettling of conventional views relating to gender. The most famous and perhaps the greatest of the day was "the Divine Sarah," Sarah Bernhardt

(1844–1923), whom Cather first saw in 1892, when she was not quite twenty years old. "Sarah the Grand," as Cather referred to her, was then almost fifty but still successfully portraying women much younger. Cather praised Bernhardt's ability to convey strong passion "genuinely," without lapsing into conventionalism or mere sentimentality (W&P, p. 39). In 1901 she saw four performances by Bernhardt in Washington, DC, and wrote an adulatory review emphasizing her "grand manner" (W&P, p. 815).

Bernhardt may have been a prototype for Cather's conception of Thea Kronborg, in *The Song of the Lark*, at least with respect to temperament. In 1894, more than two decades before publication of the novel, she commented that "very few of the world's great artists have been desirable acquaintances" and added, "Heaven preserve me from any very intimate relations" with Bernhardt – an amusing remark, since there was little likelihood that that would happen anyway (W&P, p. 49). Thea, too, is more great than pleasant.

Bernhardt's chief rival was the Italian actress Eleanora Duse (1854–1924). Cather admired both, though their styles were quite dissimilar, Bernhardt's being more flamboyant, Duse's more restrained (restraint being a relative matter, of course, since late-nineteenth century acting was far more florid than today's.) Even more restrained in style was the celebrated Helena Modjeska (1840–1909), whom Cather interviewed over lunch in 1898 (WC to Mariel Gere, March 7, 1898; *Calendar*, no. 48). She had first seen Modjeska in 1892 in *As You Like It*, then in 1893 in *Henry VIII*. After she began writing reviews, she referred to Modjeska frequently, calling her "grand," "queenly," and able to convey an "undercurrent of passion" with "naturalness and simplicity" and "freedom from exaggeration" – terms that go far towards enabling us to understand Cather's own artistic (and literary) standards (W&P, pp. 36–7, 458). She considered Modjeska, in her "freedom from exaggeration," to be "a realist in the best sense of the word" (W&P, p. 458) – a phrase that could serve as one of the best possible summaries of what Cather herself would attempt to be in her fiction. Modjeska makes a cameo appearance in Cather's brief novel *My Mortal Enemy*, where she embodies the quality and depth of a life devoted to art, in contrast to a New York social set given to socializing and extravagance.

Another cameo appearance, this one in *My Ántonia*, is made by the actress Clara Morris (1848–1925), a performer not even in the same league as Bernhardt, Duse, and Modjeska, and one we would not expect Cather to admire, since contemporaries described her style as "extravagant," "bizarre," and at times "hysterical."[7] And indeed in reviewing Morris's performance in *Camille* in November 1893 – the basis for the tear-jerking performance that Jim Burden and Lena Lingard see in *My Ántonia* (WC to Chilson Leonard, March 19, 1936; *Calendar*, no. 1306) – Cather found her style to be so violently emotional that it became "grotesque" (*W&P*, p. 44). Yet once again she proves herself flexible on these matters. She was convinced that Morris did generate real dramatic power on stage, projecting passion and making her audience *care* about the character she was portraying. That was what mattered.

Cather's interest in actresses was not a gossip-column kind of curiosity but a fascinated attention to their professional techniques and their ability to bring that skill to bear by investing a depth of emotional energy in each performance. Such an investment of self, combined with intelligent preparation and polished techniques, was what gave a performer "power" – a term that occurs with notable frequency in Cather's comments about actors, men as well as women, in letters as well as reviews and articles. She used the term "power" in writing about singers as well, praising the soprano Lillian Nordica for her "powerful," "all-conquering" voice (*W&P*, p. 645) but writing that another singer lacked "power to portray emotion of any kind" (*W&P*, p. 393). Her standards for singers and for actors, then, had much in common. Compelling stage presence was a major consideration, and a great singer, like a great actor, could so captivate an audience that they would forget where they were (*W&P*, p. 526). Basically, then, Cather seems to have meant by the word "power" the authority, passion, and credibility of a performer's projection of character, an ability to compel audience members' attention and emotional investment. She was quite ready to understand that the techniques through which a performer demonstrated "power" could vary, but the "power" itself had to be in evidence for her to find a performance or a production memorable.

Involvement in the character being portrayed was, to her, the essence of drama. She once flatly told her friend Zoë Akins, a successful playwright, that she disliked her new play because there was "not a single character one [could] care about," and on another occasion said she did not care for Akins's new play because she did not like the leading actress – comments that show how central a consideration character and the performance of character were for her (WC to Zoë Akins, February 15, 1940, and January 15, 1931; *Calendar*, nos. 1474 and 1034). When she praised another of Akins's plays, she said the leading actress was "as powerful as a fine car" (WC to Zoë Akins, November 21, 1922; *Calendar*, no. 647).[8] Character and the power and credibility of an actor's projection of character constituted, for her, good theatre. On this point, there was a great deal of carry-over between her thinking about theatre and her thinking about literature, since there, too, it was mainly character that mattered to her.

The sheer bulk of Cather's journalism during her college years and early post-college career makes it hard to generalize about her formulation of aesthetic principles or theories. (The collection in *The World and the Parish* runs to 964 pages and yet, with an end date of 1902, stops far short of her full activity as a journalist.) Even so, we can identify some recurrent ideas that emerge.

Even as a very young person she quickly developed a notion of honesty in art. What she meant by this is not always clear, but it had something to do with perceived sincerity as well as an avoidance of trite or calculated devices for wringing audiences' emotions. Excesses of bombast (often called "chewing the scenery") could usually be counted on to evoke her scorn. On the other hand, as her response to Clara Morris's performance in *Camille* demonstrates, she could forgive even a considerable measure of excess if the performer succeeded in compelling her emotional involvement as a member of the audience – or, as she once put it, if the performer made her "actually live in the story . . . going on before us" so that the "dangers of that heroine and the desperation of that hero" became for the moment "more impor-tant . . . than our own lives" (*W&P*, p. 957). "Power" in a performance – a combination of passionate commitment, intelligent understanding, and personal presence or authority – was the primary goal, though she preferred it to be achieved in contained and subtle ways.

Morality in art was a somewhat different matter from honesty in art, though certainly related. She was quite certain that good character could not guarantee good art, since art is a discipline in itself, but she tended to believe that bad character would somehow manifest itself in bad art. She once wrote, for example, that Oscar Wilde's "insincerity" – apparently the quality that led him to claim that nature imitates art rather than the reverse – would necessarily produce art lacking honesty (*W&P*, pp. 153–4). That is, she followed the widely circulated principles of British art theorist John Ruskin in linking bad art, bad taste, and bad morality, but did not attempt to formulate very precisely how these were connected. When she discussed performers' own morality, however, she avoided any gossipy scolding for personal peccadilloes, regarding character as a larger matter than concerns such as whether an actor was willing to do a performance on Sunday (a concern she once derided when it was expressed in print by a clergyman). In any event, she believed, it was not the business of art – whether the art of theatre or of literature – to engage in campaigns of social reform. "Art is its own excuse for being," it is "itself the highest moral purpose in the world" (*KA*, pp. 406, 378), and no form of art, whether drama or literature or music, should lapse into sermonizing or subordinate itself to advocacy of causes. If it did so it became mere "propaganda."[9]

Cather also quickly developed an expectation of honest workmanship. That is, she expected performers to take their own work seriously enough to study it, to polish their techniques, and to give it their best every time. Indeed, to do so was itself the primary moral principle for an artist, whether actor or musician or writer.

A principle that was slower to develop was Cather's noted commitment to conciseness, or aesthetic minimalism. Just as she came to resist in her own writing and to criticize in the writing of others any indulgence in superfluous words or extraneous details, so she wanted stage performers to resist extraneous gestures. She disliked excess – especially unconvincing excess. One of her severest reviews, and one of the few in which she is genuinely funny, was of an unfortunately overweight actress who played Cleopatra in a "carnival style," managing to faint "upon every possible pretext and upon every part of the stage." Appearance was not everything, in Cather's view, but it did matter, and these faints were a "regular landslide" (*KA*, p. 293). Not that she was always consistent in demanding restraint. And not that she could not enjoy spectacle. During her senior-year trip to Chicago she reveled in Verdi's *Aida*, an opera traditionally presented with elaborate stage trappings, and two of her favorite plays were *The Three Guardsmen* (an adaptation of Alexandre Dumas's novel *The Three Musketeers*) and Edmond Rostand's *Cyrano de Bergerac*, both of which are costume romances with plenty of action, including swordplay.[10] It is significant that when she wrote her well-known essay "The Novel Démeublé," which means something like "The Unfurnished [or the Disfurnished] Novel," enunciating her principle of minimalism in literature, she turned to the stage for a metaphor of what she meant: the elder Dumas's definition of drama as "four walls and a passion."

Important continuities link Cather's newspaper columns about theatre with those about books and authors. In both, she valued craft and serious workmanship, but she valued even more the indefinable something she called power: a force or intensity or authenticity she could sense but not explain, which engaged her response and lifted her out of herself into another dimension of reality. She preferred, on principle, an art of restraint and artists who conveyed dignity and assurance in both their on-stage and their off-stage presence, who did not smear their private lives over the public media. But she could also value actors or authors who violated these standards if they managed, in whatever way, to achieve a compelling result, one that caught up its audience, transported it, and engaged it emotionally. With respect to morality in art, she emphasized, both in the theater and in literature, a morality of honesty in the work. She demanded seriousness in the artistic endeavor, as well as something that might be called genuineness.

Another commonality between her columns on theatre and those on books and authors is their strong concern with gender. Interestingly, although she sometimes seemed to denigrate women writers,[11] she not only gave more attention to women actors than to males, but rejected any notion that they were somehow limited by their sex. Specifically, she rejected the traditional idea that men were more intellectual as performers and women more emotional. She praised some of her favorite male actors for their powers of emotion and "humanity," and some of her favorite female actors for their powers of intellect. Indeed, in her two notorious diatribes against women writers (a column published in the *Lincoln Courier* on November 23, 1895, in which she proclaimed that she had "not much faith in women in fiction" [*KA*, p. 409] and a review of Kate Chopin's *The Awakening* published July 8, 1899 [*W&P*, pp. 697–9]), she complained largely of certain women writers' failure to balance emotion and intellect. With respect to both male and female stage performers, beauty or appearance mattered to her, but mattered less than what we might call stage presence. The qualities she admired in actresses were essentially the same as those she admired in male actors, and she did not hold women in the theater to any higher standard of personal behavior than she did men.

After Cather became associated with *McClure's*, in 1906, and her energies became increasingly taken up with editorial activities, she produced less journalism of her own, reserving whatever time and energy she had for writing primarily for fiction. Even so, drawing on her long-established interest and expertise, she continued to write occasional articles about performing artists. The nature of this material was considerably different from her earlier reviews and columns, in that, rather than being evaluative of specific performances or centered in opinion, it was informative and based on research. Probably the most notable such article was a piece in *McClure's* called "Three American Singers." One of the three singers profiled was Olive Fremstad, who would become (along with Cather herself) one of the two major sources of the character of Thea Kronborg, in *The Song of the Lark*. In this and other work that proved preparatory for writing the novel, Cather built on her long-standing familiarity with performing artists, especially women, by studying their working methods. The technical knowledge she developed by observing rehearsals and consulting a knowledgeable music critic shows to great advantage not only in *The Song of the Lark* but in the later *Lucy Gayheart*. Though she herself was neither an actress nor a musician, she wrote, in both novels, from the position of the knowledgeable insider.

Cather's interest in performance and performers had led her to spend a great deal of time in their company from her college days on. One of the most ardent friendships of her life, with Isabelle McClung, sprang from a chance meeting backstage at a theater in Pittsburgh, in the dressing room of an actress Cather had met in Lincoln. When Isabelle ultimately married, it was to a noted violinist, Jan Hambourg, and so the connection with the arts continued. It was the Hambourgs who introduced Cather to the celebrated violinist Yehudi Menuhin, who became one of the most cherished of her few close friends in her later years. To Yehudi and his musician sisters she became "Aunt Willa." The Menuhins' concerts were always notable events in her life, and she cherished their family visits even after she no longer received much company. In short, throughout her life she not only took delight in the performing arts but took them seriously and always found performers themselves intriguing. The habit of theater-going and the intense interest in music that began during Cather's college years, or even before, continued throughout her life. Her letters make frequent reference to attendance at concerts, plays, and operas even into her final years.

One of the values that Cather saw in art was that it afforded an escape from tedious or distressing aspects of life. She once said that during the years when she was champing at the bit to get away from Nebraska and begin a career in the centers of the publishing and artistic world on the East Coast, she feared she would die out among the cornfields (WC to Elizabeth Shepley Sergeant, April 20, 1912; *Calendar*, no. 221). Why that struck her as fearful is perhaps indicated by a letter written two years later to her former editor at the *Nebraska State Journal*, explaining that if a young person sat in a cornfield and complained about never getting to hear any good music, it did not mean that the person did not like the farm, only that he or she needed some exposure to the wider world in order to be reconciled to life at home (WC to Will Owen Jones, May 29, 1914; *Calendar*, no. 283). Clearly, the statement applied to herself. She shared with her troubled character in "Paul's Case" an escape impulse combined with a yearning for the bright lights of the theater (but not his unbalanced temperament). By the time she was grown, she came to love the Nebraska prairies, but Nebraska was not enough; she also needed the wider world and, in particular, the performing arts.

Her early short stories reveal this conflict. Among the nine stories published prior to her July 1896 departure for Pittsburgh and her first real job, four are set in a rather bleakly rendered Nebraska. She would return to this bleak view of the prairies in some of her later stories, with the result that people in Nebraska and Kansas, including some among her family and friends, were offended (especially by "A Wagner Matinée"). Soon, however, she began to publish stories about artists and performers. The first of these was "The Count of Crow's Nest," in the fall of 1896, depicting a boarding house full of would-be artists; "The Prodigies" and "Nanette: An Aside" quickly followed in July 1897. The figure of the artist became the "organizing principle"[12] of her first book of fiction, *The Troll Garden*

(1905), a collection of stories. Of her total sixty-two stories (including three published posthumously), thirteen feature performing artists. They are, in addition to those already named, "A Singer's Romance" (1900), "A Death in the Desert" (1903), "Flavia and Her Artists" (1905), "The Garden Lodge" (1905), "The Joy of Nelly Deane" (1911, about an amateur singer), "The Diamond Mine" (1916), "A Gold Slipper" (1917), "Scandal" (1919), "Coming, Aphrodite!" (1920), and "Uncle Valentine" (1925). An additional two concern the visual arts: "The Sculptor's Funeral" (1905) and "The Marriage of Phaedra" (1905). Cather always regarded writing, too, as a kind of performing art, though she did not include "The Willing Muse" (1907, about writers) among the stories collected in her 1920 volume *Youth and the Bright Medusa*, a collection unified by the idea of youthful fascination with the lure of art. She did include in that volume her three best-known stories about deprivation and yearning for art – "Paul's Case," "A Wagner Matinée," and "The Sculptor's Funeral."[13] She would return to a glancing acknowledgment of the power of performance to provide relief from life's grimmer routines (but performance of a very different kind) in the late masterpiece "Neighbor Rosicky" (1930), where old Rosicky graciously takes over his daughter-in-law's household chores so that she and her husband can go to town for a movie. But this story was written at a time in her career when she had turned, or turned back, to writing about the humble and the everyday. In the middle years of her career she was, for the most part, far more interested in the exceptional and the high arts.

The stories of singers that Cather wrote and published from 1916 to 1919 are an especially interesting group, presenting women singers as persons of strength and virtuosity, but frequently victimized by their public or those close to them. Kitty Ayrshire, in particular, expresses a desire to be respected as a professional, not to be seen by men exclusively as an embodiment of "some wife or mistress," in other words, as a sex object. It is an uncharacteristic moment of overt feminism in Cather's writing. These stories of singers were part of a series about women's work and careers. Indeed, seven of the eight stories Cather published between "The Bohemian Girl" in 1912[14] and *Youth and the Bright Medusa* in 1920 are about women and work, and the eighth shows the problems caused by the lack of a career. We could see this group of stories, with their dual concern with women's art and women's professions, as works in which Cather was indirectly examining her own commitments and the nature of her profession. She had left *McClure's* in 1912 to try to make her living solely by her writing – that is, by the performance of her art, now clearly defined as the art of fiction. "The Diamond Mine," especially, includes a powerful statement of the difficult struggle that pursuit of an artistic vocation entails.

When we turn to the novels, we see that struggle explored most fully in *The Song of the Lark*, Cather's third published novel (1915), where Thea Kronborg works herself into exhaustion and deteriorated health before retreating to the Southwest (always, for Cather, a site of invigoration) to recover the strength she needs for a renewed commitment to artistic discipline. Thea pays a price in alienation from her family and erosion of the more genial aspects of her personality – just as a figure from her youth, an artist *manqué*, or frustrated artist, Juan Tellamantez, paid a price. First developed by Cather in her poem "Spanish Johnny," the Mexican laborer and talented amateur singer Tellamantez sporadically runs off from his workaday life for a binge of drinking and singing in bars and very nearly ruins his health in the process. Nor is he Thea's only exemplar of the failed or frustrated artist. Her first piano teacher as a child, Professor Wunsch, was an alcoholic itinerant devoted to music but shut outside the court of the blessed. Like her later teacher in Chicago, who identifies her genius as being for singing rather than for the piano, Wunsch finds his fulfillment in passing on his devotion to the art itself.

The figure of Thea is in many ways autobiographical. Though Cather herself did not have musical talent (apparently she greatly resembled Thea in her childhood music lessons, hanging on her teacher's talk *about* music more than she learned to produce it), she did have the stubborn commitment to an art that she dramatized in Thea, and she also shared Thea's conflictedness between a love for the open spaces of the West and a determination to reach New York, the one place in America at that time that could afford her the needed venue to practice her art. Thea was, of course, also modeled on the great singer Olive Fremstad, whom Cather knew and had written about in an article for *McClure's*, and possibly also on an actress character in Mary Austin's 1912 novel *A Woman of Genius*.

Thea was not, in fact, Cather's first artist figure in a novel. A performing artist had also played an important part in her now little-read first novel, *Alexander's Bridge* (1912). There, in the character of Hilda Burgoyne, Cather came very near to adopting a common stereotype of the actress as a loose woman. When the main character, Bartley Alexander, feels a need to recover his sense of youth, virility, and enjoyment of life, he conveniently reencounters his lost love Hilda and she quickly becomes his mistress. The association of actresses with sexual license was a longstanding notion, so deeply instilled in popular perception that the word "actress" was sometimes used as a euphemism for prostitute. Although the figure of Hilda does little to counteract such a perception, she is depicted as a person of sensitivity who sincerely cares about Bartley. She also exemplifies something of the physical vigor that would characterize Thea Kronborg. Thus, she is a positive presence in several ways, and the life of art with which she is associated does prove to reinvigorate Alexander and recharge his professional imagination, even if his sexual liaison with her serves as evidence of a moral flaw, or crack, at the center of his being, analogous to the crack in his bridge that causes it to collapse.

In Cather's second novel, too – *O Pioneers!* (1913) – the idea of the artist is of great thematic importance. Alexandra Bergson's childhood friend who ultimately becomes her intended husband, Carl Linstrum, is an artist of sorts – a wood-engraver. Wood-engraving required highly developed skill, but in most cases was practiced as a craft, that of transferring an artist's drawing on to a block that could be inked for printing. Carl himself pays tribute to his more vigorous and certainly more successful friend, Alexandra, by calling her, too, an artist, in her ability to conceive a vision and to pursue it by transforming the land to agricultural abundance and attractiveness. Neither of them, then, is literally an artist (unless we allow that term to Carl), and certainly neither is a *performing* artist, an actor or singer, but the value of art itself as that which holds the power to redeem the quotidian is again affirmed. A lesser example of this value in *O Pioneers!* enters when Alexandra's youngest brother, Emil, costumes himself in festive clothes from Mexico and plays the guitar for a gathering at a church bazaar. As an amateur performer he contributes to the enlivening of his neighbors' lives much as Cather herself had, as a youngster. Because of the origin of his costume and music, he is also an echo of the Mexican man Cather had met in 1912, in Arizona, who had sung to her and who became the original of Spanish Johnny and Juan Tellamantez. In each case, these male singers express the charm and the escape-value of the exotic.

After *The Song of the Lark*, which followed *O Pioneers!*, Cather's only other novel fully centered on a performing artist (a pianist) was *Lucy Gayheart* (1935). This novel, like the story of Thea, traces the artist's development as she first catches the vision she wishes to pursue, then loses her way, and then, in Thea's case, endures years of hard work before her ultimate triumph, but in Lucy's case, only catches once again the vision she is determined to pursue, this time more singlemindedly and through harder work. Lucy's story, then, is a tragic, or at least a pitiable, one. She is a far slighter figure than Thea, less emotionally sturdy and certainly less physically vigorous. But the story does imply that, having finally realized the work and commitment that are required (from seeing a performance by a touring opera company where a woman singer gives her full effort even though she is past her prime and the conditions are far from conducive to great art), Lucy has experienced a renewal of vision that would carry her through to a life of art whether she achieved greatness as a performer or not. That is, the worth of the vision is affirmed in *Lucy Gayheart* as well as in *The Song of the Lark*. Art is seen as a discipline and as a redeemer of life from shabbiness or inadequacy, and thus as a goal well worth the sacrifice it requires.

In several of Cather's other novels, performance plays a lesser role, but its value is always very similar to that enunciated in these two novels about performing artists. As we have seen, in *My Mortal Enemy* (1926) the presence of performing arts and artists (in the cameo appearance of Helena Modjeska) is the best aspect of life in New York. In *One of Ours* (1922), Cather's novel of World War I that is often but perhaps unfairly considered a failure, a fine violinist clarifies and confirms the rustic main character's vision of something more splendid in life than mere grubbing for land and money. In *The Professor's House* (1925) an excursion to the opera provides a jaded and disillusioned older couple who have fallen out of love a momentary breakthrough. And in the far more frequently read *My Ántonia* (1918) the performing arts enter twice – in the performance of *Camille* seen by Jim Burden and Lena Lingard, which allows them a venting of emotion they are unable to experience in their everyday relationship, and in a performance by a touring pianist called Blind d'Arnault, modeled on at least two blind African American pianists Cather had seen in concert.[15] Though unfortunately marred by racist caricature, the vignette of Blind d'Arnault's performance conveys much the same idea as the other performance episodes we have noted: the artist's enormous personal vigor, his intense investment in his art, and the power of the performance to lift the moment out of the ordinary for the listeners or viewers. In this case, even the hotel maids listening at the door are moved to dance.

This is the real meaning of the performing artist and the performing arts for Cather: that they offer transformation of life, both for the artists themselves and for others. In *Lucy Gayheart* the title character is a rather ordinary young woman whose story is one of apparent failure rather than conspicuous success. One point of the story is how hard society makes it for a woman to break out of the constraints of conventionality in order to achieve great things. But the larger point is conveyed at the very end of the book, when Lucy's one-time lover revisits her home long after her death and finds that she still lives in his memory as an embodiment of devotion to beauty. His own life has lacked beauty or tenderness, but as he thinks of Lucy he goes to the window and stands looking out at the stars. That is, even her memory has the power to lift his attention from his own disappointments to the realm of the beautiful. The pursuit of art, then, as personified by Lucy Gayheart, is redemptive for others as well as for herself. Redemption shines out of the artist like the flash of the distant star seen through the window.

NOTES

1. Cather's open letter to Harvey E. Newbranch, the editor-in-chief of the *Omaha World-Herald*, dated October 27, 1929, is reprinted in full in William M. Curtin, ed., *The World and the Parish: Willa Cather's Articles and Reviews*, 2 vols. (Lincoln, NE: University of Nebraska Press, 1970), pp. 955–8. Future references to articles in this collection will be made parenthetically following the abbreviation *W&P*. The letter to Newbranch is also reprinted in L. Brent Bohlke, ed., *Willa Cather in Person* (Lincoln, NE: University of Nebraska Press, 1986), pp. 184–7.

2. Photographs of Cather in costume for childhood performances are widely reprinted in, for example, Mildred Bennett, *The World of Willa Cather* (Lincoln, NE: University of Nebraska Press, 1951); Sharon O'Brien, *Willa Cather: The Emerging Voice* (New York: Oxford University Press, 1987); James Woodress, *Willa Cather: A Literary Life* (Lincoln, NE: University of Nebraska Press, 1987); and Janis Stout, *The Writer and Her World* (Charlottesville: University Press of Virginia, 2000).

3. Bernice Slote, ed., *The Kingdom of Art: Willa Cather's First Principles and Critical Statements, 1893–1896* (Lincoln, NE: University of Nebraska Press, 1967), p. 7. Future references to articles in this collection will be made parenthetically following the abbreviation *KA*. Along with two extremely useful essays by Slote, much of Cather's earliest journalism is compiled here, some of it overlapping that included in Curtin, ed., *The World and the Parish* (see note 1 above). Unfortunately, for the most part, neither collection reprints her reviews or columns in their entirety, and neither is organized chronologically.

4. See, for example, Joan Severa, *Dressed for the Photographer: Ordinary American and Fashion, 1840–1900* (Kent, OH: Kent State University Press, 1995). Cather's long-time companion Edith Lewis said that the short haircut was simply "the mark of a rebel." See Lewis, *Willa Cather Living: A Personal Record* (New York: Knopf, 1953), p. 27. Regarding women's move into careers in the late nineteenth century, see Carroll Smith-Rosenberg, *Disorderly Conduct: Visions of Gender in Victorian America* (New York: Oxford University Press, 1985).

5. Willa Cather to Carrie Miner Sherwood, 1928, in Janis Stout, ed., *A Calendar of the Letters of Willa Cather* (Lincoln, NE, and London: University of Nebraska Press, 2002), no. 922. Future references to letters summarized in this volume will be made parenthetically by correspondents' names, date, and their number in the *Calendar*.

6. On the performative nature of identity and gender, see Judith Butler, *Gender Trouble: Feminism and the Subversion of Identity* (New York: Routledge, 1990). Cather's evident understanding of the performative construction of selfhood, as shown both in her own life and in the frequency with which performance is involved in the development of her fictional characters, is an argument for reading her as a kind of proto-postmodernist.

7. William Winter, *Vagrant Memories* (New York: Doran, 1915), pp. 239–40.

8. Cather's letters to Akins are a particularly valuable series because Akins's status in theatre evoked more searching comments about performance than Cather usually made in letters.

9. See Cather's essay "Escapism" in *On Writing* (1949; Lincoln, NE: University of Nebraska Press, 1988), p. 23.

10. *Cyrano*, she enthused, "made the world some years younger and a little happier" (*W&P*, p. 497). The comment is itself an indication of what she believed theatre could do: transform, if not the world, at least one's feelings about the world.

11. I have argued elsewhere that her seeming condemnation of female writers and of anything that might be called a feminine style in literature is not so simple a matter as it may seem; see "Willa Cather's Early Journalism: Gender, Performance, and the 'Manly Battle Yarn,'" *Arizona Quarterly* 55.3 (1999), pp. 51–82.

12. Susan A. Hallgarth, "The Woman Who Would Be Artist in *The Song of the Lark* and *Lucy Gayheart*," in John J. Murphy, ed., *Willa Cather: Family, Community, and History* (Provo, UT: Brigham Young University Humanities Publication Center, 1990), p. 169.

13. The eight stories making up *Youth and the Bright Medusa*, several of them already collected in *The Troll Garden*, are: "A Death in the Desert" (about a pianist), "A Wagner Matinée" (about a midwestern farm wife's yearning for the world of art she knew in her youth, featuring an afternoon symphony concert during her visit back to Boston), "The Sculptor's Funeral" (about a talented sculptor's rejection by his benighted home town), "Paul's Case" (about a feverish boy's longing for a life of glamour), "The Diamond Mine" (about a fine singer's manipulation by the people close to her, who see her as a source of money), "A Gold Slipper" (about Kitty Ayrshire, an operatic singer), "Scandal" (also about Kitty Ayrshire), and "Coming, Aphrodite!" (about two aspiring artists, one serious and the other basically an entertainer, but a successful one).

14. "The Bohemian Girl" notably uses as its title, verbatim, the title of a popular opera that Cather had seen in her youth, *The Bohemian Girl* by Balfe. A major turning point in *Lucy Gayheart* comes when Lucy and her father and sister attend a touring production of *The Bohemian Girl*.

15. In a letter to Chilson Leonard written on March 19, 1936, Cather acknowledged that Blind d'Arnault was modeled on Blind Boone, a well-known figure in the late nineteenth century, and that she had heard of two other such pianists, Blind Tom and Blind Noah (*Calendar*, no. 1306). The implication is that she had seen only Blind Boone. In another letter she said that Blind d'Arnault was a composite of several musicians, including Blind Boone, but that she had no recollection of Blind Tom (*Calendar*, no. 1807). She had in fact reviewed a performance by Blind Tom on May 18, 1894 (*W&P*, pp. 166–7).

7

SUSAN J. ROSOWSKI

Willa Cather and the comic sense of self[1]

"Everything in Nature is lyrical in its ideal essence, tragic in its fate, and comic in its existence."

Santayana[2]

My interest in the comic Cather began with a question at a plenary session of an international seminar. "Does Willa Cather have any sense of humor at all?" After a long silence, someone gamely replied that she must have, though at the moment he couldn't think of an example. The question remained with me, initially alerting me to the one-liners in Cather's writing and eventually taking me to the most basic questions about her art and its relation to life. Art begins in feeling seeking form, Cather believed, anticipating the philosopher Susanne Langer's argument that feelings arise from premises about life that are so fundamental that they are structural. Does one celebrate the uniqueness of an individual asserting himself, or herself, against the world? If so, tragedy provides the form. Or does one celebrate life's continuities, blurring distinctions between the self and the not-self in order to do so? Such a feeling finds an outlet in comedy.

Of course, circumstances of time and place play a role, such as growing up in the United States, where a sense of self is a byproduct of a much-heralded celebration of individualism. The westward movement, the pioneer heroic, and the women's movement are variations of the assertive self writ large in the national stories familiar to Cather, as to Cather's critics. Laughter is, Cather understood, the time-honored antidote to self-importance in nations as well as individuals. I might add that laughter serves as an antidote also to the self-absorption of some literary criticism in recent decades. From the consciousness-raising of the 1960s to the identity politics of the 1990s, the general tendency to treat fiction as a psychobiographical document[3] has been exacerbated in Cather studies. Noting that she drew closely upon lived experience in writing her stories, critics go to them to get at the "real" Cather, then record her resistance to such attempts, whether admired as the complexities of her art or denounced as the evasions of Cather herself. I propose we return to aesthetic principles underlying Cather's art to recognize that something different is at play – a comic sense of self that blurs boundaries and honors indeterminacies. To do so I begin with the back stories of Cather's literary life, then focus on the first decade of Cather's novelistic career, from *Alexander's Bridge* (1912) to *One of Ours* (1922).

Accounts of Cather's life before she began writing novels describe two distinct and contrasting periods, or life narratives. Cather's childhood story begins in Virginia and moves to the frontier town of Red Cloud, Nebraska. Images of play mark these years: Willa listening to her grandmother read from the Bible and *The Pilgrim's Progress* at Willow Shade, riding her pony to visit immigrant neighbor women in Webster County, creating a play town of packing boxes in her family's yard in Red Cloud, staging plays in the attic of their home, and reading in her attic bedroom. Cather's childhood story ends and her success story begins when she enters the University of Nebraska in Lincoln, where she awakens to ideas and ambition. Images of focused will and competitive drive mark these years, with Cather editing the campus literary magazine and working for the city papers, gaining "a reputation as the incomparable roaster, the 'meatax critic,' ... partly because she liked a good fight";[4] moving on to Pittsburgh, then to New York City, where she became managing editor of *McClure's Magazine*, arguably the most influential position in America for a woman in journalism. Cather's success story climaxes with a letter she wrote to Sarah Orne Jewett in 1908. Though she was getting ahead in executive work, she felt dispossessed and bereft of her self, Cather wrote. In the supposed pleasure of the chase (which was like the stock market), one can lose the feelings that bring real pleasure; more of this and she would be ill-tempered and assertive, which is what happens when one focuses upon performing feats and never thinks. Is there not something the psychologists call a split personality? She had not had six-months of leisure since she was fifteen; surely, one should save one's soul.[5]

Cather's letter – the most important she ever wrote – is about understanding how feelings about one's self are affected by the form (or plot) of one's life: executive success versus leisure to write; focused assertion of will versus time to think; the adult she had become versus the child she was. Before long Cather took a leave from *McClure's* and wrote her first novels (there were two, she explained) that launched her as an artist. They were as different as it is possible for two novels to be in the sense of self each explored – one tragic, the other comic.

Alexander's Bridge (1912) is a modern version of the self-asserting hero (the bridge-building engineer Bartley Alexander) who suffers greatly from a flaw in his nature, and whose suffering ends in catastrophe (his bridge collapses and he, going down with it, drowns). Singlemindedly focused on ego and will, *Alexander's Bridge* is utterly lacking in humor; or (more precisely) it is only unintentionally funny. *O Pioneers!* (1913) is another matter altogether, with its narrator's cosmic consciousness and its central character's tendency to lose herself "in the great operations of nature." Rather than an assertion of ego, self-negligence was Cather's byword: "The country insisted on being the Hero [of her story] and she did not interfere," she explained to Elizabeth Sergeant.[6]

She was finding the road that was right for her, Cather later remarked about writing *Alexander's Bridge* and *O Pioneers!*. And the different roads she was trying out – one "congenial" and the other "wrong"[7] – had to do with the radical differences that are fundamental to tragedy and comedy. Whereas the tragic vision poses an individual in contest with the world, the comic vision posits life as an everlasting stream embodied briefly in individual form. Whereas tragedy celebrates the heroic of a great but doomed assertion of ego, comedy celebrates the capacity of human beings to lose themselves in the regenerative and adaptive rhythm of life.[8] Whereas tragedy features a consolidation of self, comedy requires a blurred, indeterminate sense of self.

I can scarcely overstate how deliberately Cather was addressing distinctions fundamental to these great literary forms. Whereas she wrote *Alexander's Bridge* by prototypically tragic principles, Cather aligned *O Pioneers!* with two of comedy's most influential writers. By naming her book after a poem by Walt Whitman, she recalled the poet who, writes comedy scholar Edward L. Galligan, provides American literature's "densest, most cognitive, most comprehensive account of the comic sense of the self."[9] "Self negligence" is at the heart of Whitman's comic sense of self, Galligan continues: "a cheerful lack of concern about drawing boundary lines between the self and the not-self, and a full acceptance of one's own identity" (p. 133). A century earlier than Galligan, Cather had celebrated this very quality of joyful freedom from boundaries in her 1886 essay about Whitman. Though she found his "reckless rhapsodies" sometimes ridiculous, Cather was attracted to the "primitive elemental force about him," she wrote. She explained, "He is so full of hardiness and of the joy of life. He looks at all nature in the delighted, admiring way in which the old Greeks and the primitive poets did."[10] Such an embrace of nature means that delimiting boundaries cease to exist: "He was neither good nor bad, any more than are the animals he continually admired and envied . . . He has no code but to be natural, a code that this complex world has so long outgrown . . . To live was to fulfill all natural laws and impulses" (pp. 280–1). "Lines of demarcation between the self and the not-self are neither important nor interesting, and they are confining," Galligan writes about a comic sense of self. "Drawing them, one becomes cautious and self-protective, ignoring them, one is free to become adventurous and curious" (p. 124). Only his academic prose distinguishes Galligan's description of Whitman from the undergraduate Cather's.

Whereas by titling her book *O Pioneers!* Cather recalled Walt Whitman, by naming her pioneer family "Bergson" she recalled philosopher Henri Bergson, whose *Le Rire* was translated into English as *Laughter: An Essay on the Meaning of the Comic* in 1911.[11] This was precisely the moment when Cather was completing *Alexander's Masquerade* (to become *Alexander's Bridge*) and conceiving the stories that would become *O Pioneers!* In his influential theory of laughter, Bergson aligns comedy with the vitalism of a life spirit by distinguishing those who embody the flexibility and spontaneity of life from those who impose a mechanical rigidity on the flow of experience. Cather created her Bergson family as fictional versions of Henri Bergson's theory, with Alexandra the happy embodiment of the life force and Lou and Oscar the hapless examples of mechanical rigidity. In Bergsonian terms, Alexandra is a maker of comedy, and her brothers are comic butts. But what is significant to a comic sense of self is the extent to which Cather absolved Alexandra Bergson of any taint of Bartley Alexander's consuming self-absorption. Alexandra has a "blind side," Cather writes, then explains by distinguishing personality from a personal self:

> Her personal life, her own realization of herself, was almost a subconscious existence; like an underground river that came to the surface only here and there . . . Nevertheless, the underground stream was there, and it was because she had so much personality to put into her enterprises and succeeded in putting it into them so completely, that her affairs prospered better than those of her neighbors.[12]

The distinction between "personality" and "self" is fundamental to a comic sense of self. "Personality" is the totality of qualities and traits, the pattern of collective character; it is that which underlies all else; it is mnemonic. "Self" is that which is particular and distinctive; it has to do with individuality and ego, and it involves one's self-consciousness, or one's consciousness of one's own being or identity. Comedy has to do with personality, tragedy with self.

So far, so good. In writing *O Pioneers!* by principles from the poet Whitman and the philosopher Bergson, Cather found the road for her and she knew it had to do with comedy and the self-negligence of personality. But Cather was neither a poet nor a philosopher, and the challenge before her was to bring the comic sense of self to the novel. *The Song of the Lark* records her first attempt at doing so. Cather's plot traces Thea Kronborg's coming into her own as an artist by freeing her personality from her personal self, with scenes serving as catalysts for mini-essays on personality. Thea's music lesson provides an occasion for her teacher to glimpse "her personality . . . under her crudeness and hardness";[13] bathing in a stream evokes her epiphany about "a lightly worn, loosely knit personality" of a stream of life "that reached back into the old time" (p. 304); and her performance in *The Ring of the Niebelungs* prompts a discussion on "that 'gold' quality that makes her *Fricka* so different." "How does she manage it, Landry?" Fred Ottenburg asks, and Thea's accompanist explains:

> "Oh, it's a question of a big personality – and all that goes with it. Brains, of course. Imagination, of course. But the important thing is that she was born full of color, with a rich personality . . . You've heard her *Elizabeth*? Wonderful, isn't it? . . . *It's unconscious memory, maybe; inherited memory, like folk-music. I call it personality.*" (pp. 448–9; emphasis added)

Scenes such as these prepare for Thea's performance as Sieglinde, when she enters the kingdom of art by freeing her personality from her personal self. Cather's description is Whitmanesque in its blurring of self and other, Bergsonian in its vitalism and flexibility: "All that deep-rooted vitality flowered in her voice, her face, in her very finger-tips. She felt like a tree bursting into bloom. And her voice as flexible as her body; equal to any demand, capable of every *nuance*" (p. 478).

Yet as I argue elsewhere, *The Song of the Lark* is not actually comic so much as it is about comedy.[14] Thea's struggle is to consolidate, secure, and protect identity, which is something fundamentally different from the self-negligence at the heart of *O Pioneers!*, as of comedy broadly. Rather than blurring boundaries between the self and not-self, Thea opposes her self to the world, where "things and people . . . were lined up against her," bent on denying her the ecstasy of feeling in art (p. 201). Her success is measured by the growing numbers of her "natural enemies" (p. 59) – the small-minded, timid, officious, foolish, insincere, sentimental and ordinary characters who comprise the abundance of life celebrated in comedy. Cather came to feel that this full-blooded narrative was not for her, and she took another tack in her next book. The result was *My Ántonia*, one of the great comic narratives of American literature.

Rather than consolidating identity, Cather fractured identity in *My Ántonia*, a principle she established in her introduction. There, Cather appears as herself to describe meeting Jim Burden, her fictional friend from childhood; their conversation returns to Ántonia, a girl they knew while growing up. Each agrees to set down on paper recollections of her. Some months later Jim Burden appears with his manuscript. "'I finished it last night – the thing about Ántonia,' he said; 'Now what about yours?'" To which Cather replies, "My own was never written, but the following narrative is Jim's manuscript substantially as he brought it to me."[15] In the aesthetics of a comic sense of self, the introduction brilliantly frees the narrative from restricting lines of demarcation by blurring fact and fiction, self and other, female and male.

When author and narrator agree to remember "the adventure of our childhood" (p. xii), the introduction also announces the spirit of sympathetic play that is the fundamental principle of comedy. Play is a motif joining the episodes that follow as Jim remembers riding with Ántonia to a prairie-dog town, making a calico picture book at Christmas, dancing with the hired girls at Vannis's tent, playing tag and rolling popcorn balls at the Harlings's, going with Lena Lingard to the theater in Lincoln, to name a few of myriad examples. The motif comes full circle with Jim's concluding reflection, "There were enough Cuzaks to play with for a long while yet. Even after the boys grew up, there would always be Cuzak himself!" (p. 358). Bergson's theory of comedy again figures in the background. "The comic character is often one with whom, to begin with, our mind, or rather our body, sympathizes," Bergson believed. "By this is meant that we put ourselves for a very short time in his place, adopt his gestures, words, and actions, and if amused by anything laughable in him, we invite him, in imagination, to share his amusement with us; *in fact, we treat him first as a playmate*" (pp. 193ff; emphasis added).

My Ántonia's circular, regenerative structure reinforces its expansive comic spirit. Jim's stories provide the classic reversals of humor involving youth versus age, rural versus urban, and ideal versus reality. The young Jim had come to Nebraska filled with myths of a wild frontier instilled by the Jesse James novel he had been reading; the adult Jim remembers that he actually found not desperadoes but gentle ranch hands. The young Jim imagines himself rescuing a damsel by slaying a dragon; the adult Jim understands that his was a mock adventure with an old rattlesnake. At the university in Lincoln, the undergraduate Jim (imagining himself the sophisticate in the city) believes that Lena Lingard (newly arrived from the country) expects him to marry her, only to have her tell him that she had chosen to remain independent. These might be the stock reversals of burlesque, but they aren't when distinctions are blurred, and that is the wonder of My Ántonia. When the adult Jim returns to the middle-aged, grizzled Ántonia, the child has become the man, and the man has retrieved the child. The expansive spirit of self-negligence means that Jim fully accepts Ántonia as she is, rather than imagining her as a romantic heroine; in the same manner, Jim fully accepts in himself the follies of his youth. The expansive spirit of comedy also lies behind the regenerative quality of storytelling. By the last book Jim has relinquished his assertive self ("my" Ántonia) to serve as witness to the shared humor of a family telling stories about themselves. To say distinctions are blurred is to understate a scene in which the fictional narrator (informed by the real-life experiences of his actual author) is witnessing a fictional family (drawn from the real-life family of Annie and John Pavelka) tell stories on themselves in which they appear as characters.

As for Jim Burden, so for Willa Cather, who demonstrated the maturity of her comedy by telling stories on herself when she wrote *My Ántonia*. Emigrating to Nebraska, living briefly in Webster County before moving to town, holding forth in a high-school commencement address, awakening to ideas at the University of Nebraska, feeling transported by a performance of Camille in Lincoln, are only a few examples. Beyond the specifics, Cather's youthful self-absorption informs Jim's, as does her growth into self-negligence. Cather too has retrieved childhood through memory by drawing upon her Nebraska experiences, prepared to encompass them into the humane vision of high comedy. By writing of herself as a youth in ways recognizable to those who knew her then, Cather proved her talent for comedy by standards she may have learned from George Meredith, whose *The Egoist: A Comedy in Narrative* (1879) she had included in her childhood library. In *An Essay on Comedy*, Meredith wrote, "You may estimate your capacity for comic perception by being able to detect the ridicule of them you love without loving them less; and more by being able to see yourself somewhat ridiculous in dear eyes, and accepting the correction their image of you proposes."[16]

Cather confirmed principles of comedy for herself and for America when she wrote *My Ántonia*: of finding faith in the life spirit's adaptability, and flexibility; of celebrating that faith with full knowledge of individual mortality; of blurring boundaries between the self and the not-self and, in doing so, fully accepting one's own identity. In her next novel Cather put those principles to the test. "Comedy is an escape, not from truth but from despair: a narrow escape into faith," writes Christopher Fry. "It believes in a universal cause for delight even though knowledge of the cause is always twitched away from us, which leaves us to rest on our own buoyancy."[17] And such is *One of Ours*, where within a plot that moves towards troops marching to war, Cather created an enduring description of comedy's liberating sense of self.

Feelings of loss were the catalyst for *One of Ours*. When Cather's cousin, G. P. Cather, was killed while fighting with the American Expeditionary Force, she had to write about him before she could go on to other things, she explained to her friend, Dorothy Canfield Fisher.[18] National disillusionment sharpened Cather's feeling of personal loss when, shortly after she began the book she was calling "Claude," events began to disprove her country's naive jingoism about a war to end all wars.[19] Hitler announced his 25-point program at the Hofbrauhaus, Munich (1920), his storm troopers began to terrorize political opponents, and the German mark fell, beginning inflation (1921); Mussolini marched on Rome and formed a Fascist government (1922). "The world broke in two in 1922, or thereabouts," Cather later reflected about the year *One of Ours* was published.[20]

"In tragedy we suffer pain; in comedy pain is a fool, suffered gladly," continues Fry (p. 17). When Misrule rules, Everyman is a fool, I might add, remembering that Cather originally titled her final section "The Blameless Fool by Pity Enlightened."[21] Indeed, *One of Ours* could be subtitled "A Fool's Progress": it begins with its hero's playing the fool, traces his escape from the fear at being laughed at, and celebrates his release into the folly of pursuing something splendid. The fool is a familiar figure in Cather's fiction, appearing as the hermits Lou in "Lou, the Prophet" and Crazy Ivar in *O Pioneers!*, the eccentric Aunt Tillie in *The Song of the Lark*, Mahailey in *One of Ours*, and Mandy in "Old Mrs. Harris." But Claude is the only fool Cather moved to the center of the stage as Everyman enacting his part in the play of life. The result was one of American literature's most sensitive portrayals of a comic sense of self.

"It was a fine day to go the circus at Frankfort, a fine day to do anything; the sort of day that must, somehow, turn out well,"[22] Claude feels upon waking in the opening scene of his novel. Yet instead of enjoying the show as a spectator, Claude finds himself a clown in the parade. Having washed the car to drive into Frankfort, where the circus is playing, he is told by his father to take the hired men and drive mules pulling a wagon with stinking cowhides to sell in town.

> Probably his father had looked out of the window and seen him washing the car, and had put this up on him while he dressed. It was his father's idea of a joke.
>
> Mrs. Wheeler looked at Claude sympathetically . . . Perhaps she, too, suspected a joke. She had learned that humour might wear almost any guise.
>
> (pp. 4–5)

And so in a day that began with such hope, "Claude and his mules rattled into Frankfort just as the calliope went screaming down Main street at the head of the circus parade" (p. 9).

The opening scene announces the premise underlying *One of Ours*. Life is a joke; it is only the form of the joke that varies, whether orchestrated by Claude's father looking out the window upon him washing a car, governments declaring a war into which young men are swept, a captain ordering a soldier to death defending an undefendable bit of land, or life creating in mortal beings a yearning for something splendid. Given such a premise, the question concerns how one responds – by asserting one's will against Fate, as in tragedy, or by losing one's self in the stream of life, as in comedy. In *One of Ours* Cather explores the difference.

In the Nebraska scenes Claude is an innocent who plays the dupe. He is fooled by his mild-mannered younger brother Ralph into executing mischief for which he (Claude) would be caught red-handed; he imposes meaningless physical tests and hardships upon himself, and when told about a joke played by his best friend upon Bayliss (the brother he despises), he challenges his best friend to fight. He attends a denominational college though he knows he is learning nothing; he runs a farm when he wants to be studying at the university; he marries a woman who warns him she's not suited for marriage; and in search of something splendid, he sails off to save France. Complicating the standard reversals of comic situations is the fact that Claude, so foolishly duped by the appearances of others, is most of all duped about himself. "He was exactly the sort of looking boy he didn't want to be," Cather writes, then describes Claude's debilitating self-consciousness, as if from a mirror reflecting mockingly back at him: "He especially hated his head, – so big that he had trouble in buying his hats, and uncompromisingly square in shape; a perfect block-head. His name was another source of humiliation. Claude: it was a 'chump' name, like Elmer and Roy; a hayseed name trying to be fine" (p. 17).

In short, Cather gave to Claude the body–spirit duality of the sad clown, within whose awkward, oafish body resides a sensitive spirit struggling to emerge. Then she liberated her clown in the classic manner of comedy, which involves submitting to forces beyond one's control and drifting, literally rendered as "The Voyage of the Anchises." On board the troopship Claude thrills to feelings he shares with twenty-five hundred boys at first glimpsing the Bartholdi statue; and when a band from Kansas begins playing "Over There," two thousand voices join in "booming out over the water the gay, indomitable resolution of that jaunty air" (p. 273). Cather expands her description of individuals joining an everlasting stream of life by reflecting that while these were American boys, "the scene was ageless . . . youths were sailing away to die for an idea, a sentiment, for the mere sound of a phrase" (p. 274).

Happiness is being "dissolved into something complete and great," Jim Burden realized while sitting in his grandmother's garden (*My Ántonia*, p. 18). In a like manner, Claude Wheeler's happiness comes from being dissolved into something splendid, not the war effort of fighting an enemy (of which he knows almost nothing), but the life spirit of youth's energy and idealism. The paradox of comedy, as of life, is that humans experience joy in the face of certain death. "It looks like we're all going do die out here" (*One of Ours*, p. 295), one of the men says on the troopship, and we know that he speaks truthfully whether referring to the scourge of influenza on board the transport, to the trench warfare lying ahead in France, or to the death awaiting each mortal being. Yet in uniform and one of the troops, Claude realizes he "was enjoying himself all the while" (p. 311). In explaining, Cather describes comedy's liberating sense of self. Until now he had been "so afraid of showing what he felt," she writes, "but he was on the right road at last, and nothing could stop him" (p. 311). The "right road" has to do with looking outward rather than inward, giving up the self-consciousness of an individual ego and conceiving of oneself as part of life. "Their youth seemed to flow together, like their brown uniforms. Seen in the mass like this, Claude thought, they were rather noble looking fellows. In so many of the faces there was a look of fine candour, an expression of cheerful expectancy and confident goodwill" (pp. 280–1).

Freed from debilitating self-consciousness, Claude responds flexibly, buoyantly. In France he is one of the doughboys who stumble upon history and culture, as when (for example) they stub their toes on a sunken step, examine it "with interest, and [go] in to explore the church" (p. 327). Similarly, when he sets out to look for the cathedral in Rouen, he finds himself at the Church of St. Ouen; he enters and sits quietly, earnestly trying to remember something about Gothic architecture. "When Claude joined his company at the station, they had the laugh on him. They had found the Cathedral" (p. 344). This is the stuff of stock regional humor, with Claude the rube from rural Nebraska. Yet rather than feeling himself the butt of the joke, Claude has a liberating epiphany of cosmic consciousness. The light of stars shining through the church window had traveled through space for hundreds of years, and was going through him and, farther still, to his mother in Nebraska.

Sharpening comedy's celebration of an ongoing life spirit is the awareness of the fallibility and vulnerability of each individual separately. Sympathetic identification creates the vulnerability of the comic fool, and Cather identified with her character to an exceptional degree. For broad details of Claude's life she drew upon that of her cousin, G. P. Cather, who grew up in Bladen, Nebraska, married unhappily, and then, with the American Expeditionary Force sailed for France, where he was killed. For Claude's feelings, she drew also upon memories of herself growing up. Cather gave to Claude her own awkwardness, naivete, and vulnerability, as well as her bravado, earnestness, and envy. For the Nebraska scenes she gave to him her yearning to escape provincial Red Cloud and discover the world; and the feelings of many of the French scenes "came from her memories of how she felt when [she and Dorothy Canfield] had been together in France in 1902" (Woodress, p. 329). Over two decades later Cather sought to heal a rift with her friend (now

Dorothy Canfield Fisher) by recalling that time in a series of letters written in the months she was preparing her new novel for publication. Reading proofs was hard; Claude's feeling about David's violin was the feeling of inferiority she had felt with Dorothy when they were together in France; trying to convey that feeling was a kind of revenge for how Dorothy had made her feel, albeit a revenge without anger; Cather's feeling of closeness to Claude's mind was exceptionally strong; this was something she had to write before she could do anything else; she is glad her character can help Dorothy understand how she was feeling at that time (Stout, pp. 574–96). "You may estimate your capacity for comic perception . . . by being able to see yourself somewhat ridiculous in dear eyes, and accepting the correction their image of you proposes," Meredith had written (p. 133). Cather extends his principle by giving feelings of her younger self to a character she loved, then recalling herself in her character to a friend she loved, trusting that detecting the ridicule of that image will enable them to love more.

One of Ours concludes with its hero's death as a fortunate escape from the narrow world he (and we) occupy, leaving us readers with questions about that world. In this, too, Claude acts as a ritual clown, a version of a sacred fool. "The ritual clown acts out a forbidden social role for the general good of the community," writes Maurice Charney in *Comedy High and Low*.[23] Humble, anonymous, and insignificant, he and the fool "merely act their role according to the prescribed forms and in an unsophisticated and unselfconscious way" (p. 173). Because they do, they are truth-speakers, and speaking the truth is the central concept of the sacred fool.

As she prepared her manuscript for publication, Cather revised her title from *Claude* to *One of Ours*. In telling Claude's story, she was telling a nation's story: his self-consciousness is his country's; Frankfort's insularity is that of the United States. Beyond the "joke" on Claude, Cather was writing of America's great joke, the classic discrepancy between the ideal and the real heightened by the promise of a land of opportunity in which a Declaration of Independence promises equality to all. Beyond national ideals, however, the fool reflects the folly of all human endeavor to achieve something splendid. Such folly is, writes Susanne Langer of comedy, "a quality of brainy opportunism in the face of an essentially dreadful universe" (p. 331).

By releasing Claude Wheeler into the folly of pursuing something splendid, Cather affirmed hope out of despair and celebrated life in the face of death. Hers was not Hemingway's code of an individual stoically confronting *nada*; instead, she wrote of the goodness of life as it is experienced day by day. On the ship crossing, veteran flyer Victor Morse tells novice Claude "what life at the front was really like. Nobody who had seen service talked about the war, or thought about it; it was merely a condition under which they lived. Men talked about the particular regiment they were jealous of . . . Everybody thought about his own game, his personal life that he managed to keep going" (*One of Ours*, p. 289). With only minor adjustments, Morse could be describing a comic sense of self.

Things seemed essentially dreadful to Cather during the time she was writing *One of Ours*, that much we know from her famous reference to the world's breaking in two. What is significant to comedy is the form her concerns took. While visiting in Nebraska in late October 1921 she denounced the national move towards standardization in lectures that criticized language laws, boxing regulations, and "Americanization." As a reporter wrote, "Miss Cather denounced the language law vehemently, declaring that no child born in Nebraska can hope to gain a fluent speaking knowledge of a foreign language because the languages are barred from the schools under the eighth grade. 'Will it make a boy or a girl any less American to know one or two other languages?' she asked. 'According to that sort of argument, your one hundred percent American would be a deaf mute.' "[24]

In denouncing standardization Cather was denouncing a country's inflexibility and mechanization – a Bergsonian idea of comedy as cultural critique. "Life is a struggle or a torpor. All art must be serious, and comedy is the most serious of all," she said in 1921 while she was writing *One of Ours* (Bohlke, p. 149). Art that sustains is flexible in reflecting the particularity of its place and time. Don't try to imitate New York, Cather cautioned Nebraskans. Anticipating the lament of certain urban planners of today, she urged cities to develop individuality. "'I wish that I could see across the continent a string of cities having their own particular kind of life, as the cities of the old world,' she declared. 'Does Marseilles try to be like Paris? Does Bordeaux try to be like Paris? Do Venice and Naples try to be like Rome? The people of Bordeaux are proud of their own dinner hour. They are proud of their own cooking'" (Bohlke, p. 150).

By the time she wrote *One of Ours*, Cather was well traveled on the road that was right for her. What lay ahead for her provided variations upon a comic sense of self. In her next two books she relinquished the individual ego of first-person narrators, creating Niel Herbert as a peephole character and Nellie Birdseye as a reflector of experience. Only after acknowledging that they will never "get at" the secrets of women they knew (which is to say, only after acknowledging that it is impossible to resolve the contradictions of Marian Forrester and Myra Driscoll Henshawe), do they finally achieve the hard-won maturity of being glad that the women had a hand in breaking them in to life. After writing about letting go of the accidental, personal self and recovering original identity in *The Professor's House* and letting go of Ego in *Death Comes for the Archbishop*, Cather explored a comic sense of self directly in "Old Mrs. Harris." Three generations from Cather's immediate family sat as models for her characters: her grandmother Rachel Boak as Grandmother Harris, her mother Mary Virginia (Boak) Cather as Victoria Templeton, her father Charles Cather as Hillary Templeton, and herself as Vickie Templeton. Boundaries are blurred and indeterminacies are honored: individual and group, fact and fiction, self and other. Each character is fully realized both as an individual and also a member of a family. Lived experience is unmistakably recognizable to all who know even the outlines of Cather's biography: Red Cloud appears as the town of Skyline and Cather's childhood home as the Templeton home, so faithfully drawn that first-time visitors to Red Cloud today often describe an overwhelming feeling of familiarity upon walking into the front door of an actual house they had previously inhabited only in fiction. The regenerative spirit of comedy informs the story and provides its coda when the narrator, who is unmistakably Cather and also storytellers throughout the ages, reflects:

> Thus Mrs. Harris slipped out of the Templetons' story; but Victoria and Vickie had still to go on, to follow the long road that leads through things unguessed at and unforeseeable. When they are old, they will come closer and closer to Grandma Harris. They will think a great deal about her, and remember things they never noticed; and their lot will be more or less like hers. They will regret that they heeded her so little; but they, too, will look into the eager, unseeing eyes of young people and feel themselves alone. They will say to themselves, "I was heartless because I was young and strong and wanted things so much. But now I know."[25]

"I am large, I contain multitudes," might describe Cather's oeuvre, as it does Whitman's. Like his, Cather's was the encompassing spirit of comedy. The comic spirit expresses itself in play and sympathetic identification; it involves the freeing of personality from the personal self; it is shape-changing, encompassing varied experiences and of multiple identities.

> Art is a concrete and personal and rather childish thing after all . . . it is no good at all unless it is left alone to be itself – a game of make-believe, of reproduction, very exciting and delightful to people who have an ear for it or an eye for it.[26]

NOTES

1. I am grateful to Dr. Kari A. Ronning for reading the manuscript of this essay, and to Vicki Martin for her assistance with the notes.
2. George Santayana, "The Comic Mask and Carnival," in Robert W. Corrigan ed., *Comedy: Meaning and Form* (San Francisco: Chandler, 1965), p. 57.

3. Susanne Langer, *Feeling and Form: A Theory of Art* (New York: Charles Scribner's Sons, 1953), p. 326. Future references will be made parenthetically.
4. Bernice Slote, "First Principles: Writer in Nebraska," in Slote, ed., *The Kingdom of Art: Willa Cather's First Principles and Critical Statements 1893–1896* (Lincoln, NE: University of Nebraska Press, 1967), p. 17.
5. Willa Cather, "Letter to Sarah Orne Jewett," 17 December 1908, Houghton Library, Harvard University. Cather's will prohibits direct quotation from her letters, so I observe the scholarly convention of paraphrase when referring to them.
6. Elizabeth Shepley Sergeant, *Willa Cather: A Memoir* (Philadelphia: Lippincott, 1953), p. 92.
7. Willa Cather, "My First Novels [There Were Two]," in *Willa Cather on Writing: Critical Studies on Writing as an Art* (1949; New York: Knopf, 1968), pp. 93, 96.
8. Drawing upon Langer for principles underlying tragedy and comedy, I discuss these differences in "The Comic Form of Willa Cather's Art: An Ecocritical Reading," in Susan J. Rosowski, ed., *Cather Studies* v (Lincoln, NE, and London: University of Nebraska Press, 2003).
9. Edward L. Galligan, *The Comic Vision in Literature* (Athens, OH: University of Georgia Press, 1984), p. 128. Future references will be made parenthetically.
10. Willa Cather, "Whitman: 'keen senses do not make a poet,'" in William M. Curtin, ed., *The World and the Parish: Willa Cather's Articles and Reviews, 1893–1902,* I (Lincoln, NE: University of Nebraska Press, 1970), p. 280. Future references will be made parenthetically.
11. Henri Bergson, *Laughter: An Essay on the Meaning of the Comic,* trans. from the French by Cloudesley Brereton and Fred Rothwell (London: Macmillan, 1911).
12. Willa Cather, *O Pioneers!* (1913); Scholarly Edition; Susan J. Rosowski and Charles W. Mignon, eds., with Kathleen Danker; historical essay and notes by David Stouck (Lincoln, NE: University of Nebraska Press, 1992), p. 183. Future references will be made parenthetically.
13. Willa Cather, *The Song of the Lark,* 1915 (Lincoln, NE: University of Nebraska Press, 1978), pp. 189–90. Future references will be made parenthetically.
14. Susan J. Rosowski, "Thea Kronborg, a Distinguished Provincial in New York; or Willa Cather's Cultural Geography of Humor," in Merrill Maguire Skaggs, ed., *Willa Cather's New York: New Essays on Cather in the City* (Madison, NJ: Fairleigh Dickinson University Press, 2000), pp. 289–305.
15. Willa Cather, *My Ántonia,* 1918; Scholarly Edition; Charles Mignon, ed., with Kari Ronning; historical essay and notes by James Woodress (Lincoln, NE: University of Nebraska Press, 1994), p. xiii. Future references will be made parenthetically.
16. George Meredith, *An Essay on Comedy and the Uses of the Comic Spirit,* ed. Lane Cooper (1918; New York: Charles Scribner's Sons, 1897), p. 133.
17. Christopher Fry, "Comedy" (1951); reprinted in Robert W. Corrigan, ed., *Comedy: Meaning and Form* (San Francisco: Chandler, 1965), p. 17. Future references will be made parenthetically.
18. Janis Stout, ed., *A Calendar of the Letters of Willa Cather* (Lincoln, NE: University of Nebraska Press, 2002), p. 589. Future references will be made parenthetically.

19. Cather had written to her aunt rejoicing over the war's end on November 11, 1918, describing her cousin G. P.'s death the previous May 23 as for a noble cause. Shortly thereafter she began writing *One of Ours*. As her biographer James Woodress writes, however, "Cather, like other writers of her generation, suffered sharp disillusionment when it soon became apparent that the war had neither ended all wars nor saved the world for democracy" (p. 303).

20. Willa Cather, "Prefatory Note," in *Not Under Forty* (New York: Knopf, 1936), p. v.

21. James Woodress, *Willa Cather: A Literary Life* (Lincoln, NE, and London: University of Nebraska Press, 1987), p. 328. Future references will be made parenthetically.

22. Willa Cather, *One of Ours*, 1922 (New York: Knopf, 1979), p. 2. Future references will be made parenthetically.

23. Maurice Charney, *Comedy High and Low: An Introduction to the Experience of Comedy* (New York: Oxford University Press, 1978), p. 172.

24. "State Laws are Cramping," in L. Brent Bohlke, ed., *Willa Cather in Person: Interviews, Speeches, and Letters* (Lincoln, NE: University of Nebraska Press, 1986), pp. 147–8. Future references to speeches in this volume will be made parenthetically following the editor's surname.

25. Willa Cather, "Old Mrs. Harris," in Frederick M. Link with Kari A. Ronning and Mark Kamrath, eds., *Obscure Destinies* (1932); Scholarly Edition; historical essay and notes by Kari A. Ronning (Lincoln, NE: University of Nebraska Press, 1998), pp. 156–7.

26. Willa Cather, "Light on Adobe Walls," in *Willa Cather on Writing*, p. 125.

8

MARK J. MADIGAN

Cather and the short story

> Pater said that every truly great drama must, in the end, linger in the reader's mind as a sort of ballad. Probably the same thing might be said of every great story.
>
> Willa Cather, "The Best Stories of Sarah Orne Jewett"

> Like many intelligent authors, she had a shrewd idea of the relative value of her own work . . .
>
> Alfred Knopf, "Publishing Then and Now: 1912–1964"

Pulitzer Prize-winning short-story writer Katherine Anne Porter once wrote that she liked Willa Cather's short fiction better than any of her novels.[1] More than fifty years later, Porter's opinion runs counter to critical consensus, as Cather is mainly known for her twelve novels published between 1912 and 1940.[2] Her long fiction, which she intended to be her enduring literary legacy, should not, however, obscure her achievement as a short-story writer. Her fiction-writing career began with a short story in 1892 and ended with one over fifty years later. In all, she published sixty-two stories, some of which rank among her most accomplished fiction of any length.

One commonplace view is that Cather used her stories first to gain a foothold in the literary world and later to get money from magazines. Once she established her name and achieved financial independence, the interpretation goes, she all but abandoned the short story for the novel. Cather's stories, however, amount to far more than apprentice or hack work. Her short-story collections published during her lifetime, *The Troll Garden* (1905), *Youth and the Bright Medusa* (1920), and *Obscure Destinies* (1932), shaped the contours of her career in significant ways. The first brought her to her first literary publisher, S. S. McClure, the second brought her to Alfred A. Knopf, and the third took her back "home" imaginatively to the West. She applied a novelist's sensibility to each collection, treating them not as collections of unrelated parts, but rather as coherent units of literary art. *The Old Beauty and Others* (1948), published one year after Cather's death, offers a coda to her short fiction. I argue here that Cather did care about the artistry of her stories while never losing sight of their worth in the literary marketplace. That is, she at once sought to write the great stories referred to in the first epigraph above and proved the second to be true through her involvement in the promotion of her work. This essay will situate Cather's short-story collections in her career and discuss their importance to both her artistic development and the construction of her literary reputation, in which she had an active hand.

Cather played a central role in the fashioning of her reputation as a writer of short stories. She carefully limited the reprinting of her stories and included just ten in the Autograph Edition of her work.[3] Her legacy-controlling impulse ran deep. As Marilee Lindemann has posited, she was continually "engaged with, in, and against the American literary history that was being invented all around her."[4] She was also engaged against her biographers. Cather instructed her confidants to destroy her letters and in her will she forbade quotation of those extant. This "mania for privacy," as Joan Acocella has called it, was in large part driven by a desire to focus attention on her art.[5] Not only did Cather restrict access to information about her life, she created her own version of it by writing biographical sketches for her publishers.[6] One such note on the dustjacket of *Youth and the Bright Medusa* begins, "Willa Cather wrote her first story some fifteen years ago. It was published in *McClures* [sic], having been accepted by correspondence with the author, who was in the West." That she wrote these lines herself is made likely by the fact that *Youth and the Bright Medusa* was her first Knopf-published book. The publisher's eagerness to please his new author and his penchant for details make it highly improbable that such an erroneous claim would have gone uncorrected had it not been initiated or approved of by Cather.

Cather's biographical statement is curious because she was then living in Pittsburgh (hardly "the West") and her first *McClure's Magazine* story, "The Sculptor's Funeral" (1905), was actually the thirty-third she had published. In effect, the note rewrites her personal history and disowns all of her fiction written prior to the year in which *The Troll Garden* was published. Most of these early efforts appeared in university-sponsored publications and small magazines. Some are notable for their experimentation, while others are of interest as precursors to her mature work dealing with life on Nebraska's Divide. Her early influences, including Daudet, James, Kipling, Poe, and Stevenson, are often detectable. To the author, though, these stories displayed little more than the artistic deficiencies of an apprentice writer.[7]

As Curtis Bradford has observed, "there is in [Cather's] treatment of her short fiction . . . an effort to contrive and set before us a picture both prettier and simpler than the actuality."[8] Her effort did not stop at the suppression of her early work, for the truth is that her "first" story was not simply accepted "by correspondence" at S. S. McClure's popular magazine. After graduating from the University of Nebraska in 1895, Cather worked as a newspaper journalist in Lincoln and Pittsburgh. In 1901, she began teaching high-school English in the latter city. The new job was attractive because it paid relatively well and allowed her more time for creative writing. Her stories had appeared in magazines since her college days and her book of poems, *April Twilights*, was published in 1903. *McClure's* had rejected her submissions, however, and she had given up hope of ever being published in it.

What changed her fortunes was a visit to Lincoln by the magazine publisher's cousin, H. H. McClure, who was looking for new writers for his newspaper syndicate in early 1903. After Cather's former newspaper editor, Will Owen Jones, recommended her, H. H. passed her name along to his cousin in New York. Cather responded to S. S. McClure's invitation to resubmit her work by sending a packet of stories. McClure's next correspondence came by telegram. He wanted the author to come to his New York office for an interview on May 1. Six days later, Cather wrote to Jones that the meeting had changed her life. McClure had been so impressed by her stories that he offered to publish everything she wrote. He had even called in his manuscript readers to admonish them for rejecting her stories in the past.[9] A letter from Cather's friend Dorothy Canfield Fisher to Céline Sibut, a mutual friend in Paris, reports that Cather was elated. Her years of struggle were over and her literary fortune was made, Fisher wrote. Just two months earlier, Cather had written to Fisher in despair over a collection of stories, which needed weeks of work. She told Fisher they constituted a cycle about artists. The title, derived from a poem by Charles Kingsley, would be *The Troll Garden*.[10] Among these were undoubtedly the stories she had sent to McClure. Her weeks of work on them had proved to be fruitful indeed.

The Troll Garden was published by McClure, Phillips & Company on April 5, 1905, containing "Flavia and Her Artists," "The Sculptor's Funeral," "The Garden Lodge," "'A Death in the Desert,'" "The Marriage of Phaedra," "A Wagner Matinée," and "Paul's Case." Reviews in major publications such as the *New York Times Book Review*, *Harper's Weekly*, the *Dial*, and *Atlantic Monthly* affirmed Cather's talents and held out high expectations for her future work. Closer to home, a reviewer for the *Pittsburgh Gazette* concluded that "the book will bring distinction to its author and reflect honor upon Pittsburgh."[11] "The Sculptor's Funeral" was praised in nearly all of the contemporary reviews, with "Paul's Case" ranking a close second.[12] When *Youth and the Bright Medusa* was published fifteen years later, including revised versions of both, the dustjacket copy (again, probably Cather's own) asserted: "'The Sculptor's Funeral' and 'Paul's Case' are the stories that first won a reputation for their author. 'Paul's Case' has been studied, imitated, plagiarized by young writers as perhaps only O. Henry's 'The Unfinished Story' has been." The plots of the two Cather stories may be summarized briefly for further comment.

The focal point of "The Sculptor's Funeral" is Harvey Merrick, a sculptor who dies of tuberculosis at forty. At his request, he is buried in the "dead little Western town" where he was born: Sand City, Kansas.[13] Merrick's body is returned from Boston accompanied by a devoted pupil, Henry Steavens. Arriving by train, he is met at the station by a group of citizens, who reassemble at the Merricks's home for the sculptor's wake. There, Steavens is surprised to find that his world-renowned mentor is disparaged by the people among whom he spent his youth. Of them, the sculptor's only vocal defender is Jim Laird, an alcoholic lawyer who was his college classmate in the East. Laird berates his provincial and hypocritical neighbors for failing to recognize Merrick's talent and fine character.

"Paul's Case" is set in turn-of-the-century Pittsburgh. Its teenaged protagonist loathes his working-class background and acts out his frustration in school. He seeks refuge in the "delicious excitement" of Carnegie Hall (CS, p. 174), where he works as an usher, but finds that the romantic illusions of the theater cannot be sustained beyond its doors. Expelled from school and fired by the theater, he is forced to take a position as a real-estate office clerk. In an attempt to escape his bleak neighborhood, his strict father, and his mundane job, he steals $1,000 from his employer and sets out on a week-long revel in New York, staying at the Waldorf. Finally, this, too, proves illusory, as Paul throws himself in front of a train in Newark and falls "into the immense design of things"(CS, p. 189).

"The Sculptor's Funeral" and "Paul's Case" illustrate the range of sources and prototypes Cather used in composing her short stories. They were founded upon personal experience, memory, and history, which she found to be her richest materials. The opening train-station scene of the former was drawn from her Nebraska youth and used previously in her poem "The Night Express." Biographer James Woodress has established that Cather saw the body of a Red Cloud man similarly returned to his hometown in a baggage car in 1901 (p. 167). The prototype for Jim Laird was a Nebraska attorney and congressman of the same name who was well known in the state's southern region where Cather had lived.[14] The sculptor Merrick was based on artist Charles Stanley Reinhart. Born near Pittsburgh in 1844, he became a well-known American magazine illustrator and painter. When he died in New York City in 1897, his body was returned to his hometown, as he had wished. Cather attended his burial and memorial service a year later, both of which were sparsely attended (March, p. 482). She registered her anger at Pittsburgh's disregard for one of its most distinguished artists in "The Sculptor's Funeral."

For the setting of "Paul's Case," Cather used what she knew from her years of living in Pittsburgh and from her visits to Manhattan. Paul's schoolroom and neighborhood were the stuff of her days; New York was that of her dreams. The theft-and-escape plot elements were drawn from an actual crime that had been reported in the Pittsburgh newspapers. In the real case, two teenagers stole money from an office where one of them worked. They treated themselves to a week of high living like Paul, although in Chicago, not New York. Unlike their fictional counterpart, they did not commit suicide, but rather were returned to their parents when apprehended. Paul was a composite character. Cather claimed she modeled him after two of her Pittsburgh students and herself. His desire to flee to New York was based on her own.[15]

Applying her imagination and narrative skills, Cather turned this raw material into two of her most highly regarded stories. Both exhibit her descriptive abilities and selective use of detail. In 1922, she would write in her essay "The Novel Démeublé" that the artful use of suggestion, of the "inexplicable presence of the thing not named" on the page yet still felt, was what gave "high quality" to literature.[16] In "The Sculptor's Funeral" and "Paul's Case," she struck a fine balance between artistic revelation and omission. The stories earned immediate comparisons to the work of Guy de Maupassant, Edith Wharton, and Hamlin Garland.[17] Cather's critique of small towns and small-mindedness, valorization of art, and exploration of psychology in the stories would become familiar to readers of her fiction in ensuing decades.

In spring 1906, S. S. McClure became Cather's employer as well as publisher, as she accepted an editorial position at his magazine. The job was rewarding for several reasons. Cather was living in New York, well-paid, working on interesting projects, and meeting some of the most important literary figures of the period. Finding time for her own writing, though, was difficult. Observing her creative struggles, Cather's literary mentor Sarah Orne Jewett told her in 1908 that she needed her own "quiet centre of life" from which to write and that she would never find it as long as she worked at a busy magazine (Woodress, pp. 202–3).[18] Three years later, Cather finally took the Maine author's advice and left McClure's to write full-time. Her first novel, Alexander's Bridge (1912), was imitative of Henry James; it focuses on the romantic interests of a famous engineer and his attempt to build a bridge across the St. Lawrence Seaway. In O Pioneers! (1913), Cather turned her attention to Nebraska's Bohemian immigrants. The idea for the second, more autobiographical novel, came when she combined elements of two unpublished short stories, "The White Mulberry Tree" and "Alexandra."[19] Having found her own voice and fictive parish, two of her most successful novels followed: *The Song of the Lark* (1915) and *My Ántonia* (1918).

Cather's first four novels were published by Houghton Mifflin to increasingly strong reviews. She was nevertheless dissatisfied by their sales. Her publisher's advertising was too conservative and the design of the books was dull, she contended. Adding to her frustration was a substantial bill for author's corrections to *My Ántonia*, which arrived in spring 1919. If Houghton Mifflin was taking Cather for granted, as she believed, other publishers were not. Three tried to lure her away in 1919 alone (Woodress, p. 306). Despite her complaints, she was reluctant to leave until Alfred A. Knopf, an ambitious New York publisher, made her a tempting proposition. If he could not have her next book, he would be happy to reprint *The Troll Garden*. She had proposed the same idea to Houghton Mifflin, but was met with no interest.

Cather had become aware of Knopf through one of the early bestsellers on his list, W. H. Hudson's *Green Mansions* (1916), the advertising and design of which she admired.[20] Her interest in Knopf grew, she claimed, as she observed his regular attendance at matinee performances of the Metropolitan Opera and saw the care he took in choosing the color of a book cover during an unannounced visit to his office.[21] The finer points of these accounts are open to question, but what clearly did appeal to Cather was Knopf's enthusiasm about advertising and promoting her as a nationally significant author.[22] In a letter of December 28, 1919, Cather informed her Houghton Mifflin editor Ferris Greenslet that she had agreed to let Knopf reissue *The Troll Garden*. Rather than simply reprinting the book, however, she gave Knopf a collection of both old and new stories, all centering on art. She revised "Paul's Case," "The Sculptor's Funeral," "A Wagner Matinée," and "'A Death in the Desert'" and dropped the other *Troll Garden* stories. In their place, she included three stories about opera singers, "The Diamond Mine," "A Gold Slipper," and "Scandal," which had appeared in magazines in 1916.

One of the most important decisions Cather made regarding *Youth and the Bright Medusa* was to open it with another story involving an opera singer, "Coming, Aphrodite!" Cather's correspondence with Greenslet establishes that she either wrote the story with Knopf in mind or decided to use it as her first original fiction to be published by him very soon after its completion. On January 7, 1920, she wrote to Greenslet that she had just finished writing a 15,000-word story begun in late December. This was during the same period that she was negotiating with Knopf. On February 1, she signed a contract for *Youth and the Bright Medusa* with her new publisher, little more than three weeks after finishing "Coming, Aphrodite!"[23] Her break with Greenslet was then nearly complete.

For Houghton Mifflin, Cather wrote of Bohemian immigrants on the Great Plains; in "Coming, Aphrodite!," she wrote of turn-of-the-century bohemian artists in Greenwich Village. The protagonist Don Hedger is a painter, poor and unwilling to conform to artistic trends in pursuit of sales; Eden Bower is a singer, hungry for recognition and material reward. They occupy adjoining loft apartments in Greenwich Village and fall in love. Their relationship is complicated by the transience of Bower's stay in the city, where she is taking voice lessons. She is awaiting a wealthy bachelor friend from Chicago, who will take her to Paris to study. When Hedger learns that Bower has asked a more popular painter of lesser talent for professional advice, their romance is tested. Hedger is so insulted by her failure to appreciate his art and integrity that he leaves for several days. When he is ready to reconcile, it is too late; she has left for Paris with the Chicago millionaire. Nearly twenty years later, Bower returns to New York as a prima donna. Visiting her old neighborhood in her limousine, she asks an art dealer about Hedger. She learns that her former suitor has become an important painter, respected by his avant-garde colleagues, if still unappreciated by the monied patrons of the art world.

In transferring from Houghton Mifflin to Knopf, Cather left a long-established Boston publisher for a New York firm that was barely five years old, innovative, and decidedly modern (Lindemann, p. 86). In *American Moderns*, Christine Stansell identifies Knopf as one of a group of independent New York publishers interested in authors whose "literary oddities or youth or radicalism made them risky for the established publishers."[24] "Coming, Aphrodite!," then, was perfectly suited to lead off Cather's first Knopf-published book. Hedger's modernist aesthetic and values ("I'm painting for painters – who haven't been born," he declares [CS, p. 94]) aligned him with the vanguard image of the Knopf publishing house. The sexual content of "Coming, Aphrodite!" marked a more radical departure for Cather. In one scene, for example, Bower performs her daily calisthenics naked while Hedger peers at her through a knothole in his closet. Cather describes what the painter sees, including the singer's thighs and "lifted breasts" (CS, p. 72). Hedger crouches on his knees and mentally draws her figure; he may be masturbating as well (Woodress, p. 314). Later, he tells Bower a sexual and violent tale, "The Forty Lovers of the Queen," which involves an Aztec princess, her slaves, rape, gelding, mass murder by drowning, and a dual execution by fire. That same night, Hedger takes Bower into his arms and kisses her passionately; the scene ends with their physical relationship only moments away from consummation.

"Coming, Aphrodite!" is not only Cather's sexiest story, but also an unabashed tribute to New York, where she had lived for nearly fifteen years and was now being published. Its subterranean oyster houses, hurdy-gurdies, Tammany Hall, Washington Square Park, Central Park, Fifth Avenue, Little Italy, Brevoort Hotel, Metropolitan Museum of Art, Art Students League, New York Aquarium, Metropolitan Opera, Lexington Opera House, Flatbush, Coney Island, and Long Island are all present. Other stories in the collection portray New York sympathetically; glamorous singers Cressida Garnet ("The Diamond Mine") and Kitty Ayrshire ("A Gold Slipper," "Scandal") live there, while another, Katharine Gaylord ("'A Death in the Desert'"), lies on her deathbed in Wyoming longing for the city. "Oh, let me die in Harlem!," she exclaims (*CS*, p. 217). Pittsburgh and points west, conversely, are derided in "Paul's Case," "The Sculptor's Funeral," and "A Wagner Matinée."

The richly detailed setting of "Coming, Aphrodite!" is but one of its many strengths. Against this vividly rendered New York backdrop, Hedger and Bower stand out as memorable protagonists involved in a plausibly complicated relationship. The minor characters, including the cleaning woman "old Lizzie," model/stuntwoman Molly Welch, art dealer M. Jules, and even Hedger's dog Caesar, add depth without stalling the well-plotted story. "The Forty Lovers of the Queen" inset narrative, furthermore, is engaging enough to have been expanded into a separate tale. For all of these reasons and more, "Coming, Aphrodite!" is one of Cather's best short stories.

In leading her first title under Knopf's imprint with "Coming, Aphrodite!," Cather not only showcased her latest and best work, but also made plain her strong identification with the country's literary capital. The story defied the notion of Cather as a "regionalist" writer of the West. It certainly appealed to its most important New York reviewer, Edmund Lester Pearson, who wrote in the *New York Times Book Review*: "If Willa Cather had written nothing except 'Coming, Aphrodite!' . . . there could be no doubt of her right to rank beside the greatest creative artists of the day."[25] Knopf must have been delighted. According to him, the *New York Times Book Review* notice was the only one that mattered when it came to book sales ("MC," p. 214). Almost all of the reviewers agreed that "Coming, Aphrodite!" was the outstanding story of the collection.[26] Next in line for praise were the revised *Troll Garden* stories, which were judged to be improved by Cather's pruning of superfluous detail and description. Of the 1916 singer stories, "The Diamond Mine" rated highest.

"Coming, Aphrodite!" got *Youth and the Bright Medusa* off to a strong start, and *Youth and the Bright Medusa* got Cather off to a strong start with Knopf. Published in September 1920, it sold through its first printing of 3,500 copies by the end of the year and was into its fourth printing by June 1921. Cather was so pleased by the collection's success that she never sought another publisher. Thus, *Youth and the Bright Medusa* was pivotal in her career, for it confirmed what Edith Lewis, Cather's live-in companion of nearly forty years, called the most important professional decision the author ever made.[27] Cather appreciated Knopf's loyalty, seriousness, and artistic sensibility. His business acumen, moreover, gave her the financial security to write what she wanted without pressure to produce bestsellers.[28]

In the dozen years following the publication of *Youth and the Bright Medusa*, Cather won the Pulitzer Prize for *One of Ours* (1922), published four other novels and a book of essays, and became a celebrity. In a 1922 letter to Dorothy Canfield Fisher, she referred to herself as a slow-selling author who had to pay close attention to her expenses.[29] A decade later, her financial worries were gone. Her literary agent Paul Reynolds had negotiated good prices for her stories and novel serializations from the country's leading magazines, and royalty income from Knopf was sizable. In August 1931, she was famous enough to be featured on the cover of *Time* magazine.

Obscure Destinies capped this auspicious period in Cather's career, but was born of personal grief. It was the last collection Cather arranged herself and contains the last of her stories to be published during her lifetime: "Neighbour Rosicky," "Old Mrs. Harris," and "Two Friends." According to Woodress, they were composed between late 1928 and late summer 1931, during which time Cather's father died and her mother suffered through a long illness. These events "turned her mind to family and friends of her youth"" (p. 438), evidence of which runs throughout the book. The protagonist of the lead story, Anton Rosicky, was most likely modeled after Cather's father and a Nebraska farmer of Czech ancestry who was also the model for Ántonia's husband in the earlier novel (*OD*, pp. 201, 208). Mrs. Harris, who rescues her granddaughter's chance of a college education, was based upon Cather's maternal grandmother, Rachel Boak. "Two Friends" records the nightly conversations of two small-town businessmen who were based on men Cather knew from her early years in Red Cloud (Woodress, p. 445).[30]

Cather made wise choices in conceiving of *Obscure Destinies* from the perspectives of both literary art and marketing. Documentary evidence establishes that she did so at about the time she completed "Old Mrs. Harris," more than a year before the volume was published (*OD*, p. 207). For one, she chose not to publish "Old Mrs. Harris" as a short novel; the story is longer than Cather's 1926 novel *My Mortal Enemy* and could have been issued separately (Woodress, p. 441). Kari Ronning has theorized that "Depression-era economics" may have deterred the author from opting for a separate publication, since readers might not have been willing to pay full price for such a slim book (*OD*, p. 226). "Old Mrs. Harris" was widely praised in *Obscure Destinies'* contemporary reviews, as was "Neighbour Rosicky." "Two Friends," the shortest story in the collection, was estimated to be the weakest of the three. Cather variously identified each of the stories in the volume as her favorite (*OD*, p. 232).

Publishing the three Western stories together and leaving uncollected two Pittsburgh stories which had appeared in magazines, "Uncle Valentine" (1925) and "Double Birthday" (1929), was another advantageous move by Cather. It unified *Obscure Destinies* in place and time, and gave Knopf a strong selling point, for in its pages Cather was revisiting the site and period associated with her early literary triumphs: the Western plains of her youth. One did not need to read very far to discern the locale. Beneath the title the dustjacket read "Three Stories of the West." An ear of corn was depicted on the title page and a headpiece of a sunflower adorned the lead story, "Neighbour Rosicky." There is no reason to doubt that Cather still had final approval of design matters such as these intended to influence the reception of her books – in this case, by accentuating *Obscure Destinies'* agrarian focus.

Another prudent marketing decision Cather may well have suggested was the linking of "Neighbour Rosicky" and *My Ántonia* in *Obscure Destinies'* dustjacket copy. There, the protagonist of the story is compared to Ántonia's husband, Anton Cuzak. In the novel, Cuzak is a Czech immigrant who sacrifices his social life for an isolated farm and a large family. It is, on balance, a trade-off he is happy to have made. Rosicky, too, is a Bohemian farmer. After spending impoverished and lonely years in London and New York, he appreciates his farm for the sustenance and stability it provides. At sixty-five, he has "a special gift for loving people" (*CS*, p. 57), but is troubled by heart problems. His beloved family consists of his wife and five sons, the eldest of whom has married a townswoman. She finds farm life difficult, and Anton fears that she will persuade his son to move to town. In the scenes that follow, Cather shows the salutary effect of Anton's love for his family and land on his daughter-in-law. He finally succumbs to a heart attack, but not before she tells him that she is pregnant with his grandchild. To his doctor, Rosicky's life seemed "complete and beautiful" (*CS*, p. 261).

Many reviewers drew the suggested comparison to the novel, which had been in print with Houghton Mifflin for almost fifteen years.[31] One commented that "Old Anton Rosicky . . . is the natural product of the pen that wrote *My Ántonia*," while another wrote that "Neighbour Rosicky" "seems to be the going on to his death of the husband of *My Ántonia*."[32] By implying that *Obscure Destinies* could be read as a sequel to the earlier work, Cather and Knopf made good use of the title on Houghton Mifflin's backlist. Also printed on the dustjacket was a list of seven Cather titles headed by the question, "Have you read them all?" Cather had complained to Greenslet that Houghton Mifflin did not sufficiently promote her previous works with each new publication. Knopf did not make the same mistake.

Regarding the publication of *Obscure Destinies*, the *New York Times Book Review* announced "The Return of Willa Cather."[33] Readers responded enthusiastically to the author's homecoming. Published in a first printing of 25,000 copies on August 5, 1932, *Obscure Destinies* went into a second printing of 5,000 by the end of the month, and a third of 3,000 in September (Crane, pp. 170–1). The volume's appeal during the Depression may have been partly due to its evocation of a simpler time when neighbors and family were the antidote to personal economic crises. (A number of influential critics would soon cite this as an example of Cather's "escapism.") Above all else, *Obscure Destinies* owes its popularity to Anton Rosicky and Mrs. Harris. Through direct description, dialogue, and incident, they emerge as characters of remarkable depth. In "My First Novels – There Were Two," an essay published a year before *Obscure Destinies*, Cather observed that she had once mistakenly believed that fiction ought to be based on "interesting material."[34] As she developed as a writer, she focused less on plot and more on character. "Neighbour Rosicky" and "Old Mrs. Harris" display her consummate skill in this regard.

The novels *Lucy Gayheart* (1935) and *Sapphira and the Slave Girl* (1940) were the last major works Cather completed before her death in 1947. *The Old Beauty and Others* collects her final stories: "The Old Beauty," "Before Breakfast," and "The Best Years."[35] Written in fall 1936, summer 1944, and summer 1945 respectively, the tales meditate on aging and mortality. In the title story, an English socialite's beauty has declined so dramatically since the 1890s that an old friend can barely recognize her in the French Alps thirty years later. "Before Breakfast" records the morbid reflections of a businessman in seclusion on the Canadian island of Grand Manan, where Cather herself vacationed late in life. "The Best Years" centers on a first-year teacher who dies of pneumonia while trapped in a Nebraska schoolhouse during a blizzard. Cather's age and health problems, the anguish of watching her friend Isabelle McClung suffer through an ultimately fatal kidney disease, and, more generally, the catastrophic events of World War II have all been cited as influences upon her as she composed these stories.[36]

By the time *The Old Beauty and Others* appeared, Cather's critical reputation had fallen considerably. Granville Hicks's 1933 essay, "The Case
Against Willa Cather," relegated her fiction to the category of "supine
romanticism."[37] His contention that she was principally an escapist gal-
vanized critics who found her work to be far removed from the pressing
concerns of the time.[38] Reaction to *The Old Beauty and Others* ranged
from Fanny Butcher's reverence for the recently deceased author's "truly fine
prose" in the *Chicago Tribune* to John Farrelly's derogatory comments about
her "nostalgic primitivism" in the *New Republic*.[39] The extent to which her
critical stock had dropped can be judged from the latter's declaration that
the collection did nothing to "revive her name." In "The Best Years," the
last fiction Cather ever completed, the protagonist's mother observes that
"our best years are when we're working hardest and going right ahead when
we can hardly see our way out" (*CS*, p. 394). As she wrote the line, Cather's
own years as a creative writer were coming to a close.

In the two decades following her death, Cather's critical standing improved
little. Her fiction was difficult to categorize and she had not courted the
literati to champion her cause. Her tenuous position in the canon was owed
mainly to her achievement as a prose stylist and her evocation of a particular
place and time (the Great Plains of the pioneer era). In the 1970s, though,
her stature began to grow as feminist critics turned their attention to under-
estimated women authors. Since then, Cather has come to be regarded as
one of the premier writers of the twentieth century. Ironically, one of the
primary reasons that her work has attracted a wide range of critics is that
it defies categorization. Cather herself identified this very quality as one of
the marks of a great writer in an essay lauding the short stories of Katherine
Mansfield:

> The qualities of a second-rate writer can easily be defined, but a first-rate writer
> can only be experienced. It is just the thing in him which escapes analysis that
> makes him first-rate. One can catalogue all the qualities that he shares with
> other writers, but the thing that is his very own, his timbre, this cannot be
> defined or explained any more than the quality of a beautiful speaking voice
> can be. (*NUF*, pp. 134–5)

While most critics agree that Cather's novels are the cornerstone of her literary reputation, her short fiction enters the twenty-first century a vital part
of her oeuvre. As a professional author who knew the publishing business
well, she maneuvered smartly to achieve both of these ends. As a literary
artist, she produced a body of stories that rates with the best of her contemporaries. Any serious estimation of her work must take their measure.

NOTES

1. See John J. Murphy, ed., *Critical Essays on Willa Cather* (Boston, MA: G. K. Hall, 1994), p. 36.

2. Margaret Anne O'Connor's *Willa Cather: The Contemporary Reviews* (Cambridge: Cambridge University Press, 2001) shows that Cather's short-story collections garnered fewer (though generally positive) reviews than her novels (p. xxiv). Three commendable studies of the short stories counter the critical focus on the novels: Marilyn Arnold's *Willa Cather's Short Fiction* (Athens, OH: Ohio University Press, 1984), Loretta Wasserman's *Willa Cather: A Study of the Short Fiction* (Boston, MA: Twayne, 1991), and Sheryl L. Meyering's *A Reader's Guide to the Short Stories of Willa Cather* (New York: G. K. Hall, 1994).

3. For stories reprinted through to 1980, see Joan Crane, *Willa Cather: A Bibliography* (Lincoln, NE, and London: University of Nebraska Press, 1982), pp. 239–49. Knopf reports that Cather refused to authorize the publication of a Viking *Portable Willa Cather*. See his "Miss Cather," in Bernice Slote and Virginia Faulkner, eds., *The Art of Willa Cather* (1974; Lincoln, NE: Department of English, University of Nebraska Press, 2001), p. 220; hereafter cited as "MC." Published in 1937, the sixth volume of the Autograph Edition, *Youth and the Bright Medusa*, omits "'A Death in the Desert.'" The twelfth volume, containing *Obscure Destinies*, was published in 1938 and includes the three stories from the original collection.

4. Marilee Lindemann, *Willa Cather: Queering America* (New York: Columbia University Press, 1999), p. 91.

5. Joan Acocella, *Willa Cather and the Politics of Criticism* (Lincoln, NE: University of Nebraska Press, 2000), p. 28.

6. For example, Cather wrote an author's profile for a Houghton Mifflin advertising pamphlet in 1915 and a biographical sketch for a Knopf promotional booklet in 1926 (Crane, *Willa Cather: A Bibliography*, pp. 314–15). David H. Porter argues that Cather also wrote an author's profile that was tipped-in her book of poems, *April Twilights* (Boston, MA: Richard C. Badger, 1903). See his "Cather on Cather: Two Early Self-Sketches," *Willa Cather Newsletter and Review* 45 (Winter/Spring 2002), pp. 55–60.

7. Cather's early stories are published in Virginia Faulkner, ed., *Willa Cather's Collected Short Fiction, 1892–1912* (Lincoln, NE: University of Nebraska Press, 1965). For additional commentary on the early stories, see the studies mentioned in note 2 above and note 8 below.

8. Curtis Bradford, "Willa Cather's Uncollected Short Stories," *American Literature* 26 (1955), pp. 537–51.

9. James Woodress, *Willa Cather: A Literary Life* (Lincoln, NE, and London: University of Nebraska Press, 1987), pp. 170–1.

10. Ironically, *The Troll Garden* became the subject of a feud between Fisher and Cather. Fisher objected when she learned that Cather planned to include in the volume "The Profile," a story about a woman with a facial scar who was modeled after their mutual friend Evelyn Osborne. Cather argued that if she dropped the story, *The Troll Garden* would be too slight to publish. Fisher prevailed, but their friendship was breached for many years. For further details, see my essays "Willa Cather and Dorothy Canfield Fisher: Rift, Reconciliation, and *One of Ours*,"

MARK J. MADIGAN

in Susan J. Rosowski, ed., *Cather Studies* 1 (Lincoln, NE, and London: University of Nebraska Press, 1990) and "Regarding Cather's 'The Profile' and Evelyn Osborne," *Willa Cather Newsletter and Review* 44 (Spring 2000), pp. 1–5. The letters cited in this paragraph are Dorothy Canfield Fisher to Celine Sibut, May 11, 1903, and Willa Cather to Dorothy Canfield Fisher, March 29, 1903. Both are housed in the Special Collections Department, Bailey/Howe Library, University of Vermont.

11. Review of *The Troll Garden, Pittsburgh Gazette* (April 16, 1905), pp. 1–2.
12. O'Connor, *Willa Cather*, pp. 27–34.
13. Willa Cather, *Collected Stories* (New York: Vintage, 1992), p. 210; hereafter cited as *CS*.
14. John March, *A Reader's Companion to the Fiction of Willa Cather*, ed. Marilyn Arnold with Debra Lynn Thornton (Westport, CT: Greenwood Press, 1993), p. 415. Further references will be made parenthetically.
15. George Seibel, "Miss Willa Cather from Nebraska," *The New Colophon* 2 (September 1949), pp. 195–207.
16. Willa Cather, *Not Under Forty* (New York: Knopf, 1936), p. 50; hereafter cited as *NUF*.
17. "The Sculptor's Funeral" and "Paul's Case" were for many years the only stories Cather allowed to be anthologized. Her short fiction has helped to sustain her readership, especially through its inclusion in school anthologies. Ironically, she never allowed her stories to be reprinted in such collections because she did not want students to be forced to read them (Knopf, "MC," pp. 211, 218). This restriction was eased after her death, since which "The Sculptor's Funeral," "Paul's Case," and "Neighbour Rosicky" have introduced generations of readers to her work in this format. "Coming, Aphrodite!," recently emerged from copyright protection, is now anthologized as well. Additionally, "Paul's Case" has had a second life through cinematic adaptation. The only Cather story to have been made into a film, it was originally broadcast in the PBS television series "The American Short Story" in 1980.
18. In 1925, Cather edited *The Best Stories of Sarah Orne Jewett* for Houghton Mifflin. In the preface, she named *The Scarlet Letter*, *The Adventures of Huckleberry Finn*, and Jewett's short-story collection *The Country of the Pointed Firs* as "three American books which have the possibility of a long, long, life." Cather's preface to the Jewett edition is reprinted in *Willa Cather on Writing: Critical Studies on Writing as an Art* (New York: Knopf, 1949), p. 58; hereafter cited as "OW."
19. Elizabeth Shepley Sergeant, *Willa Cather: A Memoir* (Philadelphia: Lippincott, 1953), p. 96.
20. Willa Cather, "Portrait of the Publisher as a Young Man," *Alfred A. Knopf: A Quarter Century* (New York: Plimpton, 1940), pp. 9–26; hereafter cited as "Portrait."
21. Fanny Butcher, *Many Lives – One Love* (New York: Harper, 1972), p. 366; Cather, "Portrait," p. 1.
22. Crane, *Willa Cather: A Bibliography*, p. 61.
23. Knopf, "MC," pp. 205–24.
24. Christine Stansell, *American Moderns: Bohemian New York and the Creation of a New Century* (New York: Holt, 2000), p. 157.

144

25. Edmund Lester Pearson, "Latest Works of Fiction: Miss Cather's Stories," *New York Times Book Review* (October 3, 1920), p. 24. Reprinted in O'Connor, *Willa Cather*, pp. 101–2.
26. See O'Connor, *Willa Cather*, pp. 99–115.
27. Edith Lewis, *Willa Cather Living: A Personal Record* (New York: Knopf, 1953), p. 115.
28. Willa Cather, *Obscure Destinies*; Scholarly Edition; Kari A. Ronning, ed. (Lincoln, NE: University of Nebraska Press, 1998), p. 184; hereafter cited as OD.
29. Willa Cather to Dorothy Canfield Fisher, February 6, 1922. This letter is housed in the Special Collections Department, Bailey/Howe Library, University of Vermont.
30. For a detailed account of Cather's sources for these stories, see the Historical Essay to *Obscure Destinies* in the Scholarly Edition, pp. 199–241.
31. In O'Connor, *Willa Cather*, see Fanny Butcher (p. 414), Dorothea Lawrence Mann (p. 416), and Howard Mumford Jones (p. 428).
32. "Three Stories of the West," *Christian Science Monitor* (September 17, 1932), p. 12, reprinted in O'Connor, *Willa Cather*, pp. 425–6; Hazel Hawthorne, "Willa Cather's Homeland," *New Republic* 71 (August 10, 1932), p. 350, reprinted in O'Connor, *Willa Cather*, pp. 422–3.
33. John Chamberlain, "The Return of Willa Cather," *New York Times Book Review* (July 31, 1932), p. 1, reprinted in O'Connor, *Willa Cather*, pp. 412–13.
34. Willa Cather, OW, pp. 89–98.
35. The stories in *The Old Beauty and Others* were culled from Cather's manuscripts after her death and arranged in book form by her literary executrix Edith Lewis and publisher Knopf. Given her attempts to suppress her early work and her overriding concern for her literary reputation, it is easy to imagine that she would have disapproved of the volume. The title story was rejected by the *Woman's Home Companion* in early 1937 and Cather chose not to pursue publishing it elsewhere (Woodress, *Willa Cather*, p. 475). There is no evidence that she tried to publish the other two stories or that she even considered them worthy of publication. The issue of authorial intention aside, the publication of the stories does add to the tableau of her late creative phase.
36. Meyering, *A Reader's Guide*, p. 160; Woodress, *Willa Cather*, p. 499.
37. Granville Hicks, "The Case Against Willa Cather," *English Journal* 22 (November 1933), pp. 703–10, reprinted in O'Connor, *Willa Cather*, pp. 436–41.
38. Cather responded to Hicks in a letter to the *Commonweal* in 1936, which is reprinted under the title "Escapism" in *Willa Cather on Writing*. She argued that "the world has a habit of being in a bad way from time to time, and art has never contributed anything to help matters – except escape" (p. 19).
39. Fanny Butcher, "Three Long Stories by Willa Cather," *Chicago Sunday Tribune* (September 12, 1948), p. 5, reprinted in O'Connor, *Willa Cather*, pp. 413–14; John Farrelly, "Fiction Parade," *New Republic* 119 (September 13, 1948), pp. 24–6, reprinted in O'Connor, pp. 534–5.

9

SHARON O'BRIEN

Willa Cather in the country of the ill

Two years ago, while spending a sabbatical in California, I decided to reread Willa Cather's letters to Zoë Akins, collected at the Huntington Library. As Cather scholars have long known, doing biographical research on Cather is a challenging task: her letters are scattered in collections all over the country, and no *Collected Letters of Willa Cather* exists because of the provision in her will banning publication. Now we have the invaluable *A Calendar of the Letters of Willa Cather* (2002) edited by Janis Stout, but this useful summary and chronology of Cather's correspondence is no substitute for reading the original documents.[1] Some libraries interpret her will liberally and will either allow you to make Xerox copies or will send you copies. The Huntington policy, however, is to adhere strictly to the terms of the will. No photocopies.

My original notes on the Akins collection, made while I was researching my biography of Willa Cather in the early 1980s, were detailed for the letters up to the early 1920s, then sketchier: my biography was going to take Cather up only to the publication of *O Pioneers!* (1913), so I provided myself just with quick summaries of the later correspondence ("reprimands Zoë for thinking *A Lost Lady* could be adapted," "raves about Grand Manan," "criticizes her new play," "complains about Prohibition," "struggles to write *Lucy Gayheart*"). One index card, titled "Thanks Zoë for the Flowers and Plants," listed the flora that Akins sent her friend over the years ("Thank you for the English stock . . . apple tree . . . mimosa tree . . . Roman hyacinths . . . peach blossoms . . . chrysanthemums . . . rose bush"). Many of these gifts arrived in December – for Cather's birthday and Christmas – but others, as I would discover when I reencountered the collection, were sent to Cather during or after one of her many illnesses and hospital stays.

When I reread the collection, concentrating on the letters from 1920 to 1946, I saw a side of Willa Cather I had overlooked when I was a younger reader. Interested then in the first half of Cather's life, I had missed what now seems to me – an older and different reader – a central theme in the collection, as in the later life: Cather's frequent references to illness and what we would now call depression. More attuned, in my mid-fifties, to the restrictions and losses that accompany later life, more familiar with what the poet Jane Kenyon calls the "unholy Ghost" of depression[2] than I had been twenty years before, I could see in Cather's letters not only her struggles with illness, disability (her frequently injured hand and wrist), and deaths of friends and family, but also the despairing moods sparked by these losses. As she wrote to Zoë Akins in 1932, responding to news of the death of Akins's husband Hugo Rumbold,

> It's a brutal fact that after one is forty-five it rains death. And after fifty the storm grows fiercer. I never open the morning paper without seeing the death of someone I used to know staring me in the face. In the days when I used to know you, people didn't used to die: the obituary page never had the slightest connection with our own lives.
> Death becomes a deep, benumbing fact in one's life long before it ends one.[3]

What interested me in my second reading of this letter was the way in which Cather described the impact of loss and death on herself, rather than on Zoë (it's an odd letter of consolation). Her strong language – it's raining death, the fact of death benumbs one's life long before one dies – suggested depression; not everyone responds to loss and mortality in this way. Reading further in the Akins collection, following Cather through illnesses and deaths in the 1930s and 1940s, I could see depression weaving in and out like a black thread.

What I would like to do in this essay is to use Cather's letters to Akins in order to describe the ways in which she experienced the "benumbing fact" of depression in her later life. A key issue to keep in mind is the fact that Cather never gave her despairing moods a clinical name. "Depression" would not have yet been the preferred medical term; more likely, given the period, would have been "nerve exhaustion" or, harking back to George M. Beard's classic work *American Nervousness*, "neurasthenia." Cather does not use this language in her letters to Akins: she describes her bleak moods but does not name them. On the one hand, she was spared the associations of stigma Americans now associate with clinical depression. On the other, she felt shame and anger when she was brought low by illnesses considered physical.

Central to understanding the presence of depression in Cather's later life is her frequent experience of illness and physical impairment. Cather mentions many physical illnesses in her letters (influenza, infection, a torn tendon in her left wrist, lumbago, a "chill," bronchitis) as well as referring to her operations (gall bladder, appendix) and lengthy recoveries from surgery. She never gives a medical classification for her periods of depression, but the language of physical illness – and that of fatigue and exhaustion – gave her a way of communicating emotional as well as bodily distress. During periods of depression she was more prone to illness, and when she was ill or unable to write (as she often was because of her injuries to her hand), she was prone to depression. We should think, then, of the interplay between what our insurance plans now separate as "physical" and "mental," categories that mask the interweaving of mind and body. Reflecting this interplay, Cather's use of rest cures, clinics, and hospitals offered relief for mental as well as physical ills, and played an essential part in her creative and emotional life.

Cather's biographers and critics have already described the many illnesses she dealt with in her life. It is worth remembering that Cather's numerous and lengthy bouts with illnesses such as pneumonia, bronchitis, flu, blood poisoning, and mastoiditis would lay her low for long periods, ranging from two weeks to several months, and often require hospitalization. Penicillin would not be widely available until the 1950s, and so bacteria-caused illnesses and infections could drag on for weeks, leaving the recovering patient weak and exhausted. What we would now think of as routine surgeries, requiring only a few days in the hospital – such as removals of appendix or gall bladder – were major ordeals, requiring long hospital stays, often followed by recuperation for the patient who could afford such care (Cather could) in a secluded hotel or vacation retreat.

After 1912 Cather's experiences with physical infirmities – both illnesses and injuries to her hand and arm – became so frequent that I think a brief chronology will be helpful to keep track of them.[4]

February 1914	Infection from hatpin scratch turns to blood poisoning. Spends several weeks in Roosevelt Hospital and two months recuperating in New York and Atlantic City.
Winter 1921–2	Suffers digestive problems and consults head of Stomach Clinic at St. Luke's Hospital.
Spring 1922	Ill with infection doctors first diagnosed as mastoiditis, then tonsillitis. Has tonsils removed. After hospital stay goes to Galen Hall in Wernersville, Pa., where she spends two weeks recuperating and reading proofs for *One of Ours*. Does not feel well again until June.
September 1922	Appendicitis.
Winter 1922–3	Suffers from two attacks of appendicitis and the flu. Hospital stay followed by recuperation at resort in Lakehurst, NJ.

Summer 1923	Spends summer in France, visiting Hambourgs and having portrait painted. Suffers from exhaustion, depression, and neuritis in right arm and shoulder. Spends several weeks at spa at Aix-les-Bains.
March 1924	Influenza. Recuperates at Pocono Manor Inn, Pennsylvania.
November 1924	Neuritis.
Spring/summer 1928	Visits Mayo Clinic for two weeks for unspecified reasons. Upon return to New York, contracts severe case of flu and needs nursing care at home.
Winter 1929	Bronchitis.
Winter 1932	Influenza.
Winter 1933	Bronchitis.
Spring 1934	Sprained tendon and painful inflammation of left wrist; hand and wrist in splints for weeks. Stops work on *Lucy Gayheart*.
Spring 1935	Attacks of appendicitis. Exhaustion. "Nervous strain." (*CLWC*, p. 190)
Spring 1936	Influenza. Doctor tells her to stay in bed.
Spring 1937	In bed with lumbago, later with bronchitis. Feels worn out.
Spring 1938	Influenza. May, injures hand in accident.
Spring 1939	Unable to work on *Sapphira and the Slave Girl* and suffers from flu for three months. Goes to Atlantic City for a month of recuperation.
Summer 1940	In hospital (influenza?) and doctor forbids her to go to Philadelphia in June for honorary degree from University of Pennsylvania.
Fall 1940	Hand is painful (sprain). Improves gradually.
December 1940	Decides to spend Christmas at the French Hospital so she can be taken care of well. One of my happiest Christmases, she writes to Akins on December 30.
Fall 1941	Hand in brace and cannot travel alone. Lewis accompanies her west, where brother Roscoe is ill.
Spring 1942	Inflamed gall bladder. Spends two weeks in hospital.
Summer 1942	Gall bladder surgery and Presbyterian Hospital, long recovery. Edith Lewis brings meals by taxicab. In fall, goes to Williams Inn with Lewis.
Spring 1943	Sprained tendon of right hand.
December 1943	Hand in brace again.

Spring 1944   Inflamed tendon of right thumb. Hand in brace.
Winter/Spring 1945 Writing hand in a brace, but takes off the brace for
                         two hours a day to write.

The increasing tempo of Cather's illnesses and injuries to her hand and wrist as she aged was accompanied by the deaths of her two closest siblings, Douglass in 1938 and Roscoe in 1946, as well as the death of her beloved Isabelle McClung Hambourg in 1938. In her letters to Zoë Akins, Cather's descriptions of illness, loss, and death are intertwined with descriptions of fatigue and depression.

> *June 30, 1937*
> *I have been terribly over-driven and overworked ever since Christmas, besides having bronchitis and other things . . .*
>
> *November 13, 1938*
> *I have had a bad summer and not very well. On the thirteen of June the brother I loved beyond all my family* [Douglass] *died of a heart seizure . . . Two months later the oldest and dearest friend I had in the world, Isabelle McClung Hambourg, died . . . Then I came up here alone* [to the Shattuck Inn] *in a comatose state. The power to feel seems utterly gone, and God knows I don't want it back, not for a long, long time, if ever.*
>
> *May, 1939*
> *I cannot recover from the loss of my brother, or from the death of Isabelle, the one person for whom I wrote. I have been too sick to work at all. When I am not working I cannot even write letters. I am hundreds of letters behind. I do not want you to feel that I do not think of you, just because I do not write. I am silent because I am dull.*
>
> *April 28, 1942*
> *I got word that my brother was improving* [Roscoe Cather had been ill] *and then I went into a hospital myself and stayed there for two weeks. I was just worn out by anxiety and fright. This brother is really all the family I have left.*
>
> *January 3, 1946*
> *You will not have heard from me for a long time. In the middle of this past summer brother Roscoe died. I have been ill and lifeless, only half of myself. This* [death of her brother] *has made a great change in me and I want a few, a very few, of my old friends to know it.*[5]

In her groundbreaking book *Illness as Metaphor*, Susan Sontag defined illness as both the landscape of biological disease and a socially constructed system of meanings. Together, biology and culture created another country, "the kingdom of the ill," a country one could enter at any time, perhaps never again receiving the return ticket to the "kingdom of the well."[6] Following

Sontag, in *At the Will of the Body: Reflections on Illness*, Arthur Frank developed an important distinction between "disease" and "illness" that can help us to understand Willa Cather's sojourns in the kingdom of the ill. Disease is the supposedly objective phenomenon of the malfunctioning body – defined, Frank says, by "medical talk" that "uses disease terms that reduce the body to physiology"; disease makes "*my* body, my ongoing experience of being alive, [become] *the* body, an object to be measured." Illness, in Frank's definition, is the subjective "experience of living through the disease," an experience shaped both by medical treatment and cultural attitudes.[7] Thus, in order to describe his experience of cancer as illness, Frank devotes one chapter to chemotherapy (required by the disease) and another to stigma (socially constructed and connected to the illness).

> Whenever I told someone I had cancer I felt myself tighten as I said it. Saying the word "cancer," my body began to defend itself. This did not happen when I was having heart problems. A heart attack was simply bad news. But I never stopped thinking that cancer said something about my own worth as a person. The difference between heart attack and cancer is stigma. (p. 91)

When Cather was ill, whether in bed with influenza or bronchitis, or recuperating from surgery, in addition to being fatigued and unable to work, she was frequently disgusted with herself and sometimes depressed. And so her felt experience of *illness* (in Arthur Frank's definition) was marked by shame and stigma. Elizabeth Sergeant recalls such a moment during one of Cather's early bouts with the flu.

> Some time before I went abroad I had seen my friend during a moment of convalescence and consequent gloom and self-disparagement. Indeed, I had shepherded her back from Boston on a Pullman in this typical down-hearted state of mind in which, through physical illness, she had, in a way that was baffling to me, lost her own self-respect.[8]

In her late sixties, after years of dealing with illness, Cather was no more accepting of physical frailty than she had been in her youth. Writing to Irene Miner Weisz in April, 1942, after a hospital stay for an inflamed gall bladder, Cather told her how she hated "feeling defective" (*CLWC*, p. 243). In a letter to Zoë Akins the following year, Cather acknowledged that as she grew older, she had become even less accepting of herself.

> *Something physical which I could not understand, was making me more and more short-tempered and irritable, unable to bear my own short-comings and those of my friends.*[9]

Looking back through the Akins collection and Cather's life-long experiences of disease and illness, I find it impossible to separate out "physical" and "mental": because she felt worthless when ill, she could easily descend into depression; similarly, it is likely that depression left her more vulnerable to illness, and that her low moods may have expressed themselves through her body. We can see this interplay most dramatically in Cather's last years. She never recovered fully, either emotionally or physically, from her gallbladder operation in the summer of 1942. Writing to Irene Miner Weisz on December 31, 1943, she admitted that "any kind of pleasure or emotional excitement is exhausting. Nerves seem messed up since the operation. Would be impossible to go to Red Cloud, where there would be such emotional strain" (CLWC, p. 258). Over a year later, in April 1945, she told Carrie Miner Sherwood, according to Janis Stout's paraphrase, that she had been "emotionally weak ever since her operation . . . With any emotional excitement has physical symptoms, can't sleep, and cries uncontrollably" (CLWC, p. 269).

This interplay between depression and physical illness, soul and body, strongly marked an earlier period in Cather's life when her writing life seemed in crisis. In 1920, Cather began working on the novel she then called *Claude* (retitled *One of Ours* by Knopf). This was her most ambitious novel yet, she felt – for she would be entering the supposedly masculine territory of the war novel – and it was deeply personal at the same time. Cather felt compelled to write by the death of her cousin G. P. Cather, killed at the battle of Catigny in 1918. She had read his letters home and felt a powerful emotional and spiritual kinship with the dead soldier. For several months she had resisted the pull of this project, not sure if she wanted to make the risky attempt to write a war novel. But finally she gave up: the story would not let her alone.

Cather threw herself into the project eagerly. It was the first novel for which she did research and interviewing: reading the diary of a World War I physician and talking with him about his time on a troopship; reading the letters of another fallen soldier, David Hochstein; talking with servicemen. A former student from her Pittsburgh days was posted in New York, and he would bring enlisted men to 5 Bank Street to speak with her.

Cather's letters to Dorothy Canfield Fischer describing the writing of *One of Ours* show the strength of the emotional and imaginative bond she shared with Claude Wheeler and with the novel in which he lived and died. *Dorothy, the writing comes from a very deep place inside . . . Claude's energy helps me to write. I have him in my blood. I love the feeling of resting myself in his younger, stronger body.*[10] The language Cather uses to describe her creative process suggests that her work on the novel, and with this character, provided physical and emotional healing for the writer, who gained rest and energy from her encounters with Claude, precisely the results doctors would have hoped patients would gain from rest cures.

Cather enjoyed such a rest cure in the spring of 1922 while reading the proofs for *One of Ours*, staying at Galen Hall in Wernersville, Pennsylvania, after her tonsillectomy. Cather had lost 15 pounds (7 kg) in the hospital, as well as a lot of blood, and found Galen Hall a good place to recover, despite the terrible food. Writing to Zoë Akins on April 20, Cather described the sanatorium:

> It's in beautiful forest country just coming green, with all the fruit trees and dogwood and redbud in flower. The place is luxuriously comfortable and the food is vile. That's America for you. I pay sixty dollars a week and can have the use of a ballroom, billiard room and six sun parlors, but I can't get one vegetable that is not canned.
>
> I'm reading page proofs out here – at least I work two hours a day on them. There are beautiful walks all about, but I'm limited to two miles a day. I do walk a little more than that, but I am rather spent afterward. I shall stay a week longer if I can endure the food. It is an awful good thing to get off alone with your book before other people get at it.
>
> I begin to feel that I want to live in a hotel. I'd like to live in a hotel in high mountains, with just such a drench of light as there is here – the light seems to pour through one and almost takes the place of food.[11]

Spending time alone with her book, reading proofs quietly in a sunny Pennsylvania spring, enjoying her restorative relationship with Claude, Cather healed her body and spirit as she walked down paths lined with redbud and dogwood. When the reviews for *One of Ours* appeared – some quite negative, including H. L. Mencken's, which charged that Cather had written the war scenes like a "lady novelist" – Cather's journey back towards health was interrupted.[12]

In the summer of 1923, her spirits low, she went to visit Isabelle and Jan Hambourg in France and experienced neuritis in her right arm and shoulder. Discouraged by the poor reviews for *One of Ours* – even winning the Pulitzer Prize for the novel did not cheer her up – Cather felt dispirited and exhausted. Ironically, she then had to deal with the rewards of fame: the Omaha Public Library had commissioned a portrait, sending a check to Cather for $1,000 to give to the artist of her choice. Cather selected the Russian émigré painter Leon Bakst, then living in Paris. She went into the city for sittings for several weeks in the summer and fall of 1923 (interrupted by her sojourn at Aix-les-Bains). The portrait took almost twenty sittings – far more than Bakst had anticipated, but he was seeking a psychological likeness, not simply an external resemblance. The sittings were pleasant; Cather enjoyed Bakst's company, and savored this honor from Nebraska even more than the Pulitzer. But the portrait that emerged, in Edith Lewis's words, was "stiff, dark, heavy, lifeless – everything Willa Cather was not."[13] Cather agreed with Lewis, thinking Bakst's work a good painting but not a good likeness.

Yet in many ways the portrait *did* resemble Cather in the summer of 1923. Bakst had caught the depression below the writer's surface, the "stiff, dark, heavy, lifeless" mood Cather brought with her from America. A good portrait-painter will sense the intangible or hidden self of the subject, and that may explain why Bakst kept painting much longer than he had anticipated, trying to bring his subject to life, while all the while his paintbrush told another story.[14]

Cather's letters do not say exactly when her depression began to lift. I imagine this process beginning at Aix-les-Bains, when the idea for a new story began to emerge, one about a man, a professor, caught in the heavy darkness of a mid-life depression. Cather's imagination returned to life, and as it did her spirits brightened and energy returned. Writing *The Professor's House*, she was once again the portrait-painter and shaper, not the subject, active rather than passive, transforming life into art and so regaining the power she had lost when ill. She maintained that power of shaping in writing *My Mortal Enemy* (1926), her next novel, referring to her creative process as "painting a portrait of Myra" – taking over Bakst's active role and leaving her role as the ill, fatigued subject far behind.[15]

My reencounter with the Akins Collection and rethinking the issues of health, illness, and depression in Cather's life has led me to think that further exploration of both her experience and representation of illness would be useful for us, particularly in understanding her later life and work. In his book *Illness and Culture in the Postmodern Age*, David B. Morris observes: "Chronic illness has almost no place in popular self-representations of the postmodern world. It is nearly absent from network television, which prefers to focus on acute illness that is curable."[16] One can make the same comment about American culture more generally: stories of illness, particularly chronic and continuing illnesses, are often silenced, perhaps because illness itself – with its accompanying dependence, powerlessness, and restricted abilities – is ideologically un-American, clashing as it does with our "up-by-the-bootstraps" myth of the power of the self to overcome all obstacles. (Why do we need universal healthcare, since if we were really in charge of our own destiny, we would not become ill in the first place?) What this suggests, of course, is that when one enters the country of the ill, one takes on a stigmatized and marginalized identity – paradoxical, since almost everyone will take up at least temporary residence there.

The illness story that most Americans want to hear, view, or read is the recovery story. We like the "Once I was sick, but now I am well" narrative that duplicates the structure of the Puritan conversion story ("I was blind, but now I see") and the upward-mobility story codified by Benjamin Franklin and Horatio Alger. Even writers as daring as William Styron, who spares nothing in showing the horrors of depression in *Darkness Visible*, adopts the form of the recovery narrative. He ends his memoir with the requisite return from darkness to light, giving us the narrator's full, and seemingly permanent, emergence from despair into "serenity and joy."[17]

In her novel of depression, *The Professor's House* (1925), Cather gave her readers a challenging ending. Unlike Styron's narrator, even though he has left behind suicidal despair, the Professor has resigned himself to living "without joy." In her later life Cather may well have had experiences of joy; certainly her letters show that she often felt the quiet pleasures of what Jane Kenyon calls "ordinary contentment" ("Having It Out with Melancholy"). (In Kenyon's view, it is not joy but ordinary contentment that is depression's opposite.) The years from 1922 to 1947 were filled with many pleasures and contentments – among them her restorative stays at Whale Cove cottage on Grand Manan, her growing delight in the role of aunt (both to her nieces and to the Menuhin children), her continuing creativity, slowed but not broken by ill health, and her sustaining partnership with Edith Lewis.

But Cather's later years were, as the above chronology suggests, also marked strongly by illness and disability, periods during which she felt herself defective and marginal. Despite her bold ending to *The Professor's House*, where she shunned the easy comforts of complete recovery, she could not escape American cultural attitudes towards illness, and she also may well have associated illness with the weakness culturally associated with the traditional feminine role that she had repudiated.[18]

Focusing on issues of health and illness can give us more questions to ask about the interplay between her work and life, particularly after 1922. How did illness and, later, disability affect her sense of self and identity? How are illness and disability represented in her work? How might our understanding of Cather's creative process be deepened by taking these issues into account?

Giving full weight to the substantial presence of depression, physical illness and disability in her later years can also illuminate her continuing commitment, in the face of such challenges, to living life as fully as she could: starting new novels and friendships, keeping up old attachments through letters, taking off her splint so that she could write, for an hour or two a day, slowly and maybe even painfully, stories that demanded to be written. And then dictating a letter to Zoë, thanking her for the roses.

NOTES

1. Janis P. Stout, ed., *A Calendar of the Letters of Willa Cather* (Lincoln, NE: University of Nebraska Press, 2002). Referred to in the text as *CLWC*.
2. See Jane Kenyon, "Having It Out with Melancholy," in *Constance* (St. Paul, MN: Graywolf Press, 1993).
3. Willa Cather to Zoë Akins, November 21, 1932 (Akins Collection, Huntington Library, San Marino, California). In accordance with the practice of Cather scholars, I have paraphrased Cather's letters rather than quoting directly.
4. I have created this chronology by drawing on my own work for The Library of America edition of the works of Willa Cather as well as Janis P. Stout's *A Calendar of the Letters of Willa Cather* and James Woodress, *Willa Cather: A Literary Life* (Lincoln, NE: University of Nebraska Press, 1987).
5. All letters to Akins from the Akins Collection, Huntington Library.
6. Susan Sontag, *Illness as Metaphor* and *AIDS and Its Metaphors* (New York: Doubleday, 1988), p. 3.
7. Arthur W. Frank, *At the Will of the Body: Reflections on Illness* (Boston: Houghton Mifflin, 1991).
8. Elizabeth Sergeant, *Willa Cather: A Memoir* (Lincoln, NE: University of Nebraska Press, 1963), p. 90.
9. Willa Cather to Zoë Akins, December 4, 1943 (Akins Collection, Huntington Library).
10. Willa Cather to Dorothy Canfield Fisher, n.d. [April 1922?] (Fisher Collection, University of Vermont).
11. Willa Cather to Zoë Akins, April 20, 1922 (Akins Collection, Huntington Library).
12. H. L. Mencken, *Smart Set* (October, 1922), pp. 140–2.
13. Edith Lewis, *Willa Cather Living: A Personal Record* (Lincoln, NE: University of Nebraska Press, 1953), p. 132.
14. James Woodress also finds the Bakst portrait an accurate reflection of Cather's inner life at this time. "Bakst's sitter was a middle-aged woman going through a profound physical, emotional, and spiritual crisis. The portrait bares the soul of Professor St. Peter, whose similar problems Cather had already begun to describe" (p. 339).
15. Willa Cather to Mr. Hogan, February 5, 1940 (Barrett Collection, University of Virginia).
16. David B. Morris, *Illness and Culture in the Postmodern Age* (Berkeley: University of California Press, 1998), p. 221.
17. William Styron, *Darkness Visible: A Memoir of Madness* (New York: Vintage Books, 1992), p. 84.
18. As Diane Price Herndl observes, illness and its concomitant powerlessness seem "antithetical to feminist goals" of power and agency. See *Invalid Women: Figuring Female Illness in American Fiction and Culture, 1840–1940* (Chapel Hill: University of North Carolina Press, 1993), p. 2.

II

STUDIES OF MAJOR WORKS

10

ANNE E. GOLDMAN

Rereading *My Ántonia*

> What brains they must have in Christminster and the great schools, [Jude]
> presently thought, to learn words one by one up to tens of thousands! There
> were no brains in his head equal to this business; and as the little sun-rays
> continued to stream in through his hat at him, he wished he had never seen a
> book, that he might never see another, that he had never been born.
>
> Somebody might have come along that way who would have asked him his
> trouble, and might have cheered him by saying that his notions were further
> advanced than those of his grammarian. But nobody did come, because nobody
> does.
>
> Thomas Hardy, *Jude the Obscure* (1896)

Though Hardy's *Jude the Obscure* and Cather's *My Ántonia* begin with
boyhood – Jude is eleven, Jim ten – neither book is remotely for young
people. Both writers focus upon the tension between youthful idealism and
the less highly colored vision of middle age; both also accord the latter's
pragmatism more novelistic interest than the former's energy. Each author
explores the gap between what we expect of the world and what we obtain
from it, only to close by assuming the impossibility of ever making these ideas
equivalences. "Nobody did come, because nobody does": this is a striking
tack away from the high-spirited inventiveness that characterizes so much
of fiction-writing, where, of course, the novelist may direct anyone at all to
rescue, enlighten, or waylay the protagonist.

A variation on *Great Expectations* or *Oliver Twist*, *My Ántonia* is not.
Still, the novel is most admired where its heroine is most consistently senti-
mentalized. Read as if peopled with Rosie-the-Riveter prototypes – strong,
crude, and patriotically inclined – the book is often framed as the novelistic equivalent of the country's "great expectations" for itself. It serves, that
is, as an anthem for the "melting-pot" plot: the Ellis Island-give-me-your-
tired-your-poor story without which no American schoolchild can finish the
fifth grade. What Helen Hunt Jackson's *Ramona* and Ansel Adams's photographs of Half Dome have done to dignify and legitimate California's
statehood, Cather's *My Ántonia* has accomplished for Nebraska and the
Plains. Ántonia, in this account, is an ennobling and civilizing metaphor,
dignifying the transition from wild land to fertile farm as perhaps the most
distinctively "American" story.

This version of Cather's pioneer novels we know; it is the reading that by the mid-1930s established her – notwithstanding her contemporary critical refashioning as a liminal figure – as one of the nation's most celebrated authors. In a 1926 lecture series at Bowdoin College, she took her place alongside Robert Frost, Edna St. Vincent Millay, Irving Babbitt, John Dos Passos, and Carl Sandburg. Five years later, she became the first woman to be awarded an honorary degree by Princeton University. Calling attention to her "early novels of pioneer life on the frontier," the citation equated her work with the Turner thesis, lauding her representation of "the land of opportunity and the school of character, built on hardships endured and overcome."[1] If her standing within the confines of the academy fell slightly and then leveled off, her popularity with the country as a whole swelled. By the mid-1930s, she "felt completely besieged" and resorted to "having her telephone shut off during her working hours and having her secretary write formal letters in place of the personal responses she would rather have made" (Bohlke, p. xxv). In the words of a 1940 reviewer for the *New York Herald Tribune Books*, both her work and her person were "civilized and very American" (Bohlke, p. 137). So much for marginality.

The tendency to read *My Ántonia* as an addition to "America the Beautiful" has lately been scrutinized by Cather scholars, who have alternately apologized for this assumption, denied it, censured it, modified it, and supplanted it with other equally sublime icons for a variety of political positions. Until recently I had not looked closely at this most celebrated novel, considering instead the southwestern fictions – *The Song of the Lark, The Professor's House* (to my mind her best novel), and *Death Comes for the Archbishop*. Like Elizabeth Ammons, however, I have called attention to the "significant exclusions" in Cather's work, as well as to the ways in which it "is clearly invested in master narratives of Western cultural dominance and white superiority."[2] While such criticism corrects blandishments that oversimplify her writing in the service of a reductive nationalist history, I suggest we rethink the time and energy we are committing to such interpretations of Cather's midwestern novels. The fact that these books so "clearly" support a conservative reading of American political life is an argument for not spending too long on such a corrective. Joseph Urgo has asserted that, save for a realization of the "political costs" of migration, Cather's Plains fictions would be "no more than nationalistic polemic."[3] To my mind, however, these books really *are* nationalist polemic, and so – from a purely *political* point of view – boring.

If Cather's textual politics is unremarkable, so also is her prose. Limpid and lovely at its best, it possesses neither the sinuous virtuosity of the Faulknerian sentence nor the abstract intelligence of Stein nor the panache of metaphor that dazzles in Hurston. In her conscious and unrelenting insistence on representing middle-aged women, however, the people most consistently underrepresented across a wide range of arts, then and now, Cather's work remains distinctive. How many celebrated paintings figure women over thirty-five? How many films, from the silent era to the present day, establish middle-aged women as their central characters? How many novels focus primarily on the emotional lives of women who have reached their fourth or fifth decade?

Cather's choice of representational objects has wider implications as well. Through it, she critiques the theory of the novel more largely, a form that has from its inception magnified the erotic longings of its central (and typically youthful) characters to the exclusion of many of the other feelings that move us. The pull of memory, an undertow against forward motion, the occasional or sustained yearning for a different life regardless of one's present circumstances, the paralyzing effects of boredom as a drag against flight, the quickened respiration that accompanies curiosity, the myriad attractions and repulsions that make the web of relations encircling children, adults, and the elderly vibrate: so much is shrunken in favor of a single-minded focus upon our romantic lives, as if such attachments were not interconnected with all of these other feelings. In Cather we see the language of sexual desire, certainly, but it is not the only language that drives her characters, or the "official" mechanism that moves the plot. Acknowledging the remarkable quality of Cather's widened literary attention indicates that the novel may be a less elastic genre than we typically suppose.

What the writer says of *Madame Bovary* ("One can hardly discuss that book; it is a fact in history. One knows it too well to know it well"[4]), we can equally say of *My Ántonia*. To foreground what seems most compelling about this novel requires sidestepping the ongoing critical arguments about the book, and approaching it from a different vantage point. Just as any genuine introduction of a person means assuming as little as possible, any productive rereading of a novel means asking questions of it that are not merely rhetorical. Clearly we cannot simply jettison longstanding critical habits of mind – nor would we wish to – but we can try reading without disingenuousness. A reconsideration of the novel also means avoiding the tendency to approach it as if it were the sole vertical on the literary horizon line. While readers indict the book for its Horatio Alger-like impulses, they tend to lend it a similar autonomy.

What might the book read like if I were to consider, instead, its affiliations within the design of her work as a whole? To hear what echoed previous books and what might anticipate the novels published after it, I jettisoned the regional divide between the Plains novels and the southwestern fictions that I and many other readers had taken for granted. Once I relinquished the confines of this literary zoning, I noticed affiliations across the writer's work that had been invisible. From this perspective, *My Ántonia*, like any number of novels (*Lucy Gayheart*, *The Professor's House*, *The Song of the Lark*, *O Pioneers!*), turns over the large concerns sustaining Cather throughout her career: the abiding love for the land despite the intellectually stifling and socially repressive small towns encircling it, the capacity to make art as compensation for the lost "fullness of heart that comes from being too young to see that one's desires will inevitably pattern themselves after experience and circumstance" (Goldman, p. 137), the difficulty of living with disappointment, the choice between the costs of social acceptance and the fulfillment of desires unlicensed by custom or institution.

When I read the novel this way, Ántonia's profile looked different. She appeared to resemble Augusta, the seamstress who saves St. Peter from asphyxiation at the close of *The Professor's House*, as closely as she did the stalwart Alexandra of *O Pioneers!* Her stoicism in the face of abandonment by her lover Larry Donovan recalled Alexandra's bleak assessment near the close of the book that "what was left of life seemed unimportant,"[5] but it also mirrored Augusta, who sympathizes with the Professor's despair without pity, unyieldingly resuscitating him only to face the question of "what to make of a diminished thing."[6] Ántonia possesses the resolute dignity of Frost's speaker in "The Oven Bird," who "says that leaves are old and that for flowers / Mid-summer is to spring as one to ten." Like him, she "knows in singing not to sing," recognizing middle age for the lopsided ratio it is, an uneven fraction that witnesses age approach much faster than youth recedes. Her quiet acknowledgment of this diminishment provides a means to connect these two figures, which an unquestioning acceptance of the regional divide estranges. From this perspective, the Professor and Alexandra both seem to echo Frost's songless bird, which echoes, "loud," the desire to be free of desire – or, as Cather frames Alexandra's hopeless recognition near the close of *O Pioneers!*: "longing itself was heavy: she yearned to be free of that" (p. 282).

Other literary relationships coalesced as well: the likeness between Jim Burden and St. Peter, both disaffiliated, intellectual, stuck in unhappy marriages, yearning for "home" but suffocated and restless in it, for instance. Or the shared sense of adventure Cather develops through the stories Tom Outland tells of life on the mesa and those Ántonia, Otto, and Jake recount to Jim so that he imagines his own life as richer in exploit and romance than that of "The Swiss Family Robinson" held up as the standard of youthful fantasy. More largely, I saw the resemblances of characters that are essentially different variations on a theme. In this way the outlaw-wanderers of the 1918 novel, Otto and Jake, recall Tom Outland (killed as a young soldier), Ray Kennedy (torn apart in an accident by the train in which he rode as a conductor), and Emil Bergson (murdered by his love's husband, Frank Shabata), all of whom – like Otto and Jake, abandoned by the novelist when they board the "west-bound train" and are "never heard from" again[7] – pay dearly for their insistence on remaining unconfined.

Cather's recycling of words and tag phrases to designate character and idea from the earliest novels to the latest works is striking. The lightness of heart that characterizes both the wordless joy of a connection to the land and the epiphany of art she frames in similar terms in the 1913 *O Pioneers!*, where Marie Shabata's quashed dreams find her walking on, "her face lifted towards the remote, inaccessible evening star" (p. 248), and the 1935 novel *Lucy Gayheart*, where the title character's hopes are likened to the feeling she experiences when "in the darkening sky she had seen the first star come out; it brought her heart into her throat."[8] Likewise, the energy and warmth Jim sees in the young Ántonia – "I remembered what the conductor had said about her eyes. They were big and warm and full of light, like the sun shining on brown pools in the wood" (p. 23) – echoes the lively beauty of other Cather heroines, women with amber eyes all (consider Lucy Gayheart, whose "golden-brown eyes . . . flashed with gold sparks" [p. 4] and Marie Shabata, whose "yellow-brown eyes" "everyone noticed": "the brown iris had golden glints that made them look like gold-stone, or . . . like that Colorado mineral called tiger-eye" [p. 11]). Cather describes the erotic appeal of these women lovingly, only to chasten them for their emotional extravagance.

Recognizing this patterning requires a different kind of literary attention. Readers often attack each novel's images the same way that Jim pins the head of the rattler Ántonia sees on the prairie. We triumphantly fix their symbolic registers, that is, like so many critical snakes we have to subdue, dragging their skins behind us like the puffed-up boy Cather affectionately teases in his "mock adventure" (p. 49). Instead, we might approach such representations more watchfully and respectfully, appraising the way their contours and colors shift with changes in position and different lights. In a 1931 *Good Housekeeping* interview, Cather described the layered rhetorical structure of *The Professor's House* as prompted by seventeenth-century Dutch paintings that possess an interior scene within their frame, a house door half open, the tiled floor visible in its shadow, a broom and mop angled within an alleyway. Like these "double scene[s]" (Bohlke, p. 125), her story of the sun-lit mesa is similarly recessed within the gray roll-top scholar's desk, crowded with the scraps and scrawled notations of everyday life.

By the same token, we might enrich Ántonia's portrait: the play of expressions across her face, the inflections of her accented English, the animated brown eyes, by seeing her over and against the other portraits of women Cather honors in her fiction. This way of reading is at once comparative and accretive: as when we walk through a Vermeer exhibition and study how the painter uses blue and yellow hues variously in different canvases until we understand their clarity of expression and emotional depth across his work as a whole, we can see Cather as modeling a variety of middle-aged and elderly female characters to depict all the nuances of quiet strength she so admired. Rather than see the title character of *My Ántonia* as an isolated portrait, let us understand her as one illustration for the feminine strength and dignity Cather consistently wishes to evoke, the woman who remains in possession of a natural curiosity and a "relish for life" (p. 180) despite its vicissitudes. Accordingly, we can assess Ántonia over and against "The Hired Girls" of the novel, and as she resonates with the grandmother figure Cather invokes not only in this novel (a woman of "lively intelligence," who "was then fifty-five years old, a strong woman, of unusual endurance" [p. 11]), but throughout her work more generally.

As frequently as Jim is inclined to romanticize Ántonia as alternately his muse, his love, and his youthful compatriot, he recalls to himself that it is really the qualities she possesses that attract him, qualities shared by the "score . . . of country girls who were in service in Black Hawk" (p. 198). Ántonia is compelling, not as the image either of the narrator's (heterosexual) fantasy or of the writer's (lesbian) desire, but, less romantically, because she is the most famous example of a figure Cather honored again and again in her fictions as well as in interviews and lectures: the woman who, despite personal tragedy, summoned the courage to try to live well throughout middle age and beyond. I want to distinguish this quality of receptiveness from that of endurance – although stoicism is a quality Cather clearly respects. While she chooses not so much to plumb the depths as to praise from a distance, her most admired characters never stop trying to live richly, either through the compensations art provides, or simply by remaining alert to the possibilities of learning.

For every instance in which she delineates the particular loveliness of Ántonia's features and attitudes, the writer supplies us others in which this character merely represents a collective, the "stalwart Bohemian and Scandinavian girls," "The Hired Girls" – note the collective of the title – who "are now the mistresses" of their own "rich farms" (p. 201). While critics too easily glamorize Ántonia as distinctive on the novel's horizon, Cather describes her, through Jim's contemplative eye, as a simile for strength of mind and purpose. "Like Ántonia," Jim muses, the hired girls "had all . . . been early awakened and made observant" through hard labor. "The older girls, who helped to break up the wild sod, learned so much from life, from poverty, from their mothers and grandmothers" (p. 198). Often, readers follow Jim's lead in romantically magnifying the title character – regardless of their position on the novel's sexual patterning. As if she were the plow he watches become "heroic in size" before it sinks "back to its own littleness" (p. 245), Ántonia is sized up as if she were a kind of feminine Atlas, a Titan wrestling herself out of the rock in one of Michelangelo's intentionally half-carved sculptures.

But if scholars have leaned on the proprietary address of the title to establish the bond between narrator and title character, Cather's echoing of this phrase towards the book's close undermines this relationship's presumed intimacy and exceptionalism. Here, the affection of the narrator for Ántonia cannot be mistaken as that of star-crossed lovers, but broadens and pools into a slower complacency for the hired girls more generally: "I always knew," Jim recollects, "I should live long enough to see my country girls come into their own" (p. 201). Jim's nostalgia, which Cather chides as unrealistic, is mirrored by her own affection for women like Ántonia, who themselves refuse the consolations of sympathy (recall the wall of privacy Ántonia establishes upon her return with her young daughter). Like Thomas Hardy, who is similarly enamored of his heroines but schools them to understand, as Cather remarks in "A Chance Meeting," that "conditions and circumstances, not their own wishes, dictate the actions of men" (p. 40), Cather cherishes a sentimental attachment to her characters but subjects them to suffering on behalf of this principle. Caroline Franklin-Grout, the woman commemorated in "A Chance Meeting," may not be "visionary," but she is instead a person who "jusqu'à la plus extrême vieillesse, avait conservé l'intelligence et la bonté souriante" ("until the most late age, had retained her intelligence and her smiling goodness") (*Not Under Forty*, p. 42).

As a "spirituelle femme du monde" (a woman of the world who possesses faith), the elderly Caroline seems a character far removed from the middle-aged farm wife Ántonia, but, like many of Cather's feminine representations, the two survive personal disaster with an equal grace. In *The Mayor of Casterbridge*, Hardy suggests that "the secret . . . of making limited opportunities endurable" – and whose are not? – consists in "the cunning enlargement, by a species of microscopic treatment, of those minute forms of satisfaction that offer themselves to everybody not in positive pain; which, thus handled, have much of the same inspiring effect upon life as wider interests cursorily embraced."[9] While Hardy's bitter repetition ("microscopic," "minute") registers continual surprise at the smallness of possibility, Cather honors the effort to "enlarge" as a kind of faith that enables serenity.

The most compelling figures receive the writer's grace because she refuses to let them be devoured by loss. While her most memorable masculine characters possess a fine aesthetic sense and the capacity, through nostalgia, to recover the richest moments of their past, it is older women whom Cather's work most consistently dignifies. Men, in Cather's fictions, do not often have the strength of mind to recover from hurt. Consider bereaved Father Latour, who must part with his long-time companion in *Death Comes for the Archbishop*, or the brooding Professor St. Peter, a man whose day is dedicated to intellectual life but who has clearly stopped learning, or Jim himself, who is crippled (burdened) by his eternal attitude of retrospection. By contrast, the older women of her novels are more determined than thoughtful. Forgoing the attitude of contemplation, they remain connected with the world, risking its apparently never-ending capacity to hurt.

Ultimately, more than any single portrait, it is the relationship of connection to consciousness, in all its fine shadings, that Cather is most interested in exploring. This is not to say that she does not align herself with specific vantage points. Clearly, Jim's narrative comes closest to the writer's own in *My Ántonia*: in interview after interview both before and after the book's publication she attests to this, speaking of her memories of growing up in Nebraska, of her grandparents, of the stories she hears from the immigrant families living there, and in particular of the "Bohemian girl," Annie Pavelka, whose name recalls the title character's. Ántonia is a reflection of this interest, as are Alexandra in *O Pioneers!*, Augusta in *The Professor's House*, and even Lucy's stolidly narrow-minded older sister Pauline in *Lucy Gayheart*. And certainly the writer, like her narrator, loves this central figure – lavishing upon her prose that is often sensual. But Jim complains, "You'll always treat me like a kid, I suppose" (p. 224), and ultimately, the kind of desire the narrator feels for the central character remains a childish one. It is the physical and sensual recollections of a middle-aged man for the mother figure of his childhood – readers of Arturo Islas's beautiful novel *The Rain God* will remember a parallel instance of this in the affection of Miguel Chico, the narrator-professor, for his childhood nurse.[10] And while I am endorsing with this assessment readings that represent queer sexuality in general and Jim in particular as a figure for gay masculinity, I want to insist that championing a politicized queer sexuality for its own sake is not what drives this novel (or Cather's writing more largely). Yes, she writes out of her own experience – like any writer – but to frame her books as if they were speakers at a gay-pride celebration is not altogether dissimilar from equating them with heroic bronzes celebrating "The Pioneer." This is not to dismiss the representations of sexual difference in her work, which are many. It is, however, not to reduce expressions of erotic desire to any pure political metal, but instead to see them as complicated alloys, indivisible from the composite longings that characterize human sensibilities in their largest sense.

Finally, for all its resonance with Cather's other novels, the central figure of the 1918 book does not possess the same relation to its surroundings as do the protagonists of her other novels – even *Lucy Gayheart*, the 1934 novel that returns readers to the Midwest, which, like *My Ántonia*, is framed using a bifurcated and divided narrative perspective. *My Ántonia* is not really about Ántonia in the way *The Song of the Lark* is about Thea Kronborg, or the way *Lucy Gayheart* is about Lucy, or *The Professor's House* about St. Peter, or even the way that *Death Comes for the Archbishop* is about Father Latour. If Ántonia speaks for the undervalued character of feminine resolve, she is also the focal point for an exploration of our interior lives at the point when they become colored more fully by our regrets than by what we anticipate. The sum of years that makes up the difference between Ántonia's girlhood and her life at middle age is what the writer is interested in exploring, and with it the curiously productive tension that this paradox embodies – how, that is, a difference can also be a sum. Through her, Cather finds a way, like Frost, "in singing not to sing"; that is, she articulates the complicated relation between memory and desire once "the highway dust is over all." Ántonia is the novel's frame, the window on to the landscape that the narrator looks out upon when he wishes to conjure up that deeply felt connection with the land that is beyond language, what Cather calls "the incommunicable past" (p. 372) in the closing words of the novel.

Cather makes this equation of figure and ground explicit in the novel's introduction, when, as an anonymous traveling companion on the train with the middle-aged Jim, she insists: "More than any other person we remembered, this girl seemed to mean to us the country, the conditions, the whole adventure of our childhood" (n. pag.). If you recall a loved place from your own childhood, it is easy to take this statement at face value, for the recollection of such places can involve a feeling of liberty and release that is as much about the desire to repossess a less shadowed interior (emotional) life as it is a longing for a particular kind of "country." And how many of us do not have such memories of moments in which our interior composition and the external horizon line mirror each other in effortless harmony? Of playing summer games of "capture" in the evenings, the outline of trees and shrubs obsidian-black against the lighter grain of the night sky, the air just cool enough to make you comfortable in your own skin, the slow pulse of your heart thudding loud in your ears, the breeze lifting a strand of your hair with impersonal tenderness – this is the quality of memory Cather gestures towards in *My Ántonia* and what Elsa Nettles rightly calls a "longing for the sacred places of youth."[11]

Just so, Jim's picture of himself and Ántonia as children, out in the long grass of the prairie, is a kind of snapshot by which he (and Cather) retrieve the past in total, a past that is nostalgically rendered as if it were an element altogether different from and purer than the amalgam of the present. The prairie, Jim remembers, "was like the bush that burned with fire and was not consumed" (p. 40). Or, earlier in the novel: "the grass was the country, as the water is the sea," he thinks, continuing with a phrase that resonates with Homeric epithet: "The red of the grass made all the great prairie the color of wine-stains" (p. 15). Early memory is venerated not only as the origin of desire, before it is ineluctably contained and compromised, but also of artistic inspiration. Its language is connected with the vocabulary of art – recollecting it is almost a physical sensation, the wince of an indrawn breath. Listening to the artist Clement Sebastian sing is for Lucy Gayheart in the later novel of the prairie like watching "the darkening sky" of her home: both bring "her heart into her throat" (pp. 9–10).

At the same time, because home in Cather is never identified with the hummingbird inattention of city life, its fitful, quick discordances, but rather with the slower and predictable rhythms of rural America, it is paradoxically what keeps the adult imagination shackled. Joseph Urgo writes that it is "the place to which we have reluctantly returned or in which we have got ourselves stuck" (p. 56), and the mired abruptness of this word, which pulls you up short as brutally as the choke chain on a dog's lead, seems exactly right. But it is not the land that Cather equates with lack of ambition and a halfhearted directionlessness; rather, it is the suffocating closeness of life in the small towns built at its edges that she sees as hobbling.

This attention to the aborted quality of rural consciousness makes any simple political reading of "pioneer life" impossible – wherever it falls along the spectrum. If anything, in argument if not in tone, the book in such instances resembles filmic satires of suburban life such as *The Stepford Wives* or *American Beauty* (given that suburban life is the contemporary equivalent of the rural town). In *My Ántonia*, Jim takes a long walk out of town, to "where the land was so rough that it had never been ploughed up." "Out there," he muses, "I had escaped from the curious depression that hangs over little towns" (p. 370). The repressive silence is mortifying – tangible as the clammy clutch of a ghost, thick as swamp water: "That silence seemed to ooze out of the ground, to hang under the foliage of the black maple trees with the bats and shadows" (p. 196). The suffocating lack of privacy in such places is as isolating as it is stultifying. Cather censures the inhabitants of small towns as if they were the automatons of film. Jim describes the married people who "sat like images on their front porches" (p. 196); prowling outside, he sees "the houses of good people who were . . . sitting still before the parlor stove, digesting their supper" (p. 217). Lucy imagines that no one in town even possesses an interior life at odds with their surface placidity: in the city, by contrast, "if you were burning yourself up, so was everyone else; you weren't smoldering alone on the edge of the prairie" (*Lucy Gayheart*, p. 52). The language here recalls the images buried within the ostensibly celebratory opening paragraph of *My Ántonia*, where "the world lies green and billowy beneath a brilliant sky," but one is "fairly stifled in vegetation"; where "in little towns like these" you were "buried in wheat and corn" (n. pag.).

"Buried" and "stifled": the vocabulary echoes the sustaining images of Cather's prose, which underscore the extent to which she saw the "secret accords and antipathies which lie hidden under our everyday behaviour" ("Katherine Mansfield," p. 137) as defining our emotional lives. This appreciation for the subterranean quality of daily life is unsurprising for someone who desired social approval (Jim articulates this on her behalf when he says, "Disapprobation hurt me . . . even that of people whom I did not admire" [p. 228]) but whose most intensely passionate feelings as a lesbian defied it and thus needed to be at least partially submerged. But ultimately for Cather this divided consciousness is not exclusive to those censured by virtue of difference, but is instead a condition we all share. The push-pull between the desire for acceptance and the desire for liberty that her fictions explore is communicated through phrases for what in the Mansfield essay Cather calls our "double life" (p. 136), a language of hidden feeling that runs like water trapped under the surface of ice beneath "the group life" of even the most "harmonious families," as well as in figures that mime the constricted and fettering quality of the social relations we all both require and resist. Like Hardy, Cather insisted, "human relationships are the tragic necessity of human life" that can "never be wholly satisfactory." Each of us, she wrote, is "always in his mind . . . escaping, running away, trying to break the net which circumstances and his own affections have woven about him" ("Katherine Mansfield," p. 136).

In the closing pages of this essay I would like to consider two figures that echo and further this idea, the mummy and the manikin, which like Robert Frost's songless bird speak mutely of the pain involved in living this double bind. Images of "still life," they gesture towards the frozen attitudes we take to preserve respectability. Cather recalled in an interview the grave of a Native American woman whose father had buried her on land now owned by her grandfather, a grave looted for its "rich furs and beadwork" (Bohlke, p. 9), and she returned to this image in her fiction. I have argued elsewhere that this figure exploits as it confirms a raced hierarchy of aesthetic value.[12] Here, however, I wish to consider the way Cather exploits it to reflect a kind of "doubling," a curious mixture of consolation and threat,

at once punishment for refusing convention, and, in its frozen life, a talis-
man for what she calls in *Lucy Gayheart* "the far horizon line," "the fine
things of youth, which do not change" (p. 189). A darker version of the
game of statue that children play, where at the command of one they stand
frozen in midstep, this figure is a curious fusion of the central concerns of
Cather's fiction: the confining love for the "little town" (*LG*, p. 66), and the
relationship between the wide horizon of youthful hopes and adult desires,
which, whether homosexual or heterosexual, are always extramarital in her
work and always curtailed. Cather devotes considerable space to the female
mummies of *The Song of the Lark* and *The Professor's House*: the clothes
and turquoise of the mummy Ray Kennedy finds make her "handsome" as
Thea, he thinks.[13] The erotic undercurrents of this image are picked up as
well in *The Professor's House*, where the white teeth and black hair of the
body Tom and Henry call "Mother Eve" possess a physicality that is quasi-
sensual, while the mouth, open in a silent scream,[14] is a perpetual reminder
of her murder in consequence for what they imagine to be a love affair in
defiance of marriage.

The images of violent death in the midwestern novels – Emil and Marie,
shot by Marie's husband Frank; Lucy, dragged under the icy water of the
lake by a tree branch and drowned; Mr. Shimerda, shot by his own hand in
his barn – may not at first glance seem connected with the punishments suffered by those involved in the liaisons explored in the southwestern fictions,
but Cather's concern with delineating their frozen attitudes recalls both the
suffocating quality of small-town life (what Lucy calls the "heart-breaking
love" for her "own little town," which is "like loving the dead who cannot
answer back" [p. 66]), and the reprisals for transgressing its perimeters. The
death tableau of Emil and Marie, murdered as they lie resting joyfully in
one another's arms, is chronicled with a clinical focus on rigor mortis that
recalls the post-mortems of Arthur Conan Doyle's fiction. The stillness and
sprawl of their forms is also a perverse variation on the Cliff City dwellers
"preserved" as Tom Outland says "like a fly in amber" (*PH*, pp. 201–2).

This "still life" also resonates with the self-destruction of Mr. Shimerda,
whose marriage to his servant girl (again, in defiance of custom, since she is
socially far beneath him), yields only anguish: a reluctant emigration to the
United States, grief at leaving behind the masculine companions of his youth,
a deep sense of loss for his native land, all of which ends in suicide. The writer
details the rigidity of his blood-spattered body, "frozen through" (p. 102) for
days, with a grisly attention that does little to advance the novel's plot. "The
body can't be touched until we get the coroner," Jim's grandmother cautions,
"and that will be a matter of several days" (p. 98). When the coroner does
arrive, Cather returns to the still corpse, whose body must be "cut . . .

loose from the pool of blood in which it was frozen fast to the ground" (p. 114).

The extended description of Mr. Shimerda's body that follows suggests that the mummy is the primary image for this fascination with life arrested. "I slipped out from the cave and looked at Mr. Shimerda," Jim recalls. "He was lying on his side, with his knees drawn up. His body was draped in a black shawl, and his head was bandaged in white muslin, like a mummy's" (p. 115–16). Like the mercurial temperaments and quicksilver movements we associate with characters like Lucy and Marie, Mr. Shimerda's sentimentality – his love for music, his extravagant mourning for his homeland – is a defiance of convention whose punishment is a literal straitjacketing in the winding cloths of a mummy.

The rigidity of social life is also reflected in the unchanging physiognomy of the respectable self that Cather describes in *Lucy Gayheart* through this striking passage, which I would like to cite in full:

> Pauline was a much more complex person than her sister: her bustling, outright manner was not quite convincing, for all its vehemence. One felt that it had very little to do with her real feelings and opinions – whatever they might be. She was, so to speak, always walking behind herself. The plump, talkative little woman one met . . . was a manikin which Pauline pushed along before her; no one had ever seen the pusher behind that familiar figure, and no one knew what that second person was like. Indeed, Pauline told herself that she 'put up a front.' She thought it very necessary to do so. Her father was queer, and not at all like the real business men of the town; and Lucy, certainly, was not like other people. Someone had to be 'normal' (a word Pauline used very often) and keep up the family's standing in the community.　　　　　　(p. 142)

Besides the fascination of the figure itself – a twentieth-century mummy, we could say, which rewrites and extends the implications of Augusta's dressmaker's dummy that forms so integral a part of the domestic horizon at the close of *The Professor's House*, what strikes me is its punishing quality. If Pauline is a more complex figure, why not write the novel from her perspective rather than from Lucy's? Yet it is Lucy who remains the image of interest and of beauty in the novel, despite, or rather in the face of, this patronized "little woman" whose interior life is gestured at only to be quickly foreclosed upon. As with the young men of Black Hawk whom Jim dismisses because they bow down to the force of convention despite their desire for "the country girls" (p. 201) they go dancing with on Saturday nights, the "pusher" behind the manikin is never made visible. Where the housekeeper in *The Professor's House* is dignified as an illustration of reserved fortitude, this later portrait makes the figure one to be absently pitied, although Pauline, in an unusual shift to the second person, seems to appeal to us directly when she says of her sister: "You coddled her as if she were a superior being, and she treated you like the housekeeper" (p. 163). In this late and substantially darker exploration of middle-aged femininity, Cather does not provide us with the portrait of a dignified woman; rather, she considers the consequences of unjustly withholding respect, by focusing upon the "negative space" around such an absent portrait.

While Cather does not use this image of refusal explicitly in *My Ántonia*, her censure of the timorous attitudes and negations of small-town life resonate with its petrified blankness. Jim critiques "the married people" sitting "like images on their front porches" (p. 196) as if they were dummies in a store window, and the more sustained indictment that follows arraigns this "guarded mode of existence" as another illustration of life arrested. Like "living under a tyranny," such "evasions" have long-term consequences. "People's speech, their voices, their very glances, became furtive and repressed" (p. 219). The novel's representation of the cold rigidity of this kind of behavior, in which people refuse connection only to "slip over the surface of things in the dark" (p. 219), anticipates the dressmaker's figure in the darkened room at the close of *The Professor's House*, as well as Pauline's manikin in *Lucy Gayheart*.

Its vacant "front" resonates as well with the critique of married life Sylvia Plath presents four decades later in "The Munich Mannequins."[15] For the poet as for the novelist, these plastic "idols," voiceless as "snow," embody an intolerable domesticity. Recognizing the parallels between Plath's image of the manikin, "Glittering and digesting/Voicelessness" and the "good people" of *My Ántonia* sitting "still before the parlor stove, digesting their supper" (p. 217) brings the 1918 novel into a closer accord with the later Cather novels, making it bleaker in tone – but more interesting – than most conservative and progressive political readings allow.

In Plath's work, of course, there is no solace. The corrosive image of the Munich mannequins in all their "sulphur loveliness" is just bitter ash falling indiscriminately upon everything like snow. Cather begins with a similar metaphor – "the growing piles of ashes and cinders in the back yards" are "the only evidence that . . . life went on at all" (p. 219–20), but art is compensation for all this waste. In fact, art is "richer" amid these "restrictions," the "things that one must not talk about," she explained in a 1925 speech (Bohlke, p. 167). Like Katherine Mansfield, Cather "chose a small reflector to throw a luminous streak out into the shadowy realm of personal relationships," and it is precisely these "uncatalogued" (p. 135) aspects of human relation that we bump into like furniture in the dark as we navigate her prose. But what remains "incommunicable" (p. 372), as the closing phrase of *My Ántonia* asserts, need not be interpreted as an admission of failure, but as a way of gesturing towards those "intangibilities" of "feeling" too fine, as Hardy writes in *Far from the Madding Crowd*, to be caught "in the coarse meshes of language."[16] In this sense even the images of arrested life Cather writes of throughout her work are testimony as much to the quick as to the dead: like the child's sled that so famously closes out *Citizen Kane,* or those plastic globes that fit in the palm of your hand and which, with a turn of the wrist, you fill with snow, they are apt figures for the interior world of memory and the world of the novel itself.

NOTES

1. Willa Cather, *Willa Cather in Person: Interviews, Speeches, and Letters,* ed. L. Brent Bohlke (Lincoln, NE, and London: University of Nebraska Press, 1986), p. 112. Future references will be made parenthetically.
2. Elizabeth Ammons, "Cather and the New Canon: 'The Old Beauty' and the Issue of Empire," in Susan J. Rosowski, ed., *Cather Studies* III (Lincoln, NE, and London: University of Nebraska Press, 1996), p. 265. Anne E. Goldman, "All in the Family? Willa Cather's Imperial Housekeeping in the Southwest," in *Continental Divides: Revisioning American Literature* (New York: Palgrave/St. Martin's Press, 2000). Future references will be made parenthetically.
3. Joseph R. Urgo, *Willa Cather and the Myth of American Migration* (Urbana and Chicago: University of Illinois Press, 1995), p. 54.
4. "A Chance Meeting," *Not Under Forty* (New York: Knopf, 1936), p. 17.
5. Willa Cather, *O Pioneers!* ([1913] New York: Quality Paperback Book Club, 1995), p. 286. Future references will be made parenthetically.
6. Robert Frost, "The Oven Bird," *The Poetry of Robert Frost,* ed. Edward Connery Lathem (New York: Henry Holt, 1969).
7. Willa Cather, *My Ántonia* ([1918] rev. 1926; Boston, MA: Houghton Mifflin, 1981), pp. 144, 145. Future references will be made parenthetically.
8. Willa Cather, *Lucy Gayheart* ([1935] New York: Vintage, 1995), pp. 9–10. Future references will be made parenthetically.
9. Thomas Hardy, *The Mayor of Casterbridge* (1886; New York: Modern Library College Editions, 1950), p. 431.
10. Arturo Islas, *The Rain God: A Desert Tale* (Palo Alto: Alexandrian Press, 1984).
11. Elsa Nettels, "Youth and Age in the Old and New Worlds: Willa Cather and A. E. Houseman," in Robert Thacker and Michael A. Peterman, eds., *Willa Cather's Canadian and Old World Connections, Cather Studies* IV (Lincoln, NE, and London: University of Nebraska Press, 1999), p. 289.
12. See, for instance, Elizabeth Ammons's essay already cited, Deborah Karush's "Bringing Outland Inland in *The Professor's House:* Willa Cather's Domestication of Empire," in Thacker and Peterman, eds., *Cather Studies* IV, and my own chapter from *Continental Divides,* already cited.

13. Willa Cather, *The Song of the Lark* ([1915] Boston, MA: Houghton Mifflin, 1983), p. 148.
14. Willa Cather, *The Professor's House* ([1925] New York: Vintage, 1973), p. 214. Future references will be made parenthetically.
15. Sylvia Plath, *Ariel* (London: Faber & Faber, 1965), pp. 74–5.
16. Thomas Hardy, *Far from the Madding Crowd* ([1874] Oxford: Oxford University Press, 1998), p. 26.

II

JOHN N. SWIFT

Fictions of possession in
The Professor's House

The following analysis of *The Professor's House* addresses an old critical debate over the relation of Willa Cather's art to her society's realities, to the actual world experienced by her readers. In the 1930s she quarreled with the critic Granville Hicks, who had liked her early prairie novels for their "authentic" and "realistic" pictures of the hardships of midwestern pioneer and immigrant life, but deplored the later works – particularly *Death Comes for the Archbishop* and *Shadows on the Rock* – as glamorous pseudo-histories, escapist fantasies to comfort "readers who share her unwillingness to face the harshness of our world."[1] Hicks understood Cather's escapism as a moral flaw and abdication of social responsibility; other readers have seen it as an aesthetic triumph. Cather herself, in a famous response to Hicks, acknowledged it proudly as a simple necessity: "What has art ever been but escape?"[2]

Hicks's developmental narrative is useful in a general way. Cather's subjects were often remote, stylized, and tranquil in her later career (although Hicks had not had the benefit of reading the knotted politics of *Sapphira and the Slave Girl*, which, though a historical romance of sorts, is hardly tranquil). In the final twenty-five years of her life, she deliberately cultivated a persona of pained alienation from the corrosive daily worlds of commerce, politics, and social struggle: a persona focused resolutely, if nostalgically, on the simple purity of great art. But as Guy Reynolds has argued in his own consideration of Cather's argument with Hicks, a simple opposition of "engagement" and "escapism" oversimplifies her response to her contemporary history.[3] The core of Hicks's argument against Willa Cather is his charge that she "never once tried to see contemporary life as it is; she sees only that it lacks what the past, at least in her idealization of it, had. Thus she has been barred from the task that has occupied most of the world's great artists, the expression of what is central and fundamental in her own age" (Hicks, p. 144). But this seems to me simply wrong, as I shall try to demonstrate: in fact – setting aside the problematic of seeing "life as it is" – Cather responded at all times with considerable complexity to her "contemporary life," including the great systemic transformations of American society that occupied some of her fellow writers of the 1920s and 1930s more overtly. Her escapism was itself an "expression of what is central and fundamental in her own age."

The Professor's House is a particularly rich novel for understanding the tension of contemporary experience and escape in Willa Cather's thinking. Begun in late 1923 and finished in early 1925, it occupies the dead center of her career.[4] Its dual structure, the story-within-the-story, seems self-consciously transitional. In her 1922 *New Republic* manifesto, "The Novel Démeublé," Cather had denounced literary realism's catalogues of things, its overcrowded interiors, and endorsed an austere new classicism – "How wonderful it would be if we could throw all the furniture out of the window . . . and leave the room as bare as the stage of a Greek theater, or as that house into which the glory of Pentecost descended" (*On Writing*, pp. 42–3). *The Professor's House* very deliberately realizes these two opposed modes of art (and worldviews) in its two narratives, juxtaposing Godfrey St. Peter's claustrophobically material world of mean people and things against Tom Outland's empty but redemptive Blue Mesa, the "world above the world,"[5] where he "found everything, instead of having lost everything" (*Professor's House*, p. 251). That this juxtaposition is a deliberate working-out of the principles of "The Novel Démeublé" is clarified in Cather's well-known 1938 letter to Pat Knopf, echoing the language of furnishings and open windows:

> In my book I tried to make Professor St. Peter's house rather overcrowded and stuffy with new things; American proprieties, clothes, furs, petty ambitions, quivering jealousies – until one got rather stifled. Then I wanted to open the square window and let in the fresh air that blew off the Blue Mesa, and the fine disregard of trivialities which was in Tom Outland's face and in his behaviour.
>
> (*On Writing*, pp. 31–2)

In the structure of *The Professor's House*, then, we find a pivot or moment in which two worldviews or aesthetics self-consciously competed: worldliness and escapism, materialism and idealism, the overfurnished and the *démeublé*. As we shall see, neither prevailed. The competition's terms are not simple, however; as most readers have recognized, the story's multiplying ironies undermine the clear oppositions and valuations of "The Novel Démeublé" or the letter to Knopf. Materialism and idealism blur at their points of contact; Louie Marsellus and Tom Outland trade moral places disconcertingly (who is the businessman, who the dreamer?); the Blue Mesa itself acquires final significance in its status as commodity. If, as generations of readers have rightly insisted, *The Professor's House* is Cather's exploration of and protest against a pervasive materialist commodity culture (the same that she had recognized in 1922 in *One of Ours*), the novel proposes no particular alternative.[6] I believe that its internal frustrations and contradictions can be understood, not so much through Willa Cather's own personal increasing disaffection with modernity, but rather through the pervasive crisis of western liberal thought whose dimensions were emerging in the early twentieth century: a crisis having to do with fundamental ideas about political identity and the individual's relation to property. In other words, *The Professor's House* seems to me to be a work deeply engaged with what were – and still are – the central political issues of modern western society.

I

I will begin at a moment of forgetting: a trivial error or slip that nevertheless unmistakably resembles Freud's famous symptomatic parapraxes or "bungled actions." In the novel's first conversation, Godfrey St. Peter tells Augusta about his intention to maintain occupancy of their attic study/sewing room, despite his family's move to a new house. "I'm staying on until I finish a piece of writing," he explains. "I've seen your uncle about it" (*Professor's House*, pp. 19–20). But in chapter 2, on the following day, walking from new house to old, "the Professor remembered that he really must have an understanding with his old landlord, or the place would be rented over his head" (pp. 50–1). As a result, he turns aside, visits Augusta's uncle (his landlord Appelhoff), explains "that he wanted to stay on in the new house, and would pay the full rent each month" (p. 51), and negotiates a genial agreement. Has he seen Appelhoff or hasn't he when he talks to Augusta? And since he apparently has not, why does he say that he has?

This uncertainty recalls other, slightly less striking or more easily explicable, points of disturbance in the novel where Cather, or St. Peter, or both, appear uncharacteristically absent-minded, failing to keep their first stories straight in later iterations: strange lapses for a meticulous craftswoman and a prize-winning historian. The Professor is fuzzy on just how and why he came to Hamilton as a young man. In one version, "When St. Peter was looking for a professorship, because he was very much in love and must marry at once, out of the several positions offered him he took the one at Hamilton, not because it was the best, but because it seemed to him that any place near the lake was a place where one could live" (p. 31). On the other hand, in a later memory, "when he accepted almost the first position offered him, in order to marry at once, and came to take the chair of European history at Hamilton, he was thrown upon his wife for mental companionship" (p. 50). How many job offers did St. Peter in fact entertain? Did he accept Hamilton only to satisfy a hot-blooded urge appeasable only in marriage – or because of the lake as well?

Or consider St. Peter's hands-off relationship to his wife Lillian's inheritance, whose renunciation he proudly recalls early in the novel: "By many petty economies of purse, he had managed to be extravagant with not a cent in the world but his professor's salary – he didn't, of course, touch his wife's small income from her father" (pp. 28–9). Yet this income, he eventually acknowledges, has been the very foundation of his comfortable middle-class life:

> His married life had been happy largely through a circumstance with which neither he nor his wife had anything to do. They had been young people with good qualities, and very much in love, but they could not have been happy if Lillian had not inherited a small income from her father – only about sixteen hundred a year, but it had made all the difference in the world. A few memorable interregnums between servants had let him know that Lillian couldn't pinch and be shabby and do housework, as the wives of some of his colleagues did. Under such conditions she became another person, and a bitter one.
>
> (p. 257)

Has he "touched" his wife's money or not? (It is hardly a "small income" – "sixteen hundred a year" was a decent annual salary for a junior faculty member at most American universities in the early twentieth century.) If not downright dishonest, St. Peter's early boast of self-sufficiency seems evasive and legalistically nit-picking (if he's correct, the servants must have served only Lillian), as evasive as his related disavowal to Mrs. Crane of any interest in Tom Outland's legacy. "I tell you frankly," he insists, "I have never received one dollar from the Outland vacuum." She replies, unanswerably: "It's all the same if it goes to your family, Doctor St. Peter" (p. 135). From plush rooms at the Blackstone Hotel to the "dozens of the brilliant rubber casquettes he liked to wear when he went swimming" (p. 269), St. Peter enjoys the Outland vacuum's profits as surely as does the legally entitled Rosamond.

What is at stake in these forgettings and denials? What sort of anxiety do they express? In all three cases the story that undergoes revision or qualification concerns a financial relationship – a lease, a job, a bequest – and in each St. Peter confronts its terms skittishly, reluctantly, as though business relations themselves are the distasteful "trivialities" for which Tom Outland shows his admirably "fine disregard" in the letter to Knopf. And this is quite exactly the case, as St. Peter's musings on the fortunate aspect of Tom's early death demonstrate: "His fellow scientists, his wife, the town and State, would have required many duties of [Tom's hand]. It would have had to write thousands of useless letters, frame thousands of false excuses. It would have had to 'manage' a great deal of money, to be the instrument of a woman who would grow always more exacting" (p. 261). In short, Tom would have become enmeshed in just the web of contractual relations (drawn about him by his desire for an "exacting woman") that St. Peter seeks throughout his novel to deny, or at least to hover above: a man of substance, yet with no visible means of support.

The anti-materialism of *The Professor's House* thus clarifies itself specifically as a horror of *contract*, and particularly of possessive contract: while St. Peter enjoys things (including his own labor and that of others) and their uses, he shies from admitting his possession of them, preferring renting to owning, gifts to purchases, favors to paid services. He mistrusts the formal legal ties that bind humans to their things, or that allow them (since the end of possession is transmission or exchange) to maintain a commerce in things. Once we acknowledge this taboo we recognize immediately also its scope in the novel – and, consequently, the omnipresence, nearly intolerable for St. Peter, of contracts themselves: wills, patents, investments, passbooks, bills of sale, leases, terms of employment. The book's two apparently antithetical landscapes (St. Peter's Hamilton and Tom Outland's Blue Mesa) are by no means differentiated in this regard, as possession and sale invade the latter exactly as they do the former, in a common language that echoes persistently on both sides of the Cruzados River's "Dangerous Crossing." "There can be no question of money between me and Tom Outland," St. Peter admonishes his daughter Rosamond, in rejecting her efforts to include him in Tom's legacy. "Your bond with him was social, and it follows the laws of society, and they are based on property. Mine wasn't, and there was no material clause in it" (pp. 62, 63). On the Mesa, Tom breaks with Roddy along almost identical lines (and with identical words) over "possession" of the Cliff City and its artifacts: "There never was any question of money with me, where this mesa and its people were concerned. They were something that had been preserved through the ages by a miracle, and handed on to you and me, two poor cow-punchers, rough and ignorant, but I thought we were men enough to keep a trust. I'd as soon have sold my own grandmother as Mother Eve – I'd have sold any woman first" (p. 244).

In *The Professor's House*, then, contractual ownership of personal property itself (including labor and its products) elicits an anxiety sufficient to produce measurable ripples and distortions in the narrative. That this anxiety attaches to ownership and not to the owned goods themselves – that it stems from no simple anti-materialism – is underscored by the happy status of *gifts* in the novel: although Cather uniformly treats buying and selling as distasteful, disturbing processes, giving or receiving gifts, particularly rich gifts, is wholly admirable. Tom readily gives away the turquoises and pottery that he cannot bring himself to sell, and, as we have seen, St. Peter can overcome his scruples enough to accept most of Louie's gifts with genuine pleasure. Gift-giving is in fact the mark of the "sumptuous generosity" (p. 121) that connects Tom Outland and Louie Marsellus. Louie unself-consciously claims Tom "as a brother, an adored and gifted brother" (p. 166), while in St. Peter's language the two transcend the complications of their material successes and become fantastic brothers in chivalric magnanimity, purveyors of "princely gifts" (p. 121) or a "princely invitation" (p. 161). Ownership may be a pinched and grasping state, but fine things themselves, given freely, can be ennobling.

II

One way to understand Cather's contract-anxiety is by locating it in the pervasive psychological context of her personal possessiveness, in the drive towards autonomy and formal control that shaped her early career choice (as editor), left its traces on her works' titles (My Ántonia, My Mortal Enemy – even the ghost-written McClure's My Autobiography), underlay her 1921 change of publishers from Houghton Mifflin to Knopf, and led finally to her remarkable last will and testament's attempt to control her literary properties and biography – to fix immutably her historical face – past her own death.[7] Willa Cather was personally territorial, perhaps to an unusual degree, and her territorialism involved the mastery or possession of objects whose status was inherently problematic: intellectual and literary properties, impressions, histories, memories, public reputation. The question over which Tom and Roddy split – who has the right to own and sell my labor and its products? – affected Cather with particular force in her career.

Rather than pursue the problem further in Cather's personal psychology, however, I want to position it in a larger history of American social change in the twentieth century's first quarter, when legal philosophy was radically retheorizing both property and contracts in the face of a socioeconomic landscape dominated by big corporations, an emergent labor movement, and, increasingly, governmental regulation of their relations to each other. As Reynolds has demonstrated, Cather was an active though idiosyncratic observer of and participant in the ferment of Progressivism, the diffuse national project that sought to redefine and reorganize society's controlling institutions along rationally systematic, equitable, and often utopian lines (Cather in Context, pp. 11–14). Progressivism's reform spirit entered jurisprudence in the interests of justice, addressing the needs of workers, and thus focused predictably on matters of contract and ownership. But since these matters are at the very core of historical liberalism's ideas of individualism and individual rights, Progressive legal theory ultimately called into question classical liberal idealizations of the absolute sanctity of individual sovereignty itself, suggesting their increasing irrelevance to a culture of collective entities in complex relations of dependency to one another. If Willa Cather was worried in the 1920s about possessions and contractual relations, she was not the only one: her anxiety reflected a national juridical project whose implications for the most cherished traditions of American ideology were enormous.

I shall digress briefly to sketch the historical situation. In the late nineteenth century, American courts increasingly elevated "liberty of contract" – the right of individuals to enter freely into contracts with others – to a position of remarkable authority in deciding business and labor cases. This liberty was rooted in Lockean notions of the natural possessive right of all men to their bodies, their labor, and the fruits of their labor, and thus to their "perfect Freedom to order their Actions, and dispose of their Possessions, and Persons as they think fit . . . without asking leave, or depending upon the will of any other man."[8] It was reinforced in the United States Constitution by Article 1, Section 10, Clause 1, and the Fifth and Fourteenth Amendments, all of which served in different ways to discourage government from intervening in or regulating the contractual process. The famous expression of the courts' individualist position was a Supreme Court decision of 1905, *Lochner v. New York*, which declared unconstitutional a state-mandated sixty-hour maximum work week for bakers, ruling that "there is no reasonable ground for interfering with the liberty of person or the right of free contract, by determining the hours of labor, in the occupation of a baker."[9] It framed the dispute as a competition between state and individual interests: "It is a question of which of two powers or rights shall prevail, the power of the state to legislate or the right of the individual to liberty of person and freedom of contract . . . We think the limit of the police power has been reached and passed in this case" (*Lochner v. New York*, pp. 57–8). These connected impulses – a perceived sanctity of individual contractual freedoms, a mistrust of law by public legislation – constituted the philosophical kernel of what historians term the "*Lochner* era": three decades of judicial efforts to limit the regulatory powers of states and maintain the autonomy of contracts, efforts that generally supported the interests of businesses and employers. The *Lochner* era finally drew to a close in the mid-1930s, in the New Deal's triumphant empowerment of big government and regulatory legislation.[10]

In his dissent to *Lochner*, Oliver Wendell Holmes pointed pragmatically to the social and institutional realities of modern American life:

> The liberty of the citizen to do as he likes so long as he does not interfere
> with the liberty of others to do the same, which has been a shibboleth for
> some well-known writers, is interfered with by school laws, by the Post Office,
> by every state or municipal institution which takes his money for purposes
> thought desirable, whether he likes it or not.
>
> (*Lochner v. New York*, p. 75)

This common-sensical response to the idealism of the court's majority was echoed over the next twenty years by Progressive legal theorists, who, responding to Lochnerism in the courts, sought to devise a jurisprudence less abstract and absolutist, more practically "sociological" in its orientation to the times.

Thus the early arch-reformer Roscoe Pound, the Dean of Harvard's Law School (and an old acquaintance of Willa Cather's from the University of Nebraska in the 1890s), in his influential essay "Liberty of Contract" (1909), directly attacked what he saw as Lochnerist contract doctrine's unjust and unsupportable assumption of a level playing field between employees and their employers, "a fallacy to everyone acquainted at first hand with actual industrial conditions" (Horwitz, *Transformation*, p. 34). By 1922 Pound's thought had crystallized by way of pragmatism into a forthright collectivism: "Suppose," he proposed, "that instead of beginning with the individual free will we begin with the wants or claims involved in civilized society?"[11] And such a radical reimagining of law's conceptual foundation would effect a corresponding transformation in the construction of property, complicating massively the simple classical authority of the individual over his body, his work, and his possessions. Pound acknowledged that such a complication was taking place: "We are ceasing to think of [property] as a private right and are thinking of it in terms of social function" (Pound, p. 233). His Yale contemporary Arthur Corbin observed, also in 1922, that "'property' has ceased to describe any *res*, or object of sense, at all, and has become merely a bundle of legal relations – rights, powers, privileges, immunities" (Horwitz, p. 156). In short, Pound and his fellow reformers were theorizing, in the interests of social justice, a law based not in private individual rights but in public communal relations, not in immutable "natural law" (or even traditional common law) but in practical sociology.

III

This was the historical moment in which Cather wrote *The Professor's House*: a national legal landscape of deep rifts and contradictions, where a conservative judiciary, insistent on the inviolability of individual rights to property and contract, confronted an energetic reform movement determined to weigh those rights against the claims of the community. Each in its own way responded to a state or states (as Holmes pointed out) increasingly inclined to regulate human relations in the interests of the public good. Like other American intellectuals, Cather was acutely aware of these crossed energies in her society's self-construction. She understood them, properly, as marking a crisis in the history of liberal individualism, and in *The Professor's House* they represented the conditions for St. Peter's "falling out of all domestic and social relations, out of his place in the human family, indeed" (*Professor's House*, p. 275) – the utter alienation to which I shall now return.

Consider again the structure of laws that St. Peter and Tom Outland seek to evade: "the laws of society . . . based on property," and particularly on the sanctity of private property and individual contract for its disposition. Strict application of these laws leads to injustices disturbing to St. Peter's good-hearted sympathy for the disadvantaged: Augusta's loss of her savings to the Kinkoo Copper Company, or Dr. Crane's exclusion from the spoils of Tom's legacy. Each of these cases involves exactly the kind of legal question that a modern economy had made possible and necessary, the kind of question Progressive theorists were raising in the new jurisprudence: is the Lockean notion of contract as a voluntary arrangement between free and propertied individuals a useful paradigm for adjudicating relations between small investors and complex corporations? Who owns ideas and their consequences? Is the patent on an invention of great social significance really a piece of private personal property like a Mexican blanket or a cowboy's diary, something to be passed cleanly to a single inheritor? (For that matter, are Tom's blanket and diary themselves such simple properties?) These are the specific questions of equity that Crane and St. Peter explore in their frustrating interview (*Professor's House*, pp. 145–50), an interview that steals both men's nobility and reduces Crane to pinched mean-spiritedness, and St. Peter to evasion and embarrassed finger-pointing:

> The university, his new house, his old house, everything around him, seemed insupportable, as the boat on which he is imprisoned seems to a sea-sick man. Yes, it was possible that the little world, on its voyage among all the stars, might become like that: a boat on which one could travel no longer, from which one could no longer look up and confront those bright rings of revolution.
>
> He brought himself back with a jerk. Ah, yes, Crane; that was the trouble. If Outland were here tonight, he might say with Mark Antony, *My fortunes have corrupted honest men.* (p. 150)

"Getting off the boat" echoes across *The Professor's House*, a trope of escape answered and revised in St. Peter's eventual resignation to a life "full of

Augustas, with whom one was outward bound" (p. 281) and to facing "with
fortitude the *Berengaria* and the future" (p. 282). Here the "little world" that
St. Peter almost succeeds in transcending or forgetting (like the details of his
own business dealings) through gorgeous metaphor and literary reference
is plainly the world of contracts and property, a world governed by what
Roscoe Pound called "the nineteenth-century dogma that everything must
be owned" (Pound, p. 199), where Outland's fortunes have corrupted honest
men only by their necessary status as private property.

But what exactly is there about the "laws of society . . . based on property"
that is so wholly insupportable to St. Peter, filling him with the claustropho-
bic dread that finally becomes arguably suicidal? These very laws have, after
all, treated him pretty well. His problem is exactly that of Pound and other
legal reformers, and, I believe, of Willa Cather herself: the dilemma of the
traditional liberal looking with guilty unease at the historical products of the
ideology that the political historian C. W. Macpherson calls "possessive individualism," the legacy of Locke.[12] Macpherson argues that the liberal and
possessive aspects of Lockean thought – i.e., natural equality and property
ownership – were eventually bound to come into conflict with one another,
in an inevitable historical moment when possessive individualism's successes
as economic paradigm would generate a self-aware, enfranchised, articulate
working class: a moment when "an industrial working class developed some
class consciousness and became politically articulate," and "Men no longer
saw themselves fundamentally equal in an inevitable subjection to the determination of the market" (Macpherson, p. 273). In other words, the myth of
equality under property-based law could prevail only as long as those disadvantaged by that law – most strikingly, those whose sole property was their
alienated labor – had no voice. But a visible and vocal working class, such
as was developing in the United States in the late nineteenth century, could
call this myth into question – and did so, as we have seen, in the emergence
of Progressive jurisprudence.

Cather was no less aware than was Roscoe Pound of the voice of the
working class and its challenge to classical liberalism. Her career's trajectory
positioned her necessarily as an engaged observer of labor's insistent, unas-
similable emergence into American political and cultural discourse: her early
brushes with midwestern populism, her accounts of Pittsburgh's steel mills,
her time at the muckraking *McClure's*, her brother Douglass's career on
the railroad (the prime incubator of turn-of-the-century labor movements),
her life in Greenwich Village – the Village of Floyd Dell and John Reed –
in the 1910s and 1920s. Although she characteristically held the experience of the exploited working poor at fastidious arm's length, distancing
herself from the social idealism of people like her friend Elizabeth Shepley

Sergeant, to whom she dismissed leftish intellectual writers as "reforming pamphleteers,"[13] Cather nevertheless knew workers – and the national social debate that was developing around them – well indeed.

In *The Professor's House* she gave workers and their subjection a presence and troubling voice. St. Peter's first conversation with Augusta focuses his hazy anxieties about change, as she gently rebukes his easy assumption of democratic camaraderie, reminding him specifically of their class difference and the social role of "people in your station" (*Professor's House*, p. 20). More startlingly, she corrects his unthinking, patronizing equation of their two kinds of "work," represented in the interpenetration in the box-couch of her dress patterns and his scholarly manuscripts.

> "I see we shall have some difficulty in separating our life work, Augusta. We've kept our papers together a long while now."
> "Yes, Professor. When I first came to sew for Mrs. St. Peter, I never thought I should grow grey in her service."
> He started. What other future could Augusta possibly have expected? This disclosure amazed him. (p. 23)

St. Peter is "amazed" not so much at the enforced recollection that the colleague and co-worker in his study is actually his wife's servant (presumably paid for by Lillian's legacy, the income that he has disavowed), but at her claim of expectations of her own: her barely articulated protest against the terms of her servitude. Recall that in this conversation St. Peter's own complaints are practically medieval, directed at the universally "cruel biological necessities" of sex and death (p. 21). By contrast, Augusta's complaint is shockingly modern, simply that of a laborer stuck in a dead-end job. Squirming in the face of unexpected truth, St. Peter bumblingly offers Augusta his own comfortable middle-class fatalism – and praise, comical in its ineptness, for the very badge of her service:

> "Well, well, we mustn't think mournfully of it, Augusta. Life doesn't turn out for any of us as we plan." . . . Her last remark had troubled him.
> "What a fine lot of hair you have, Augusta! You know, I think it's rather nice, that grey wave on each side. Gives it character." (p. 23)

The encounter with Augusta, embarrassing and disturbing to St. Peter's sense of the world, resonates more bitterly on the Blue Mesa itself, in the destructive collapse of another fiction of collegial labor and joint ownership: Roddy Blake and Tom Outland's "partnership," which ends with Roddy's selling of the Indian artifacts to Fechtig, the German collector. In an attractive idealization, St. Peter has imagined (and envied) a working-class chivalry in some ways outside the "laws of society . . . based on property," one in

which both Tom and Roddy participate: "There is, he knew, this dream of
self-sacrificing friendship and disinterested love down among the day-
labourers, the men who run the railroad trains and boats and reapers and
thrashers and mine-drills of the world" (*Professor's House*, p. 172). Tom also
entertains "this dream" in his own narrative: "[Roddy] was the sort of fellow who can do anything for somebody else, and nothing for himself. There
are lots like that among working-men. They aren't trained by success to a
sort of systematic selfishness" (p. 185). But Roddy Blake – whom Hermione
Lee has perceptively identified as Cather's portrait of "a radical working
man"[14] – knows better: struggling in a possessive world where "everything
must be owned," he claims the right to the products of his labor, explodes
Tom's idealization of a democratically held national possession, and articulates the fundamental injustice hidden at the very core of classical liberalism,
in the relation of master and servant, employer and employee, propertied
and property-less:

> "I suppose you gave him my diary along with the rest?"
> "No," said Blake, his voice growing gloomier and darker. "That's your pri-
> vate property. I supposed I had some share in the relics we dug up – you always
> spoke of it that way. But I see now I was working for you like a hired hand,
> and while you were away I sold your property." (p. 245)

Despite the democratic stories we may tell to comfort ourselves or assuage
our guilt, Roddy suggests, the fact remains that some are masters, some
servants, and their relation is one of absolute inequality. Seeing clearly that
Tom's anger proceeds, not from his patriotism, but from his implicit assumption of his personal power as patriotism's representative to dispose of the
artifacts, Roddy discovers his own corresponding servitude. In doing so he
paraphrases the notorious moment in Locke's *Second Treatise on Government* when one catches an unexpected glimpse of the feudal underpinnings
of the inalienable right to property, as the servant's labor yields the master's
property: "Thus the Grass my Horse has bit; the Turfs my Servant has cut;
and the Ore I have digg'd in any place where I have a right to them in common with others, become my *Property*, without the assignation of consent
of any body" (Locke, p. 289).

IV

My reading so far of *The Professor's House* has examined three propositions:
that the novel's "anti-materialism" is connected to a pervasive and only
partially acknowledged anxiety over property and contracts; that this anxiety
corresponds historically to a sea-change in American legal thinking that was

underway in the twentieth century's first thirty years or so, away from law based in individual rights and towards law based in collective needs and functions; and that both the literary anxiety and the juridical sea-change arose in the uncomfortable moment when democratic liberalism began to hear the strong, assertive voice of a hitherto mainly silent population, the working class, whose only property was its labor – a voice threatening to give the lie to the foundational American ideal of a nation of equal individuals. In *The Professor's House* more than any other of her novels, Willa Cather attended to that voice, to her own dismay.

I don't mean to suggest, however, that *The Professor's House* is Cather's "labor novel," or that it responds to a social crisis in the way that Granville Hicks or Elizabeth Shepley Sergeant might have preferred. Its revulsion at the injustices of individualistic property law, its distaste for a society founded in private ownership, are pointed and real enough, and no doubt express in part Cather's genuine, acute awareness of the oppression of the working class. Despite her famous conservatism, there is no evidence that she thought this oppression trivial. But she could not make the full leap into espousing collectivism (as an alternative to individualism) that American law was to make with the advent of the New Deal; her inability to do so is quite clear in the ironies that underlie Tom Outland's "Fourth of July talk" (in Roddy's telling phrase) about national heritage (*Professor's House*, p. 245). For Tom's high rhetoric of public property and collective ownership – "they belonged to this country, to the State, and to all the people" (p. 242) – has already been undermined by his dismal experience with "the State" as possessive entity in Washington, as Roddy cannot resist reminding him: "If there was anybody in Washington that cared a damn, I wouldn't have sold 'em. But you pretty well found out there ain't" (p. 243). Although individual possession brings about a nearly insupportable culture of avarice and condition of injustice, its replacement by state or public ownership offered no acceptable alternative for Cather. Consciously loyal throughout her life to her deepest ideals of the artist's necessary autonomy, she could not imagine the leveling structures of socialism as anything other than destructive of that autonomy and thus of beauty itself: as she insisted in her 1936 *Commonweal* response to Hicks (and her condemnation of reformist art),

> The revolt against individualism naturally calls artists most severely to account, because the artist is of all men the most individual: those who were not have been long forgotten. The condition every art requires is, not so much free-dom from restriction, as freedom from adulteration and from the intrusion of foreign matter; considerations and purposes which have nothing to do with spontaneous invention. ("On Writing," pp. 26–7)

In other words, Cather's scruple against the collective or the state sprang from her unabashedly romantic aesthetic, which led her to an unshakable belief that government could no more effectively address human distress than it could erect a science building of integrity (p. 143) or design a college curriculum (p. 55). In each case, creation by committee ruinously corrupts the original intention. For the Blue Mesa's artifacts, it is in the end better that they go to Germany with a genuine collector, after all, than that they enter the trivializing bureaucracy of Washington, DC, to become souvenirs or ashtrays.

So Roddy gets the last bitter word, another affirmation of his own subjection under the laws of property – "I'm glad it's you that's doing this to me, Tom; not me that's doing it to you" (*Professor's House*, p. 248) – and vanishes from the Mesa and *The Professor's House*, presumably into the world of work. Tom also vanishes heroically but irretrievably into a collective dream of nation and culture. Willa Cather, like Godfrey St. Peter, a middle-class observer of considerable intelligence and compassion, finds herself caught: ahead, an intolerable bureaucratic future that will sacrifice beauty and passion – and even identity – to the gray, leveling demands of social justice; behind, a culture of private ownership whose manifest injustices and particular inappropriateness to an industrial and corporate culture now make human pleasure – and human intercourse – impossible.

Where could a committed liberal turn in a modern world destructive of both equality and individual dignity? Cather "escaped" down at least two paths, both paradoxical themselves, which I shall briefly describe in closing. First, given the specificity of her complaint against modernity, it is not surprising that she was increasingly tempted by visions of an overtly pre-Lockean medieval culture, where the "laws of society . . . based on property" had yet to be articulated, where the possessive individual was still submerged in a stable web of mutual loyalties and duties – and where the brute realities of feudal labor relations were masked by ideals of self-sacrifice. The pull of the medieval is ubiquitous in *The Professor's House*, in a persistent language (often ironic in its effects) of chivalry, nobility, princeliness, devoir. In a better, more feudal world, the disaffected Roddy would be "noble Roddy" indeed, a knight-errant, and Augusta as a loyal retainer would find the fulfillment and protection she needs. And Cather was not alone among liberal modernists in imagining a medieval solution to the problem of possessive individualism.

At the same time, in the summer of 1924, while exploring St. Peter's property-anxiety, she apparently made up her mind to acquire property herself, and did so two years later: her first and last purchase of personal real estate, five acres on Grand Manan Island, where she and Edith Lewis could build a summer cottage for their escapes from New York. She possessed the land obliquely, as one might expect: Lewis is vague on just when it was bought or who staked it out (Lewis, p. 130), and the deed was registered in Lewis's name, not Cather's (Woodress, p. 550). The Grand Manan cottage – "the novelist's house" that emerged from *The Professor's House*, and hangs behind my reading of that novel now in some ways as the Cliff City hangs behind Tom Outland's Virgil (*Professor's House*, pp. 252–3) – served complicated purposes. It was a literal escape from the state (Grand Manan Island is in Canada, and Cather particularly enjoyed its consequent exemption from American Prohibition, among other things). It offered "solitude without loneliness" (Lewis, p. 129) and autonomy without guilt, "a sort of summer camp where she could come and go at will – where she would not have to make arrangements in advance, keep set dates, etc. – and where she could live with complete independence" (p. 130). In Lewis's account it seems like a resolution to the Professor's dilemma: a personal property somehow outside the "laws of society . . . based on property." "It was rather a rough little place," she says, "with many inconveniences; but it came to have not only comfort, but great charm. Above the living room was a large attic from which one could look out over the cliffs and the sea, and this Willa Cather chose for her study. There was nothing in it except a few trunks, and her chair and table" (p. 131). It is the exact antithesis of "Outland" or Godfrey St. Peter's cluttered new house: and isn't this bare cottage, miraculously materialized and ownable in a world of commodities, nothing less than the "unfurnished room" of "The Novel Démeublé," the clean, uncorrupted space where "to make a drama, a man needed one passion, and four walls" (*On Writing*, p. 43)? Beside St. Peter's weary resignation, it seems a triumphant affirmation of ownership, if only for a while.

NOTES

1. Granville Hicks, "The Case Against Willa Cather," in James Schroeter, ed., *Willa Cather and Her Critics* (Ithaca, NY: Cornell University Press, 1967), p. 146.
2. Willa Cather, *On Writing: Critical Studies on Writing as an Art* (New York: Knopf, 1949), p. 18. Future references will be made parenthetically.
3. Guy Reynolds, "Introduction," in *Willa Cather in Context: Progress, Race, Empire* (New York: St. Martin's Press, 1996). Reynolds concludes, as I do, that Cather "was aware of the significant tendencies of her age: immigration, cultural transmission, and the 'new life,'" and that she was "a writer liberally attuned to the broad currents of early twentieth-century American life – race, immigration, multiculturalism" (pp. 10–11).
4. "Tom Outland's Story" had probably been begun (as "The Blue Mesa") as early as 1916 after a trip west, but was apparently completed in the summer of 1922.

See James Woodress, *Willa Cather: A Literary Life* (Lincoln, NE, and London: University of Nebraska Press, 1987), pp. 282, 323.

5. Willa Cather, *The Professor's House* (New York: Knopf, 1925), p. 240. Future references will be made parenthetically.

6. See, for example, David Stouck's influential reading in chapter 3 of *Willa Cather's Imagination* (Lincoln, NE: University of Nebraska Press, 1975), or his later "*The Professor's House* and the Issues of History," in *Willa Cather: Family, Community, and History*, ed. John J. Murphy *et al.* (Provo: Brigham Young University Humanities Publication Center, 1990), pp. 201–11. More recent critical discussions of the novel's "materialism" include Charles Crow, "The Patrimony of Blue Mesa: *The Professor's House* and Museum Theory," *The Willa Cather Pioneer Memorial Newsletter* 41.3 (1997–8), pp. 53–7; John Hilgart, "Death Comes for the Aesthete: Commodity Culture and the Artifact in Cather's *The Professor's House*," *Studies in the Novel* 30.3 (Fall 1998), pp. 377–404; and John N. Swift, "Unwrapping the Mummy: Cather's Mother Eve and the Business of Desire," in *Willa Cather and the American Southwest*, ed. John N. Swift and Joseph R. Urgo (Lincoln, NE: University of Nebraska Press, 2002), pp. 13–21.

7. Edith Lewis describes Cather's move from Houghton Mifflin to Knopf as motivated primarily by Alfred Knopf's giving "her great encouragement and absolute liberty to write exactly as she chose," in *Willa Cather Living* (New York: Knopf, 1953), p. 116. (Future references will be made parenthetically.) Cather's will prohibits, among other things, the publication of her personal letters and the transformation of her work into other media such as film, radio, or theatre. Following Cather's death in 1947, Lewis, her companion of forty years, destroyed what letters she could.

8. John Locke, *Two Treatises of Government*, ed. Peter Laslett (Cambridge: Cambridge University Press, 1988), p. 269. Future references will be made parenthetically.

9. *Lochner v. New York*, 198 U.S. 45 (1905), at 57. Future references will be made parenthetically.

10. My description of Lochnerism and the Lochner era is generally derived from Morton J. Horwitz, *The Transformation of American Law 1870–1960: The Crisis of Legal Orthodoxy* (New York: Oxford University Press, 1992), pp. 33–63, and Laurence Tribe, *American Constitutional Law*, second edition (Mineola, NY: Foundation Press, 1988), pp. 567–81.

11. Roscoe Pound, *An Introduction to the Philosophy of Law* (New Haven: Yale University Press, 1922), p. 169. I am also indebted to Leah Feria Ordonia of Occidental College, who introduced me to Pound's "sociological jurisprudence" and his important role in Progressive legal theory. Future references to Pound will be made parenthetically.

12. C. W. Macpherson, *The Political Theory of Possessive Individualism: Hobbes to Locke* (Oxford: Oxford University Press, 1962). Future references will be made parenthetically.

13. Elizabeth Shepley Sergeant, *Willa Cather: A Memoir* (Philadelphia and New York: Lippincott, 1953), p. 45.

14. Hermione Lee, *Willa Cather: Double Lives* (New York: Pantheon Books, 1989), p. 251.

12

LEONA SEVICK

Catholic expansionism and the politics of depression in *Death Comes for the Archbishop*

Although writers choose from a variety of settings and circumstances for their novels, few writers venture into religious arenas in which they have little direct experience. Cather, whose family had been Baptists in Virginia, was no Catholic, although she joined the Episcopal Church on December 27, 1922, the same year when, she famously wrote in *Not Under Forty*, "the world broke in two."[1] When she began writing *Death Comes for the Archbishop*,[2] she wanted to create a novel that reflected both her profound visual appreciation for the Southwest, which she had visited many times in her lifetime, and her respect for the contributions of the Catholic Church in that region and throughout America. That she admired the rich cultural and artistic traditions of the Church, as well as the devotion of its nineteenth-century missionary clergy, is evident in her novel. The work was inspired by a little-known biography Cather discovered in 1925 while she was visiting Santa Fe, New Mexico. *The Life of the Right Reverend Joseph P. Machebeuf*, written by Father William Howlett and published in 1908, provided the writer with her novel's heroes: Jean Latour and Joseph Vaillant are closely based on the real-life Archbishop Lamy and his vicar-general Machebeuf.[3] Cather's historical novel was a critical success, and she soon followed it with another work that also focused on the Catholic Church and another culture that she admired and enjoyed. In *Shadows on the Rock*, set in the late seventeenth and early eighteenth centuries, Cather tells a story that shares some similarities with the southwestern adventure story offered in her first Catholic novel. Like many of her stories, these two novels grapple with their characters' uneasy adjustment from the old world with its steady values and certainties to a world of unchecked advancement and undefined possibility; the Catholic Church, in both novels, seems to provide a solid anchor. *Death Comes for the Archbishop* develops both real-life figures and fictional characters, weaving them together in order to present to the reader a more complete picture of the historical past. With its interest in pre-industrial religious ritual and forms, the novel suggests a yearning for a simpler time of religious devotion and miracles wrought by faith. However, what is actually accomplished in the novel is a resignation to modernity with all of its attendant economic and social reorderings.

Some Americans, including Cather herself, were not prepared to accept either the demands or the offerings of modernity's blinding pace. According to Cecilia Tichi, Cather was "hostile" to modernity throughout her career and "declared war on modern technology" in her fiction.[4] Cather's turn to historical, seemingly remote subjects in *Death Comes for the Archbishop* may have been part of a larger movement in the late nineteenth and early twentieth centuries identified by the cultural critic T. J. Jackson Lears as "antimodernism."[5] The term, a vexed one because it has little to do with the kinds of stylistic, aesthetic doctrines that characterize modernism, is used by Lears to describe the protest against the spiritual emptiness of a modern, materialistic society. According to Lears, middle-class Americans actively responded to their psychological and spiritual emptiness in three distinct ways: through a renewed engagement in a pre-industrial work culture that accepted the tenets and philosophies of the American Arts and Crafts movement; by employing masculine correctives to an increasingly feminized culture; and by taking a therapeutic turn from a bland and static Protestantism to an exploration of older Catholic art forms and ritual – all interests that thrived in a pre-modern society and gained new vigor in the twentieth century. Through their interest in these areas, Americans waged an "antimodern protest" against capitalism and consumerism that functioned as a search for more "authentic," more *physical*, more Whitmanesque experiences – experiences that constituted a new kind of classless, plural culture: a distinctively *American* one.

Ann Douglas has observed that in the 1920s (when Cather was writing *Death Comes for the Archbishop*), "the pace of change had not only accelerated but peaked" and that "the consequent transformation of American culture was not followed by any cultural change so wide or drastic . . . Increased speed could be a temptation because it was not only a material development but an ethos, a peculiarly modern ethos of instant power and instant assimilation."[6] In 1922, the sociologist William Osborn coined the term "cultural lag" to identify the "delay, the conflict between a society's means of material production and the modernization of its sensibility, between what is available in a society and what is actually endorsed or consumed by it" (quoted in Douglas, p. 191). Such a "lag" had the power to produce devastating social and psychological anxieties. In the 1880s, the physician George M. Beard characterized the depressive illness resulting from the anxieties associated with the modern world and industrial capitalism as the psychological disorder known as "neurasthenia" or "American nervousness." Beard

believed that "American nervousness is the product of American civilization," and that "The modern differ from the ancient civilizations mainly in
these five elements – steam power, the periodical press, the telegraph, the sci-
ences, and the mental activity of women . . . When civilization, plus these five
factors, invades any nation, it must carry nervousness and nervous disease
along with it."[7] Intellectuals and artists, who possessed the most sensitive
constitutions, were believed to be particularly susceptible to the illness, and
everything from exercise to Silas Weir Mitchell's infamous rest cure was prescribed to sufferers. As late as 1931, doctors were treating patients for the
two different manifestations of neurasthenia: depression and manic activity.

Cather suffered through many periods of depression, experiencing a particularly bad bout in the years that directly preceded the writing of her 1927
novel.[8] The causes of her condition and what may have exacerbated it are
innumerable – the lingering effects of World War I, the first fully technolo-
gized war, or the artistic and publishing pressures involved in the life of a
twentieth-century woman writer, to name only a few of many possibilities.
Depression is a central theme in her 1925 novel about a restless college professor in the midst of what seems to be a mid-life crisis, and *The Professor's
House* can offer some insight into Cather's private feelings during the early
1920s. According to Hermione Lee, it was "not until [Cather's] long journey to the Southwest and her stay in Santa Fe in the summer of 1925 – a
visit that prepared the ground for *Death Comes for the Archbishop* – that
this mood of anxiety seems to have lifted" (p. 184). It was not until after
that momentous visit, which provided Cather with the inspiration for a new
kind of book, one in which there is no suspenseful plotline and incidents
follow one another like interesting ramblings, that the author seemed herself
again. What was it about the southwestern setting, the faithful Mexicans
that peopled that region, and the history of the Catholic Church that may
have relieved Cather's neurasthenia?

In the 1840s and 1850s, Protestants and Episcopalians like Cather began
adopting some of the Catholic rituals and interests in art and Gothic architecture that had once been condemned as diabolic and sensual. By the turn
of the century, this new brand of religious aestheticism could be described as
the *embourgeoisement* of Protestantism, "the increasing fondness of afflu-
ent congregations for 'sensuous luxury'" (Lears, p. 192). These interests
were thought to bring new vigor and stimulation to a mind made dull and
depressed by secular materialism. This interest in Catholic forms also worked
to ally the privileged American with the interests of the working class and
to offer him a more "authentic" and meaningful spiritual experience. Pre-
industrial ritual and acts of devotion became a kind of self-therapy for those
who were otherwise caught up in the spirit of capitalist consumption; it

offered the complicit modern a means of mitigating his guilt. However, rather than offering a strident protest against modern culture, Lears argues that "perhaps more than any other antimodern impulse, the movement toward art and ritual [in the Catholic Church] displayed a Janus face . . . By generating a cult of taste in churches as well as secular society, it promoted a consumption ethos appropriate to the coming era of corporate capitalism" (p. 184). Instead of leveling an unqualified protest against modernity and thereby undermining the capitalist structures at work in this system, the antimodern interest in Catholic forms helped to transition society into a modern culture. The antimodernist sought to escape from his neurasthenia through religious ritual and devotion, or, in Cather's case, through writing a collection of stories about the Catholic faith and the people who practiced it. Still, Lears writes, "the collecting impulse reflected the contradictory tendencies of American antimodernism. A taste for the exotic, a desire to preserve the old – these sentiments could coexist with a zeal for industrial growth, even with an ability to build financial empires" (p. 187). Despite their overt antimodernism, the novel and Cather are mired in a modern culture of consumption.

Modernity is marked historically in *Death Comes for the Archbishop* by the growing population of whites and the arrival of the railroad. The historical setting of *Death Comes for the Archbishop* and Cather's own twentieth-century circumstances straddle several tumultuous periods in the developing history of the Catholic Church in North America. In spite of significant Catholic inroads into North America, the Church remained a minority, new-immigrant religion until the mid-1800s, with the arrival of Irish and German Catholics in America. Eastern Catholics continued to acquire the wealth that would eventually transform the Church into a "respectable" religious and social affiliation. Catholics survived the violence of the Know-Nothing attacks of the 1850s, and they withstood the less violent agitation of the American Protective Association in the 1880s and 1890s. In 1891, when the world stood ready to enter a fully modern era and labor strikes threatened almost every industry in America and abroad, Pope Leo XIII issued the encyclical *Rerum Novarum*, which set out to clarify the Church's position on the labor question and class dissent. Contemptuous of any exploitation of the worker, the Church was also quick to condemn the dangerous influences of a rising socialism and its attendant hopes for an atheistic utopia, which threatened to undermine the Church's power by doing away with private property. It is important to note that the Church itself relied on the donation of wages and acquired land, and *Rerum Novarum* predicted the deleterious effects that communally held property would have on the Christian worker and the family:

The sources of wealth themselves would run dry, for nobody would have any interest in exerting his talents or his industry; and that ideal equality, about which they entertain pleasant dreams, would be in reality the levelling down of all to a like condition of misery and degradation . . . therefore the first and most fundamental principle, if one would undertake to alleviate the condition of the masses, must be the inviolability of private property.[9]

Furthermore, Leo encouraged employers to be fair and workers to be compliant – a fairly conservative stand for the Church to take. "The real purpose of the *Rerum Novarum*," writes Hales, "was not so much to introduce new teaching on the social question as to bring the Church Universal, through her authoritative voice, into line with the efforts which were coming here and there to have the generic name of Christian Democracy" (p. 198). Named officially by Leo and the Church in 1901, "Christian Democracy" identified a large Catholic movement that sanctioned the aims of capitalism while quelling the socialist threat. Catholic workers who otherwise might have been drawn to the comradeship and security of labor unions were now encouraged to come together under the protective authority of the Church (Hales, p. 206). On June 29, 1908, Pope Pius X signed the apostolic constitution that elevated the Church from a missionary territory to a fully functioning Catholic body.[10] Still, throughout Cather's lifetime, the Catholic Church countered charges that it was an "un-American" religion. Without a Protestant work ethic or notions of frugality in decoration, and led by cultured, largely European clergy, the Catholic Church was called "un-democratic." However, American bishops and even some politicians (Theodore Roosevelt was one) defended the loyalty of American Catholics and tried to span the widening distance between Catholic and Protestant America by refashioning it as a "working man's church" and thus a more democratic one.[11]

But it was in the middle of the nineteenth century, when Cather's first Catholic novel is set, that the Church first actively sought to reestablish its authority in America as it underscored its allegiance to capitalism and to democracy. After the American conquest in which the ranches, farms, and communal pueblos of the native peoples were dissolved, an entire workforce of unskilled laborers was created to facilitate the settling and growing modernization of the West. These workers faced the double bind of exploitation and the realization of their own displacement and disempowerment. As Cather's novel will show us, the Catholic Church's official policy on labor and management resembles the antimodern impulse that drew Americans to Catholic ritual and form; both create what appears to be an attractive connection between Catholicism and working-class values. Just as the historical Catholic Church's seeming alliance with the working man helped to promote the aims of an exploitative capitalist culture, so the bourgeois retreat into Catholicism as a means of combating its neurasthenia implicitly promoted the very consumer culture it sought to avoid. The Church's therapeutic, spiritual function in this novel nearly masks its (and Latour's) complicity in the expansionist enterprise. *Death Comes for the Archbishop* can be read as an allegory of antimodern protest against – and subsequent accommodation to – American capitalism and modernity.

In *Death Comes for the Archbishop*, miracles not only renew faith, they function as a means of sharpening aesthetic appreciation. Latour's carefully tended garden, Joseph's onion soup, the crafts and religious objects created by the native peoples, and finally his great yellow cathedral all function as little miracles for Latour – miracles that soothe his senses and urge him to a finer appreciation of both the natural beauty that surrounds him and what he injects into his new environment. But what Latour chooses not to see is also important. While he celebrates the end of black slavery and the restoration of Navajo land (p. 290) – two great wrongs that history never *quite* righted – he neglects to worry over his own complicity in the Catholic Church's establishment of cultural hegemony in the southwestern provinces and its cooperative role in the swelling American economy. Latour's fondness for the miracle story of the missionary Junipero Serra (1713–84) is emblematic of his own blindness. In his enthusiasm for the simple faith embodied by the missionary, Latour fails to reflect on the brutality with which Catholic missionaries such as Serra "civilized" the Indians, bringing them under the control of the Catholic Church in California, Texas, Arizona, and New Mexico. While the exploitation of Indian labor was never as prevalent in the Southwest as it had been in California, where the agricultural corporation of the friars was valued at $78 million in 1834, Indians were nevertheless drawn into the cycle of Spanish conquest and Catholic conversion throughout the territory.[12] Latour's arrival in New Mexico coincides with the end of Mexican independence in 1848 and the flagging control of the Catholic Church, but by the end of his tenure, the Church has regained its foothold in the now American region.

What this inviolate text perpetrates is a kind of *aesthetic mystification*. Dazzled by the beauty of the land and its myths and the hard work and pure intentions of two decent religious men, the novel's readers are urged, it seems, to overlook one of the most unflattering moments of America's cultural history. Still, a variety of critical approaches has shown us that texts *can* and *do* at once occlude and reveal. Although the Marxist critics of the 1930s attacked it as escapist and thus sharply disconnected from the historical circumstances that surrounded it,[13] *Death Comes for the Archbishop* can be read as a commentary on the Catholic Church's role in America's development as a modern nation. In an effort to come to terms with history, Cather's novel invites readers to look beyond its attractive mystifications to the harsher truths that lie just beyond them. *Death Comes for the Archbishop* offers us an example of Cather's proleptic resistance to the damaging effects of modernity and capitalism and her protest against its twentieth-century legacy. The Catholic aestheticism and spirituality embodied in the character of Latour, as well as the native legends and miracles that appear in the text, are offered by Cather as both correctives to the damaging effects of modernity and the means by which those effects are achieved. Although Guy Reynolds has written that Cather's Church is "akin to the immigrant peoples celebrated in the early novels and has a similar ideological significance, representing an enriching cultural pluralism,"[14] Cather's Church in the novel also works in the interest of American expansionism, and Latour is its agent. The divided character of the Church is fully realized in the divided character of Latour.

In the opening scene of *Death Comes for the Archbishop*, the Church is clearly an elitist one. The Spanish cardinal's villa overlooking Rome positively drips with wealth and culture. The splendid scenery, fine food and wine, and the elegant manners of these Europeans belie the missionary Father Ferrand's purpose. While the business of reining in the Catholics of the Southwest calls for a man with workmanlike resolve and strength, their host asks for one with "intelligence in matters of art" (p. 11). In spite of the Church's history of interest in the poor, Latour is no working man's priest. His manners, even when he was alone in the desert, were "distinguished" (p. 19). His entrance into the text, as a solitary horseman making his way across a lonely land, could very well be the description of a knight-errant in search of adventure and fortune. He is an attractive man who dislikes a variety of unattractive men who appear in the novel. From the snake-headed Buck Scales to the big-toothed Padre Martinez and his fat-faced, "irritatingly stupid" secretary, Trinidad (p. 144), the lower-class status and vulgarity of these men are marked by their appearance. Sensitive, contemplative, and easily depressed, Latour seeks to fill some void with beautiful objects and authentic experiences, gathering these stories and images as part of his private collection, and he is caught up in the consumption ethos of his time – an ethos that continues into Cather's twentieth century. Latour's appearance marks him as "a man of gentle birth – brave, sensitive, courteous." From the "thick clay walls" that "had been finished on the inside by the deft palms of Indian women" (p. 33) to the lovingly decorated altars of the devout peasants, Latour gathers insight. Other examples of this sort of commodity fetishism abound in this text as a marker of the Catholic culture of excess in decoration, and the Spanish cardinal in search of his El Greco is not the only one to be drawn to objects of value. Latour's "few rare and beautiful books" (p. 34) that he risks his life to save after his ship is wrecked on the way to Santa Fe, his skins and blankets, and his fine linen and the silver plate form a catalogue of pleasing things that soothe his senses, pique his aesthetic interest, and make him complicit in the capitalist enterprise. Perhaps Latour is the "business man" that he jokingly calls himself in his Christmas letter to his brother (p. 35).

Not all collectors demonstrated the kind of grasping and bourgeois acquisitiveness that we associate with the very rich. They often displayed both taste and discernment, qualities that Cather, whose own collecting impulse is apparent in the interpolated tales that comprise her novel, possessed and transferred to Latour. Seemingly unaware of his complicity in the modern, capitalist enterprise, Latour gathers not only objects, but also myths and interesting stories. Carson's manly exploits in battle and on the frontier, along with Serra's Holy Family and the miracle at Guadalupe, all function as a kind of spiritual, discursive therapy for Latour; like the other objects he collects, these offer him comfort and anchor. In the introduction to Book III of the novel, "The Mass at Ácoma," the bishop is "eager to be abroad" in his diocese and "to know his people" (p. 81). What he comes to know in this section is not the real life circumstances of the poor, but myths and entertaining fables such as the story of the parrot-worshipers of Isleta and the scandalous Baltazar and his rain-making picture of St. Joseph. Even his visit to Jacinto's convincingly "authentic" native home, replete with tightly swaddled baby (a dark reminder of the high infant mortality rate among the Indians and the presence of the smallpox and measles carried there by whites), is merely a short and interesting interlude. This story is a disruption that gives way to the even more compelling episode of the Stone Lips and the great snake that the natives worship, an experience that Latour savors in all of its native mysteriousness and its suggestions of diabolism. Only two years earlier, a strikingly similar collecting ethos appeared in *The Professor's House*, a novel that focuses on the clearly neurasthenic Godfrey St. Peter. His good taste, evident in everything from his choice in furnishings and furs to select stories of the Spanish adventurers, extends to the history of Tom Outland. In the midst of St. Peter's self-imposed exile and depression, he turns to Outland's journal, hoping, perhaps, to transport himself from the dull comforts of his middle-class existence to the mesa and Outland's attractive adventures. Like Latour, St. Peter is buoyed by these tales and reflections, and as a result he is better prepared to face the challenges of the future.

Like the collecting impulse, worship in the novel seems to have a regenerative, therapeutic effect on Latour. Poised to accomplish his dream of building a cathedral, Latour's neurasthenia (the domain of the privileged) seems to be worsening. At the start of Book VII, the bishop is in "one of those periods of coldness and doubt which, from boyhood, had occasionally settled down upon his spirit and made him feel an alien" (p. 210). According to Lutz, neurasthenia had "class and racial implications and was closely allied to the discourses justifying dominant American culture" (p. 6). Latour is one such "caretaker" of privileged culture as he secures American Catholic interests in the territory, but, without relief from the depressive and guilty burdens of his position of influence, Latour might abandon his enterprise. His will is fortified by his encounter with Sada, the Mexican slave of a low-caste Protestant family that has moved West to build its fortunes. Her plight is similar to that of many Mexicans who had been "dispossessed of their land and displaced from their traditional pastoral economy . . . forced into the unskilled labor market of the new, expanding American economy" (Dolan, p. 154), and Latour's unwillingness to intervene on her part also remarks the Church's problematic position on slavery. Although it viewed slavery as a sin and a social evil, it did not profess that slaves or slaveholders were "spiritually ruined" by the practice. Although "it was treated as a condition to be improved with a view to its ultimate removal," slavery was not, in the mid-nineteenth century, openly condemned by the Church (Hales, p. 167). Unwilling to threaten its influence among property-holding Americans, the Church failed to intervene, and Latour's inaction provides us with a clear example of this official policy. When Sada appears in the doorway of the sacristy, crouching and afraid, she offers him the faith-therapy he needs. He is reminded by this woman's devotion that he is a "servant" in God's house and, "kneeling beside the much enduring bond-woman, he experienced those holy mysteries as he had done in his young manhood" (p. 217). Her humble service rendered, she shuffles off, hiding in the folds of her clothes a tiny silver medal that Latour has given her. His hope is that this modest object (not unlike his own collection) will lift her spirits when she is overworked and beaten. Though he fails to intervene on Sada's behalf for fear of jeopardizing Catholic and Protestant relations in the region as well as his own position, Latour is invigorated by his democratic hospitality in the House of God.

The bishop also seeks therapy for his neurasthenia in the homes of his native friends, a move that helps to prepare him for the daunting task of building the first cathedral in the western region. Eusabio offers Latour a Navajo house, set at a distance from the rest of the community. Once again, the bishop does not come here "to know his people." Latour seeks a picturesque, authentic refuge in which to revive his depleted spirit. In this airy, sandswept hogan, he writes long letters to friends and relatives, he meditates, and he plans. When Eusabio accompanies the bishop back home, Latour notes the peculiar character of the native, though he fails to understand it. Navajos "obliterate every trace of their temporary occupation . . . just as it was the white man's way to assert himself in any landscape, to change it, make it over a little (at least to leave some mark of memorial of his sojourn)" (p. 233). The words are prophetic. His energy and enthusiasm restored, the bishop returns to Santa Fe, having recalled his vicar, Joseph, from his soul-saving abroad in order to show him something *really* remarkable: a yellow hill of rock on a ridge high over the Rio Grande valley that will become the walls of his cathedral.

The bishop's withdrawal functions as more than an effort to combat his own depression; it is the means by which he shores up his weakened will and prepares himself for a project of imperial proportions. In an effort to establish for the Church a solid foundation in a modern, capitalistic America, the bishop will "leave some mark" on the landscape, employing the help of the native peoples in the process. Amy Kaplan shows us how imperialism begins at home:

> To understand the multiple ways in which empire becomes a way of life means to focus on those areas of culture traditionally ignored as long as imperialism was treated as a matter of foreign policy conducted by diplomatic elites or as a matter of economic necessity driven by market forces. Not only about foreign diplomacy or international relations, imperialism is also about consolidating domestic cultures and negotiating intranational relations. To foreground cultures is not only to understand how they abet the subjugation of others or foster their resistance, but also to ask how international relations reciprocally shape a dominant imperial culture at home, and how imperial relations are enacted and contested within the nation.[15]

In *Death Comes for the Archbishop*, the Catholic Church constitutes a dangerous source of power precisely because of its imagined distance from political and economic discourse, and Cather engages in these disquieting suggestions throughout the text. In the early "Hidden Water" episode, after Latour has been miraculously saved from death by the cruciform tree, he finds himself in the Mexican settlement of *Agua Secreta*. Here, Benito and his family live a squatter's existence because they have no contract binding them to the land and "were afraid the Americans might take it way from them" (p. 26). The family is relieved to find that Latour is not an American, and José, a grandson, explains why:

> "They say at Albuquerque that now we are all Americans, but that is not true, Padre. I will never be an American. They are infidels . . . They destroyed our churches when they were fighting us, and stabled their horses in them. And

now they will take our religion away from us. We want our own ways and our
own religion." (p. 27)

What the family fails to recognize is that Latour, though French and an
emissary of the Catholic Church, is also an agent of the kind of American
imperialism that Kaplan describes above. In this hidden oasis, the bishop is
called on to sanctify marriages, baptize children, and hear confessions, practices that will "legitimize" the various contracts and commitments that have
already been made, thereby undermining the authority of the Mexican family that had once performed these rites themselves.[16] Latour's appearance
and ritual sanctifications, along with the building of the cathedral, mark
the dissolution of the *cofradías* and an end to an era of self-determination
for the Mexican people. The Church, irritated by the growing practice in
America of tolerating folk traditions and embracing all religions as "different roads to God," condemned this practice of "indifferentism" as hereti-
cal in the 1864 Syllabus of Errors (Hales, p. 171). In just the same way
that Latour reestablishes the legitimate authority of the Catholic Church
by offering the sacraments, defeating renegade priests like Martinez, and
building a Midi-Romanesque cathedral, Americans will continue to assert
their authority over the land, resources, and native people of the Southwest.
Though Latour's sympathy with cultural difference appears to align him with
those tolerant priests who practiced "indifference," he never betrays his mission to reestablish the Church's control, even as he is easing his neurasthenic
conscience. His mission continues the displacement process that began with
Junipero Serra and continued during the American conquest, and the result
is that many families, like Benito's, will lose their land. Later in the novel,
as Latour coaxes money from the vain widow Dona Isabella for his cathedral, the Mexican outlaw Manuel Chavez recognizes the alliance between
the padre and the Americans, and he prophesies the resulting erasure of
the Mexicans' claim to the land (pp. 182–6). Here, the novel closely follows Howlett's biography in making clear the Church's very political plan
of "detaching the church in New Mexico from its Mexican affiliations, and
making it dependent upon conditions in the United States" (quoted in Lee,
p. 266).

If Cather means in her novel to mitigate the Church's grasping interest in material concerns, then she has accomplished this feat in Latour's
connection to the beloved Joseph. Like the very different ways in which
each man admires the tamarisk tree, Jean for its unusual tints and textures,
and Joseph because it was "the tree of the people, and was like one of
the family in every Mexican household" (p. 202), Latour's ambitions and
aesthetic sensibilities are balanced by Joseph's simple desire to build faith

among the poor and his lack of interest in matters of beauty and taste. Ugly, tirelessly occupied in service to the poor, and "scarcely acquisitive to the point of decency" (p. 226), Joseph, "in order to communicate with peons [was] willing to speak like a peon" (p. 225). Here, Cather's sympathy for those who find themselves tangled in the process of modernization reveals itself in sympathetic, benevolent, and troubled human form, and, like Jean's, Joseph's temperament is described as "nervous," although his neurasthenia is of a different character. Infused with energy, a life-long restlessness and a desire to move and accomplish good works, Joseph's peripatetic nature is the perfect complement to Latour's desire to build and mark. When the bishop shares his cathedral scheme, Joseph is made visibly uncomfortable, shifting his shoulders uneasily. Latour speaks Joseph's mind when he says, "I hope you do not think me very worldly" (p. 243). Still, Cather may not have intended Joseph to serve simply as a conscientious corrective to Latour's ambitious nature. Joseph may have the plight of the native poor at heart, but he, like the real-life Machebeuf, leaves New Mexico to minister to the gold-rushers in Colorado who are depleting the land of its resources. For Joseph, these men may present the most challenging spiritual cases, but his willing-ness to minister to them may also function as a means of reconciling religion and wealth; Joseph may be unwittingly complicit in the American capitalist enterprise. Like the novel itself, each character embodies the contradictory impulses of Catholicism and the "Janus face" of antimodernism.

What completes the "protest and accommodation" model is the comple-tion of the bishop's cathedral. In spite of Joseph's gentle but pointed reminder that "everything about us is so poor – and we ourselves are so poor" (p. 241), the bishop will have his fine building, and, like the white men who came before him and who will come after him, Latour will make his mark in his-tory. Though Latour insists that the cathedral is for the "future" (p. 241), that future does not include the simple peasants whose religious, decorative needs do not stretch beyond their hand-made altar ornaments. The cathedral is built to satisfy the growing population of the region and its establishment as a center of American commerce and trade. Like the arrival of the rail-road, it marks the Southwest's entrance into the modern era. However, what is conspicuously missing from the novel is the story of how the cathedral actually gets built. Was it, as the novel tells us, like the church at Ácoma, built on the "backs of men and boys and women" by those "who built for their own satisfaction, perhaps, rather than according to the needs of the Indians" (p. 101)? Ironically, the observation is Latour's own. Like the other "Powerful men" who "draft[ed] Indian labor for this great work with-out military support" (p. 101), Latour gets his yellow rocks to Santa Fe, although we never learn just how. It is, as Latour notes, an accomplishment of "an historic period" (p. 271) in which the Catholic Church has chiseled out its place. By ministering to the poor and indebting itself to the wealthy, facilitating conquest and assuaging guilty consciences, the Church was able to establish itself securely in modern America.

In *Death Comes for the Archbishop*, Cather created characters whose multiple, competing roles in society contribute to their psychological, physical, and spiritual engagement in modernity and a culture of progress. With sensitivity and a sincere interest in the faith and devotion of American and Mexican Catholics, Cather explores the role that Catholic ritual and worship played in the transition to modernity. Both Latour and Vaillant possess traits that make them fit to survive in an increasingly modern world. With their generous missionary work and benevolent dealings with the southwestern peoples, Latour and Vaillant are able skillfully to advance the influence and power of the Catholic Church in an increasingly capitalistic and imperialistic America. *Death Comes for the Archbishop* is a novel that is at once politically engaged, aesthetically successful, and spiritually profound.

NOTES

1. Willa Cather, *Not Under Forty* (Lincoln, NE, and London: University of Nebraska Press, 1988), p. v.
2. Willa Cather, *Death Comes for the Archbishop* (1927; New York: Vintage, 1990). Page references are made parenthetically in the text.
3. For more on the historical sources for Cather's novel, see James Woodress, *Willa Cather: A Literary Life* (Lincoln, NE, and London: University of Nebraska Press, 1987), pp. 393–404.
4. Cecilia Tichi, *Shifting Gears: Technology, Literature, Culture in Modernist America* (Chapel Hill: University of North Carolina, 1987), p. 174.
5. T. J. Jackson Lears, *No Place of Grace: Antimodernism and the Transformation of American Culture 1880–1920* (New York: Pantheon Books, 1981). Future references will be made parenthetically.
6. Ann Douglas, *Terrible Honesty: Mongrel Manhattan in the 1920s* (New York: Farrar, Straus, Giroux, 1995), p. 192.
7. Beard's comments are repeated in Tom Lutz, *American Nervousness 1903: An Anecdotal History* (Ithaca: Cornell University Press, 1991), p. 4. Future references will be made parenthetically.
8. Hermione Lee, *Willa Cather: Double Lives* (New York: Pantheon Books, 1989), pp. 183–4. Future references will be made parenthetically.
9. E. E. Y. Hales, *The Catholic Church in the Modern World: A Survey from the French Revolution to the Present* (Garden City, NY: Image Books, 1960), p. 201. Future references will be made parenthetically.
10. Chester Gillis, *Roman Catholicism in America* (New York: Columbia University Press, 1999), p. 48.

11. Carl Degler, *The Age of Economic Revolution, 1876–1900* (Glenview: Scott, Foresman, 1977), p. 165.

12. Jay P. Dolan, *The American Catholic Experience: A History from Colonial Times to the Present* (Garden City, NY: Doubleday, 1985), pp. 29–30. Future references will be made parenthetically.

13. Woodress discusses this historical disconnection in his *Willa Cather*, p. 465.

14. Guy Reynolds, *Willa Cather in Context: Progress, Race, Empire* (New York: St. Martin's Press, 1996), p. 157.

15. Amy Kaplan and Donald Pease, *Cultures of U.S. Imperialism* (Durham, NC: Duke University Press, 1988), p. 14.

16. The practice of self-sanctification was common among Mexican families in the mid-nineteenth century who were visited infrequently by priests, and what resulted, according to Jay Dolan, was a civic and faith organization that blended Catholic and folk traditions: "For them the most important religious organization was not the parish, but the religious confraternity, the *cofradía* . . . The vital center of religion, they could be found in every pueblo in New Mexico and throughout the Southwest. Together with the celebration of religious festivals, they nurtured the religion of the people and helped them to maintain their identity as a people once they became part of the United States" (p. 176).

13

ANN ROMINES

Willa Cather and "the old story": *Sapphira and the Slave Girl*

Sapphira and the Slave Girl (1940), Willa Cather's last novel, is the first to be set in her birthplace, the Shenandoah Valley of northern Virginia. In 1936, just before she began work on this new book, Cather wrote an enthusiastic and reflective essay in response to two of Thomas Mann's biblical novels, based on Old Testament narratives. She praised Mann's skill in "making a new story out of an old one which is a very part of the readers' consciousness," and concluded, "What we most love is not bizarre invention, but to have the old story brought home to us closer than ever before, enriched by all that the right man could draw from it and, by sympathetic insight, put into it."[1] This essay appeared in *Not Under Forty*, a collection that Cather proclaimed was intended for "the backward," readers "over forty" whose gaze was turned toward the past. Cather herself was now in her early sixties, entering the last decade of a career that had been marked by invention. Each of her eleven novels had posed a fresh set of challenges. As Cather turned to the writing of *Sapphira*, she confronted at last her own quintessential "old story": the Virginia of her family history and early childhood.

This "backward" gaze was hardly a nostalgic retreat. Instead, it required contemplation of a family past that included slaveholding and many of its attendant abuses, troubled relations between parents and children (especially daughters and mothers), the painful losses of aging – as well as powerful ties to an intimately familiar place and to a local culture in which Willa Cather's ancestors had been rooted for five generations. In her last years, Cather marshaled all her narrative resources to write her "old story," at last. When the book was finished, she wrote to Viola Roseboro', the former fiction editor of *McClure's Magazine*, who was one of her most trusted critics (and a fellow "exiled" southerner, too), that the hardest part of writing it was conveying the horror that lay just under the pleasant surfaces of Virginian domestic life – while still getting across the reality of those pleasant surfaces, as well.[2] That is what it meant, for Cather, "to have the old story brought home," and again and again, in *Sapphira*, she explores what it can mean to come home to old stories, the sites of both solace and horror. In this novel, drawing from the resources of both personal and cultural memory, Willa Cather scrutinizes the meanings of *home* and *homecoming* in the life stories of white slave-owners and their abolitionist daughter, in four generations of escaping and remaining slaves, and – in an unprecedented autobiographical epilogue that is as close as she ever came to "bizarre invention" – in the author's own life.

Born in 1873, Willa Cather belonged to the generation of Reconstruction-born white southern children who were charged with the rehabilitation of the recently defeated South. Although most of her paternal relatives had opposed slavery and supported the Union, her mother and maternal grand-mother had been strong supporters of the Confederacy, and three maternal uncles fought in the Confederate army. One of these uncles, whom young Willa later adopted as her namesake, was killed in the war. During and after Reconstruction, women across the South worked "to redeem their fallen nation through memorial associations and Confederate women's groups." They facilitated the perpetuation of plantation mythology, "campaigned to build monumental memorials and dot the nation with markers to preserve confederate values and memories," sponsored prizes for children's essays extolling Confederate virtues, and insisted on textbooks for southern children that would provide "a truthful history of the war."[3] Although Willa Cather's parents moved the family to Nebraska when Willa was nine, much of this southern mythology moved west with them, like the Confederate sword and uniform that Willa's mother preserved, as relics of her dead brother. (A famous photograph shows a teenaged Willa wearing his Confederate cap.) The Cather family maintained close ties with their many Virginian relatives, exchanging visits and frequent letters. As suggested in the autobiographical story "Old Mrs. Harris," Willa Cather's parents and grandparents kept up many of their Virginian customs in the prairie town of Red Cloud, and, when her father died in 1928, she mourned his sweet and boyish southern ways. His favorite song remained "Carry Me Back to Old Virginny."

Willa Cather's own attitudes towards her southern origins were ambivalent in her adult life. Although she maintained affectionate relations with some of her Virginian relatives, Cather made only three documented return visits to her birthplace after her departure in 1883. When a favorite niece moved with her husband to Tennessee in 1942, Cather wrote to her friend Irene Miner Weisz that "going south" seemed to her "like regressing to a more primitive place" (Stout, *Calendar*, p. 243). In the biographical sketch that Cather wrote in the 1920s, for distribution by her publisher, she described her birthplace as

> an old conservative society . . . the Valley of Virginia, where the original land grants made in the reigns of George II and George III had been going down from father to son ever since, where life was ordered and settled, where the people in good families were born good, and the poor mountain people were not expected to amount to much. The movement of life was slow there, but the quality of it was rich and kindly.[4]

By the mid-1930s, Willa Cather had written major fiction set in virtually all the places where she had lived or made meaningful visits during her lifetime – except Virginia. Only two early, experimental stories are set there, while a series of southern characters, expatriated in the West, appear in later fiction. When she at last began writing her Virginia novel, around 1936, both her parents had died in the past decade. Feeling herself now to be a member of "the older generation," Cather – perhaps engaged in the process of life review that occupies many older persons – was much engrossed in early memories, as her companion Edith Lewis reported.[5] As she worked on the book, she was beset by further personal disasters. First, her favorite brother, Douglass, died; her first loss of a sibling. Then she lost the great romance of her life, her friend Isabelle McClung Hambourg. In addition, World War II was accelerating in Europe in the late 1930s, and Cather, with many friends in Europe, was worried and distraught. As Cather wrote to her friend and editor Ferris Greenslett, memories of Virginia, and of a time before family deaths and losses, in a "rich and kindly" "old conservative society" were – more than anything else – a solace and comfort to her during her mourning (Stout, *Calendar*, p. 231).

One of these memories was the genesis of her novel and became the heart of the epilogue, one of the first portions of the book that Cather wrote. As a small girl, she had witnessed the return to the Cathers' Virginia home of Nancy, her great-grandmother's escaped "slave girl," who, during twenty-five years as a free woman in Canada, had become a poised, elegant and successful professional housekeeper. Nancy was greeted by her mother, "Aunt Till," also a former family slave, and by Willa's maternal grandmother, who had defied her slaveholding mother by abetting the "slave girl's" escape. This was one of the most vivid and important memories of Cather's life, and, as she wrote to Alexander Woolcott, one that she inevitably recalled with a "thrill," even as a mature woman (Stout, *Calendar*, pp. 247–8).

Before her return, Nancy was already an important figure in young Willa's imagination. Her mother had told her the story of the slave girl's escape, and "used to sing me to sleep" with

> *Down by de cane-brake, close by de mill,*
> *Dar lived a yaller gall, her name was Nancy Till.*

I never doubted the song was made about our Nancy.[6]

Already the child understands that narrative may be a way of asserting ownership. Almost as if she were still a slave, Nancy is "our Nancy" because Willa possesses "her" story.

And yet this Nancy is clearly someone who has escaped the confines of Virginia ownership. Her Canadian-accented speech, her physical self-possession, even her clothes, exceed the constraints of the storied "our Nancy" that Willa has heard of. Her fur-lined coat, for example, is an object of "astonishment" to a rural, southern child; Willa says, "We had no coats like that on Back Creek" (p. 283). All this both delights and troubles Willa, who is suspicious of Nancy's un-Virginian speech. But she is reassured by the visitor's acquiescence to Virginia manners (the "visiting," the "slight shade of deference in her voice when she addressed [Willa's] mother" [p. 284], the descendant of her former owner, and her acceptance of the separate dinner seatings for whites and blacks, even in this hospitable household). Indeed, during her visit of several weeks, Nancy seems at home both as a guest in the Willow Shade kitchen – where she takes part in long afternoons of cooking, storytelling and needlework with Aunt Till and Willa's grandmother Rachel – and as a daughter in the former slave cabin that was her childhood home, where her mother still lives. When the returning Nancy embraces her mother after their long separation, "There was something Scriptural in that meeting, like the pictures in our old Bible" (p. 283). In her essay on Mann in *Not Under Forty*, Cather had emphasized the inevitable familiarity of "Scriptural" scenes for Americans of her generation: "We took it in unconsciously and unthinkingly perhaps, but we could not escape it" (p. 101). The escaped child's homecoming to a mother–daughter embrace follows a familiar, sanctioned script, as weighty and inevitable as Judeo-Christian Scripture. And yet, through it all, there is something about Nancy that cannot be possessed or read, something that is unknowable and her own. There is also the fact that she has returned only to visit, not to stay; she will return to her own life and story elsewhere, outside the borders of the United States.

The figure of Nancy told Willa Cather – both the Virginia child and the sixty-some-year-old woman now essaying a fictional return to her birthplace – that one could come back to one's ancestral home, even to "mammy's cabin," which was such a powerful site of plantation nostalgia, without loss, diminishment, or enslavement. In the elegant, resourceful figure of Nancy, young Willa Cather perhaps first glimpsed the possibilities of an urban life unimaginable in her rural birthplace, a life that was to become her own.

In studies spearheaded by Toni Morrison's groundbreaking 1992 reading of *Sapphira* in *Playing in the Dark*, many readers have noted and problematized the relatively uninflected quality of the African American characters in this novel, especially in relation to more complexly rendered white characters. Patricia Yaeger, for example, discusses "Till's and Nancy's lost complexity – a loss that becomes particularly clear at the novel's end."[7] As Yaeger suggests, that "lost complexity" is particularly evident in the epilogue, built around the almost fairytale-like scene of Nancy's return and all that it suggests about the possibilities of an expatriated African American southerner's return to the South. Harrassed by her relentless mistress, the girl suffers from a nearly fatal case of homesickness, an ailment from which Willa Cather had suffered painfully herself – sickness both *from* and *for* home. The untenable conditions of her home life as a plantation slave whose mistress has turned against her and arranged for her rape have disabled Nancy; she can imagine no alternative but suicide: "I gets no rest night nor day. I'm goin' to throw myself into the millpawnd, I am! . . . I wisht I'd never been bawn . . . I got nobody to call to. I cain't do nothin'!" (pp. 217–18). Simultaneously, Nancy ardently loves her Virginia home. In an opulent, sensuous passage that first notes the smallest details of plants, animals, weather and landscape, Nancy then exults in her home connections:

> Oh, this was a beautiful place! Nancy didn't believe there was a lovelier spot in the world than this right here. She felt so joyful that her heart beat as hard as it did last night when she was scared [of being overcome by the rapist Martin]. She loved everybody in those vine-covered [slave] cabins, everybody . . . After all, they were home folks. And down yonder was the mill, "*and the Master so kind and so true.*" . . . It was still hers: the home folks and the home place and the precious feeling of belonging here. (p. 197)

Nancy's love of home is a fantasy of perfect union with a place and a community, even though her own enslavement is one of that community's conditions. It is also the fantasy of the idealized, nurturing antebellum plantation that was fostered in the postbellum South. And it seems totally at odds with the self-obliterating fear and helplessness that consume Nancy's nights: "Maybe that fright back there in the dark hall had been just a bad dream. Out here [in the summer morning] it didn't seem true" (p. 197).

On to the relatively fragile character of Nancy, a romantic, adolescent African American girl, Willa Cather has projected two of the most persistent constructions of the late nineteenth- and early twentieth-century South: the plantation as "Sweet Home" and as a system that obliterates identity. As Yaeger suggests, the complexity of Nancy's character is lost through the process of this projection. To extricate Nancy from the enslavement implicit in her home, a controlling will is required, and the overwhelmed girl's character cannot supply it. Instead, Rachel Blake steps in and puts the machinery of Nancy's escape in motion. "I'm a-going to get you away from all this, Nancy," she says (p. 217). Although Rachel acts against slavery, her will becomes as decisive as her mother's, and she has no doubt that her decisions about Nancy's future are correct. Nancy makes a last plea for home: "Please mam, take me home! I can't go off amongst strangers. It's too hard . . . I want to go home to the mill an' my own folks." But Rachel is firm. From Nancy, she has heard only half the story of home: the story of loss and abuse. And she has acted on that partial story. She instructs Nancy: "You mustn't fail me now. I took a big risk to get you this far. If we went back, Mother would never forgive you – nor me." Rescuing Nancy, Rachel arguably reenslaves her, as well. The girl's only possible response to her instructions is "Yes'm." By this time, Nancy has shut down entirely. "She couldn't take anything in; her mind was frozen with homesickness and dread" (p. 237). In this condition, Nancy disappears, out of slavery and into Canada and a life as a free woman. She does not reenter the novel until the epilogue, as the triumphant and "thrilling" figure of the returning adult Nancy, object of young Willa's fascinated, possessive gaze. "Our Nancy," still.

Willa Cather's insistence on this experimental autobiographical epilogue for *Sapphira* – even though she was deeply uncertain about the experiment's success – suggests that this novel may have particularly intimate personal implications for her. Certainly it expresses the powerful, troubled responses to her several "home places" that ran through her life. Her first known fictional attempt to express the combination of natural beauty and ritualized abuse that young Nancy experiences is in "The Elopement of Allen Poole," a Virginia story published when she was only nineteen. Later, through the characters of Jim Burden, Thea Kronborg, and Cecile Auclair, as well as others, she returns to these issues. Elizabeth Sergeant paraphrases a letter that Cather wrote from Red Cloud around 1912: "Once there, an unreasoning fear of being swallowed by the distances between herself and anything else jumped out at her – as in childhood, again . . . She was afraid to drowse and to dream. Why did she have such feelings if she were to write about the country – unsuitable, wasn't it?"[8] Here Cather's language is remarkably similar to Nancy's. Cather fears "being swallowed" and is "afraid to drowse and to dream," while Nancy says, "He's just after me night an' day," and she "gets no rest" (p. 216). It seems possible that Cather is using Nancy to explore the "old story" of homecoming that had become increasingly freighted for her. When Nancy returns to Willow Shade in the 1880s to reclaim the Virginia cooking, places, and stories that she remembers from her childhood and to be reunited with her mother, Rachel Blake, and her owners' family, she posits that the partially rehabilitated New South can welcome and nourish an expatriated native – and that an expatriated Willa Cather can write herself back into her beloved childhood home. The problem with this project, of course, is that, put to these uses, Nancy is not a plausible African American woman. Through her overwhelmed and obliterated character – "homesick" nearly to death – it is impossible to suggest the intricacies of a slave woman's relations with her slave community, her owners, and the places she inhabits. And in the epilogue, Nancy is appropriated to enact a white girl's scenario – so deeply encoded that it seems "Scriptural" – as her return is staged for the benefit of five-year-old Willa (who is a direct descendant of the slave mistress, Sapphira).

In the larger narrative of the full epilogue, Nancy becomes a figure in a portrait of a successfully (and implausibly) reconstructed South. In this narrative, Willa Cather's birthplace has "changed very little" since the Civil War, which "made few enmities in the country neighbourhoods" (pp. 273–4), and an escaped slave can return home unfazed by the prospect of Jim Crow laws and untroubled by the decided differences in social privileges enjoyed by whites and blacks, even in the most "hospitable" of households. As Janis Stout states, *Sapphira* is "troublingly affirming of the very social systems it exposes as evil."[9]

For Cather, that paradoxical process of simultaneous affirmation and exposure *was* the old story she was trying to tell. She told Ferris Greenslet, her former editor at Houghton Mifflin, that in this book she wanted to give a balanced view of the "strange" domestic institution of slavery, to render both its pleasant surfaces and what lay beneath them – although her own Virginian household hadn't given much thought to what was underneath (Stout, *Calendar*, p. 229). This elegant novel, with its restrained style and its rapt attention to details of the natural and domestic worlds, renders pleasant surfaces masterfully – whether the blooming mountain laurel on Timber Ridge or the accoutrements of Sapphira's well-run household. But it also gives a great deal of thought to what lies under those southern surfaces, as the child Willa was *not* schooled to do – to the persistent, intimate presence of the Terrible. This is powerfully portrayed at the beginning of the novel as Sapphira's adult daughter Rachel walks down the familiar "long carpeted passage" to her mother's bedroom. She hears her mother's voice, with a tone of "cold, sneering contempt," and then "a smacking sound, three times: the wooden back of a hairbrush striking someone's cheek or arm" (p. 12). Rachel tightens her lips and knocks on the door; her mother admits her and dismisses the young slave who has displeased her, Nancy. In this pleasant house that resembles a national icon, Mount Vernon, abuse – or the potential for it – is behind every door. Rachel recognizes this; from outside the door, she knows what is passing between her mother and the slave girl. But when she enters the room, she does not say a word to indicate her knowledge. She is still silent when she sees "the red marks of the hairbrush" on Nancy's arm (p. 18). To speak would be to betray her mother, "the old story," and the home in which she (unhappily) grew up. (Eventually she will disturb the pleasant surfaces of the Mill House order by organizing Nancy's escape – but still without a word of acknowledgment or intervention to her mother.) In the epilogue, young Willa's position is similar, as she sits in the Willow Shade kitchen with the old women and hears their stories. "I soon learned that it was best never to interrupt with questions, – it seemed to break the spell." Instead, she says, "While they talked, I looked and listened" (pp. 288, 284). Will Willa ever "break the spell" of her southern home and interrupt the old story? The adult author's ambivalence about this question is one of the most powerful and equivocal conditions of *Sapphira*.

To supplement the fabulous epilogue narrative of Nancy's return, the body of this novel, set in 1856–7, is filled with other, troubling encounters with various Virginians' "old stories" of home. Sapphira herself, for example, is a woman of immense determination who, on her marriage to a man whose social standing is "certainly no match" for her own, left an established estate in Loudoun County to set up a new home and a new life on property she had inherited in an "out-of-the-way, thinly settled district" where "much of the land was still wild forest" and slaveholding was uncommon (p. 22). Her audacious marriage in this new place, coupled with her strong will and energy, would seem to be an opportunity to establish a genuinely new home. But Sapphira's Mount-Vernon-style estate is instead an old story, for she fills it with property – such as silver, portraits, and her mother's English carpet – that perpetuates her privileged past. Her most crucial property is human, for Sapphira, immobilized by her heavy, aging, dropsical body, is surrounded and enabled by the slaves who do her bidding. As Morrison writes, the slaves' "surrogate black bodies become her hands and feet, her fantasies of sexual ravish and intimacy with her husband."[10] Sapphira and her husband, Henry, conceive their home very differently; Henry tries to operate the mill as a successful independent business and to run not a plantation, but a farm, where he works alongside the (slave) men he oversees. For the most part, he eschews his wife's house; his home is a sleeping room at the mill, where he keeps his necessities, books, and a few keepsakes of his immigrant father. However, Henry is legally and financially bound to his wife's property. Her slaves are jointly his and he must use their labor to run the farm and mill; even his most trusted mill worker is a slave. Henry's and Sapphira's visions of home are deeply at odds and, while she is alive, Sapphira's vision trumps Henry's, because it is supported by more valuable property. The minute she dies, he frees her slaves, in an effort to end his wife's old story.

Henry also suggests another crisis in this book. As Sapphira's husband, he is legally bound to her slaves; they cannot be sold without his consent. Like it or not, he is the owner and overseer of slaves and the beneficiary of their labors. Yet his family has never owned slaves, and he has deep premonitions that slavery is wrong. Henry turns to his Bible, the trusted holy text of his culture and a repository of cultural memory, for guidance, but it is not forthcoming. This "old story" is equivocal; "never in his Bible had he ever been able to find a clear condemnation of slavery" (p. 110). In his isolated room at the mill, Henry pores over the Bible, hoping to find confirmation of his anti-slavery convictions, which are compromised by the fact of his marriage. But the scriptures fail him; he is still homesick.

Henry and Sapphira's daughter, Rachel, is acknowledged as the chief abettor of Nancy's triumphant adult return to Back Creek; on her arrival, Nancy says, "I never forget who it was took me across the river that night, Mrs. Blake" (p. 283). Rachel's own homecomings are far more ambivalent, however. Rachel's relations to her two previous homes is problematic; as we saw, she is at odds with her mother's household (where she grew up) because of the abuses of power she has silently witnessed there. She is also cut off from the happiest years of her life, when she lived in Washington with her Congressman husband and their children. Although loving, this adored husband was improvident, and Rachel could do nothing to deflect his careless hedonism. When he and their young son die on a pleasure trip to New Orleans, Rachel and her two surviving daughters are left without resources; their home has failed. Henry rescues the young family and builds them a house in Back Creek, near the plantation where Rachel grew up and now feels silenced and estranged. One major reason why Nancy's return is triumphant is that she is able to bring stories and images of her Canadian life to share with her mother and friends; she is also able happily to revisit her childhood home, Till's former slave cabin. For Rachel, such feats of memory and return are impossible. When asked about Washington, she says, "I hardly remember. All that is gone. I'd take it kindly of you not to bring it back to me. This is my home now, and I want to live here like I had never gone away" (p. 145). Rachel's Washington life combined joy and pain; she chooses to be estranged from these mixed memories. Confronting mixed memories of home, both cultural and personal memories, is Willa Cather's task in this novel, as she said. Although Rachel is one of the purported heroes of *Sapphira*, she also illustrates another troubled relation to the old story of her former home.

These complications are augmented in the lives of the book's African American characters. The oldest of these is Jezebel, the only one of Sapphira's slaves who was African born; she was captured "by slave-hunters," in Guinea, in the 1780s. At eighteen, Jezebel witnessed the destruction of her "native village" and the slaughter of her father and brothers. "It was all over in a few hours; of the village nothing was left but smoking ashes and mutilated bodies" (p. 90). At ninety-five, Jezebel remembers that night only dimly. After her arrival (via Middle Passage) in the port of Baltimore, she was bought by several successive owners until Sapphira's family, the Dodderidges, purchased her. "She went to the Dodderidges the year that Sapphira was born, and had been in the family ever since" (p. 96).

Jezebel has been a cornerstone in Sapphira's construction of home since her birth; for Sapphira, she is an essential premise of the old story. When Sapphira – an invalid herself – visits the dying slave woman, she emphasizes their common experiences – both were active, vigorous women who worked together to establish the Mill House gardens and have common memories: "those were good times . . . I expect you remember those things, too" (pp. 87–8). Although Jezebel appears to acquiesce, a moment later – when asked if there is anything that would tempt her appetite – she responds very differently: "The old woman gave a sly chuckle; one paper eyelid winked, and her eyes gave out a flash of grim humour. 'No'm, I cain't think of nothin' I could relish, lessen maybe it was a li'l pickaninny's hand'" (p. 89).[11]

This much-debated passage suggests that Jezebel, who lived among "a fierce cannibal people" for her first eighteen years (p. 91), has not forgotten her own, African "old story" and that she has used that story – and the horrified response that it provokes among such mid-nineteenth century Americans as the squeamish Nancy – to maintain her own distinctive persona, self-possessed and grimly humorous, to the last. In fact, the listening presence of Jezebel's great-granddaughter might be read as one reason for the old woman's startling remark. The actual and metaphoric devouring of black children, by both Africans and Americans, is a part of Nancy's family history. As Gregg D. Kimball has shown, the institution of slavery and its aftermath effectively erased much "black historical and social memory," yet slaves sometimes found covert ways – of which oral tradition was perhaps the most powerful – to create and transmit memory.[12] Old Jezebel's calculated remark may be – among other things – such a project.

Jezebel's old story obviously incorporates the Terrible on many levels, including such tabooed practices as cannibalism, and it does so in the language of the American present – "pickaninny" – suggesting that hunger for black children's flesh is a continuing condition. The naive Nancy, who hears her great-grandmother's remark, interprets it to Sapphira as a mad utterance: "Don't stay, Missy! She's out of her haid!" Nancy is not yet capable of acknowledging all that her ancestor's memory may contain (or at least she will not admit to her white owner that she does so). But Sapphira silences the girl, saying, "I know your granny through and through. She is no more out of her head than I am" (p. 89). She emphasizes her absolute possession of Jezebel: mind and body, past and present, "through and through." Yet she acknowledges their commonality as well, as old women who have confronted the full range of the Terrible in their home lives – including the literal and figurative devouring of children (as Nancy herself is currently in danger of being consumed by Sapphira). This is a commonality that Sapphira shares with no one else but Jezebel, who has always been a presence in her life story. Perhaps it is no coincidence that Sapphira's major breakdown of confidence in the novel – a panic attack during which she feels that her slaves and husband are all deceiving her and her home has become "shattered, treacherous" – occurs on the night of Jezebel's funeral.

Jezebel's long survival as an obdurate personality seems linked to her capacity to draw on even the most horrifying (to us) aspects of her own past and present homes as a sustaining resource. Another Colbert slave, the Virginia-born Sampson, Henry's able and intelligent assistant at the mill, is in a very different position. Long before Sapphira's death, Henry offers to manumit Sampson and find him a job at a Pennsylvania mill. Sampson's reaction to this offer is dismayed: "He broke down. This was his home. Here he knew everybody. He didn't want to go out among strangers" (p. 109). Despite his considerable abilities, Sampson is deeply attached, like the young Nancy, to a home where his enslavement (and that of his children) is a necessary condition. Of course, when Sapphira dies and Henry frees all her slaves, Sampson is obliged to take the position at the Pennsylvania mill. His return visit to Back Creek is also described in the novel's epilogue, forming an interesting parallel to Nancy's. Sampson has been equally successful outside the South; he and his children have "done well." Like Nancy, he is hungry for the southern food he remembers, on his return. Till recalls,

> "Sampson come to my cabin every day he was here, to eat my light bread . . . 'I ain't had no real bread since I went away.' He told me how in the big mill where he works . . . the machines runs so fast an' gits so hot, an' burns all the taste out-a the flour. 'They is no real bread but what's made out-a water-ground flour,' he says to me." (p. 289)

Although he has his freedom, Sampson has lost his home. The taste of the wheat grown, harvested, and water-ground at the Colbert farm and mill is no longer available in his new life; he is estranged from the taste that represented a direct connection with nature, mediated through his own labor. There is no longer any "real bread" for Sampson (a terrible loss for a miller and a man who, as a slave, baked the bread for his family). The industrial world has given him a new job and home, but it has cut him off from the old agrarian story, for which he still has a powerful hunger. Sampson's "success" echoes some of the facts of Reconstruction life for many former slaves. Yet another compelling feature of Nancy's parallel story of return is that she does not appear to suffer from any of Sampson's estrangement. As a housekeeper, she does work very similar to that of her mother, Sapphira's slave housekeeper, and of Till's surrogate mother, the British housekeeper Mrs. Matchem; she is apparently untouched by the encroachments of industrialization. Nancy also enjoys the remembered tastes of Virginia, on her return. "She begged to be allowed to roast the coffee. 'The smell of it is sweeter than roses to me, Mrs. Blake,' she said laughing." But Nancy is flexible enough to enjoy more than one beverage. In Canada, she says, "the coffee is always poor, so I've learned to drink tea" (p. 286). Even in the smallest details of diet, Nancy is a model construction of a successfully negotiated return.

Nancy is the daughter of Till, and the character of Till is modeled on the African American who apparently played the largest part in Cather's own story. Cather's letters refer repeatedly to "Aunt Till" as an important presence in her Virginia childhood and to Aunt Till's stories as a major source of the novel. She emphasizes the dignity and complexity of the actual Till's character. Nevertheless, Till is the character in the novel that many critics have found most unsuccessful. According to Morrison, for example, Cather posits through Till that "slave women are 'natally dead,' with no obligations to their offspring or their own parents. This breach startles the contemporary reader and renders Till an unbelievable and unsympathetic character" (Morrison, p. 21). I would argue, instead, that Till is the most complexly and problematically rendered of Cather's slave characters. As portrayed in the epilogue, Till is a prolific storyteller who showers the young white narrator with details about her family history, particularly Sapphira and Henry. Yet she withholds such stories from Nancy, even the identity of the girl's father. Obviously, as we see at their reunion, Till loves Nancy. It is almost as if she were protecting her delicate daughter from the full weight of the "old story," as it may come down to an African American girl. Young Willa, the white girl, is less protected by Till.

The central known fact about Till's own girlhood at the Dodderidge family's estate in Loudoun County, Chestnut Hill, is that she watched her mother burn to death, as the woman was dressing for a slave party. The little girl was "struck dumb" by this sight. The English housekeeper adopted her, cared for her, and trained her in the rituals and niceties of housekeeping. Housekeeping gave Till back a voice, a self, and a zone of safety – even though, within that zone, she was still a slave. Chestnut Hill, where she learned and practiced her "finer" domestic accomplishments, remains home to her; when Sapphira bought her and brought her to the Mill House, Till "felt buried in the deep woods. For years to come she was homesick for Mrs. Matchem" (p. 72). According to Morrison, Till exhibits no "maternal concern" for her daughter before Nancy's escape. I would argue, on the contrary, that Till expresses her concern for Nancy by teaching her the housekeeping skills that have been her greatest pride and protection. Although Sapphira's jealousy and anger have turned her irrevocably against Nancy, Till insists that domestic service, done just right, will reinstate the girl in her owner's favor. She instructs her daughter, "Now honey, if I was you, I'd make a nice egg-nog . . . an' I'd carry it in to the Mistress . . . on the small silvah salvah, with a white napkin . . . I'd smile, an' look happy to serve her, an' she'll smile back" (p. 44). This is what Till, who was taken out of the slave community at an early age and reared by a white surrogate mother, has to offer her daughter; it is her version of a safe "old story," with the dangerous fact of the fragility of a slave woman's life (like Till's mother's) edited away. Nancy knows that her mother's advice will not work; she has seen that Sapphira is beyond being placated by egg-nog on silver. Yet, later, when Nancy is thrown back on her survival skills as a fugitive in Montreal, her housekeeping accomplishments become a valuable commodity on which she founds her new life as a free woman – thanks, at least partially, to her mother, Till.

Till is a capable, intelligent woman. What she seems to have lost at her mother's death (if, indeed, she ever had it) is an audacious imagination. She cannot conceive of a life outside the slaveholding household. While the other Colbert slaves moved on (with varying degrees of success) when Henry freed them, Till did not. The "new miller," who succeeded Henry at his death, has "let Till stay on in her cabin behind the Mill House, work her own garden patch, and even keep a pig or two" (p. 285). At the sufferance of the white man who has taken her "Master's" place, she lives as a free (?) woman in the surroundings of her slave life, spending much of her time in the household of Sapphira's daughter and granddaughter, where she is apparently employed. When Nancy makes her return visit, she spends six weeks with her mother in these two places. We do not know what they say to each other when they are alone; Nancy and Till are portrayed in the epilogue only when white eyes are present to observe them. At one point, on the first day of Nancy's visit when little Willa is the only white person present, Till listens with delight to the patterns of her daughter's speech, "looking up into her face with idolatrous pride. 'Nancy, darlin', you talks just like Mrs. Matchem, down at Chestnut Hill! I loves to hear you'" (p. 286). Till is reconstructing the old story, and she finds herself at home, at Chestnut Hill, with her daughter – once endangered by her status as a female, mulatto slave – now in the role of the white, English housekeeper who was Till's safe, surrogate mother. Even that safety had limits, however, for Mrs. Matchem did not have ultimate power; she did not own slaves. And, despite her disapproval, she could do nothing to prevent Till's sale to Sapphira and her removal. In her postbellum reconstruction of the story, Till can believe in the safety of both her daughter and herself. In fact, she has reversed their roles. As a "little black girl," Till "would stand looking up at the tall Devonshire woman, taking [her housekeeping] precepts devoutly to heart" (p. 71). Now, Till looks up at her tall daughter with similarly worshipful devotion. Till's story is a part of the idyllic return to the reconstructed South that the novel's epilogue both posits and critiques.

For the white child Willa, Till also has a fund of stories, about her great-grandparents, Sapphira and Henry; these tales "grew more and more into a complete picture of those two persons" (p. 292). It is a far more complex narrative than we ever see Till offering Nancy, created from what is related and omitted, from "unconscious hints" as well as told tales. (And it perhaps represents much of the material from which Willa Cather built this novel, gleaned from "Aunt Till"'s stories.) In her cabin, Till has assembled a chest full of keepsakes from her former owners that she shows little Willa: the miller's shawl and books, Sapphira's "lace caps and fichus, and odd bits of finery such as velvet slippers with buckles." Her "chief treasure" is a gold-edged brooch with locks of Sapphira's and Henry's hair, "at the time of their marriage" (pp. 291–2). The objects evoke the relative prosperity and modest luxury (lace, velvet, gold) of Sapphira's household, the same prosperity that made it possible for Sapphira to own slaves. Till is still the housekeeper, caring for the Colberts' things. Her "chief treasure," with its gold setting, is among those valuables. But instead of pearls or gems, this brooch contains human hair, snippings from the bodies of the Master and Mistress. Once, they were the owners of Till's body. But now she possesses these pieces of them. And she has become the arbiter of their stories.

In her last novel, Willa Cather returned to a place, time, and history in which she was deeply, natally implicated. As she wrote to her niece Helen Cather Southwick, even in the 1930s when she met Paul Robeson, she feared that her "southern heritage" in matters of race would make the meeting difficult (although it did not, Cather thought; she was overwhelmed by Robeson's "greatness" [Stout, *Calendar*, p. 259]). Although Cather sometimes took pains not to define herself as a southerner, she was obviously aware that her own Virginian origins were still a powerfully influential presence in her life. A part of her inheritance was the white memory of slavery "produced by white southerners during the late nineteenth and early twentieth centuries," typically an idealized view that glorified "the living and faithful black slave, especially the mammy, [and] sought to conceal alternative memories of violence, exploitation, and cruelty." For Cather, much of this memory was acquired from local and family stories she heard while a child and adolescent. Indeed, as W. Fitzhugh Brundage writes, such storytelling had an important custodial function, especially in an era when professional historians were still relatively few, as they were even in 1940, when *Sapphira* was published:

> Scholarship only recently has exerted influence over social memory in the American South. Until well into the twentieth century trained historians were so few in number and so limited in influence that they could not exert broad cultural authority over matters past. Even when their influence began to increase, trained historians did not quickly discard interpretive conventions inherited from their amateur predecessors and contemporaries.[13]

It was in this climate that Cather attempted to write the old story of her Virginia origins, and, as we have seen, this book presents that story in multiples, as southerners black and white, old and young, from little Willa to old Jezebel, compete to narrate their tales of home. Describing her book to Viola Roseboro', Cather said that it drew so much from collective memory – local and family tales – that she hardly knew where her own contribution began (Stout, *Calendar*, p. 228). According to Brundage, "when appealing to a collective memory, individuals necessarily define themselves in relation to inherited conventions and hierarchies. Consequently, justifications of status, privilege, and authority, like a mnemonic device that derives its efficacy from repetition, often are recurring elements in both personal and social memory" (Brundage, p. 13). For Willa Cather, a white southerner born only eight years after the end of the Civil War, "inherited conventions and hierarchies" were an inevitable part of her project, and, by including her child-self in the autobiographical epilogue, she allows us to see her own youthful imagination as a canvas for competing "justifications of status, privilege and authority," as stories are enacted and related before her voracious eyes. This reveals the tensions and continuities between the Reconstruction-born girl and the 67-year-old novelist of 1940.

In the epilogue, the two major competitors for space in Willa's memory and imagination are the stories of daughter and mother, Till and Nancy. From Cather's letters, we know that both of them remained vividly on her mind, all her life. Nancy's return captured Willa's imagination because it made it seem possible that one could have a southern story *and* a life elsewhere, that one could enjoy pleasant surfaces and family, community ties without becoming ensnared by that something "Terrible" beneath the surfaces – that one *could* come home again, at least for a visit.

Till's story is different. And it is Till's voice that concludes the novel, as she narrates and interprets the death of Sapphira, in 1857:

> When the miller came at supper-time and went into the parlour, he found her. The strong heart had been overcome at last. Though her bell was beside her, she had not rung it. There must have been some moments of pain or struggle, but she had preferred to be alone. Till thought it likely the "fine folks" were waiting outside for her in the arbour, and she went away with them.
>
> (p. 294)

Here, what Till has to tell little Willa about her great-grandmother emphasizes fortitude (the courage to die alone), propriety (death in the parlour, with no unseemly sounds or commotion), and the importance of defining oneself "in relation to inherited conventions and hierarchies" (Brundage, p. 13). Till interprets Sapphira's death as a decision to rejoin her own class (out of which she had married), leaving her husband, daughter, and devoted slave Till, none of whom are "fine folks." It is a decision that Till apparently supports and admires. And she goes on, concluding the book:

> "She oughtn't never to a' come out here," Till often said to me. She wasn't raised that way. Mrs. Matchem, down at the old place, never got over it that Miss Sapphy didn't buy in Chestnut Hill an' live like a lady, 'stead a' leavin' it to run down under the Bushwells, an' herself comin' out here where nobody was anybody much."
>
> (pp. 294–5)

One does best for oneself, Till instructs Willa, when one stays *home*, in the place where one was born, and lives as one was raised, retaining one's social class and, in Sapphira's case, living "like a lady." (Till herself is largely living by these principles, still at home in her slave cabin.) Otherwise, things fall apart – property "runs down" and hierarchies disintegrate in a society without distinctions, where "nobody was anybody much."

Such advice, strictly followed, would have kept Nancy enslaved and would have cruelly hampered Willa Cather's own peripatetic life. Spotlighted, without comment, at the novel's end, Till's words are the old story at its most constraining. They are a former slave's defense of slavery, and they contradict the triumphant escape of Till's beloved daughter Nancy and negate many of the human stories from which *Sapphira* is woven. Cather herself, who even as a small girl unquestioningly accepted that whites always had certain privileges – such as eating before African Americans were served – understood the terrible power of Till's formulation and, as we see in this book, was sometimes constrained by it herself. But, in her Virginia novel, she took on some of the thorniest difficulties of Americans' personal and cultural memory of the nineteenth-century South, undertaking a "dangerous journey" into the heart of the "old stories."

NOTES

1. Willa Cather, "Joseph and His Brothers," in *Not Under Forty* (New York: Knopf, 1940), p. 119.
2. Janis P. Stout, ed., *A Calendar of the Letters of Willa Cather* (Lincoln, NE: University of Nebraska Press, 2002), p. 128. Future references to letters summarized by Stout will be made parenthetically in the essay.
3. Catherine Clinton, *Tara Revisited: Women, War, and the Plantation Legend* (New York: Abbeville Press, 1995), pp. 182–3.
4. *Willa Cather* (New York: Knopf, n.d.), p. 2.
5. Edith Lewis, *Willa Cather Living: A Personal Record* (1953; Lincoln, NE: University of Nebraska Press, 2000), p. 182.
6. Willa Cather, *Sapphira and the Slave Girl* (New York: Knopf, 1940), p. 281. Future references to this novel will be made parenthetically in the essay.
7. Patricia Yaeger, "White Dirt: The Surreal Racial Landscapes of Willa Cather's South," in Ann Romines, ed., *Willa Cather's Southern Connections: New Essays on Cather and the South* (Charlottesville: University Press of Virginia, 2000), p. 154.
8. Elizabeth Shepley Sergeant, *Willa Cather: A Memoir* (Philadelphia and New York: Lippincott, 1953), p. 79.
9. Janis P. Stout, *Willa Cather: The Writer and Her World* (Charlottesville and London: University Press of Virginia, 2000), p. 284.
10. Toni Morrison, *Playing in the Dark: Whiteness and the Literary Imagination* (Cambridge, MA: Harvard University Press), p. 26. Future references will be made parenthetically.
11. I discuss this scene more thoroughly in "Admiring and Remembering: The Problem of Virginia," in Susan J. Rosowski, ed., *Willa Cather's Ecological Imagination: Cather Studies* v (Lincoln, NE, and London: University of Nebraska Press, 2003), pp. 285–6.
12. Gregg D. Kimball, "African, American, and Virginian: The Shaping of Black Memory in Antebellum Virginia, 1790–1860," in W. Fitzhugh Brundage, ed., *Where These Memories Grow: History, Memory, and Southern Identity* (Chapel Hill: University of North Carolina Press, 2000), pp. 57–77.
13. W. Fitzhugh Brundage, "Introduction: No Deed but Memory," in Brundage, ed., *Where These Memories Grow*, p. 7. Future references will be made parenthetically.

SELECTED BIBLIOGRAPHY

Cather's writings

The Willa Cather Scholarly Edition project, under the general editorship of Susan J. Rosowski, began producing scholarly editions of Cather's works through the University of Nebraska Press in 1992. To date, *A Lost Lady, Death Comes for the Archbishop, My Ántonia, O Pioneers!, Obscure Destinies*, and *The Professor's House* have been published. Each volume contains a complete historical and textual apparatus. The project represents the first scholarly effort to standardize Cather's texts, although Houghton Mifflin produced an Autograph Edition of the complete works, with the author's participation, between 1937 and 1941. Cather's novels and stories are widely available in trade paperback editions; the Vintage Classics series is one of the more popular. In the following list, I give the original publisher and date of publication.

Novels

Alexander's Bridge (Boston, MA, and New York: Houghton Mifflin, 1912).
Death Comes for the Archbishop (New York: Knopf, 1927).
A Lost Lady (New York: Knopf, 1923).
Lucy Gayheart (New York: Knopf, 1935).
My Ántonia (Boston, MA, and New York: Houghton Mifflin, 1918; rev. 1926).
My Mortal Enemy (New York: Knopf, 1926).
One of Ours (New York: Knopf, 1922).
O Pioneers! (Boston, MA, and New York: Houghton Mifflin, 1913).
The Professor's House (New York: Knopf, 1925).
Sapphira and the Slave Girl (New York: Knopf, 1940).
Shadows on the Rock (New York: Knopf, 1931).
The Song of the Lark (Boston, MA, and New York: Houghton Mifflin, 1915).

Short fiction

Obscure Destinies (New York: Knopf, 1932).
The Old Beauty and Others (New York: Knopf, 1948).
The Troll Garden (New York: McClure, Phillips & Co., 1905).
Uncle Valentine and Other Stories: Willa Cather's Uncollected Short Fiction, 1915–1929, ed. Bernice Slote (Lincoln, NE: University of Nebraska Press, 1972).

Willa Cather's Collected Short Fiction, 1892–1912, ed. Virginia Faulkner. Introd. Mildred Bennett (Lincoln, NE: University of Nebraska Press, 1965, rev. 1970).
Youth and the Bright Medusa (New York: Knopf, 1920).

Poetry

April Twilights (Boston, MA: Richard G. Badger, 1903).
April Twilights and Other Poems (New York: Knopf, 1923).

Articles, Essays, Interviews, etc.

The Kingdom of Art: Willa Cather's First Principles and Critical Statements, ed. Bernice Slote (Lincoln, NE: University of Nebraska Press, 1967).
Not Under Forty (New York: Knopf, 1936).
Willa Cather in Person: Interviews, Speeches, and Letters, ed. L. Brent Bohlke (Lincoln, NE, and London: University of Nebraska Press, 1986).
Willa Cather On Writing: Critical Studies on Writing as an Art (New York: Knopf, 1949).
The World and the Parish: Willa Cather's Articles and Reviews, 1893–1902. 2 vols., ed. William M. Curtin (Lincoln, NE: University of Nebraska Press, 1970).
Writings from Willa Cather's Campus Years, ed. James R. Shively (Lincoln, NE: University of Nebraska Press, 1950).

Bibliographies and guides

The first two items listed below are standard bibliographical resources. For bibliographical updates, chiefly focused on secondary materials, consult *The Willa Cather Pioneer Memorial Newsletter and Review*, which occasionally publishes bibliographical essays, and the section devoted to Cather in *American Literary Scholarship*, published annually by Duke University Press.

Arnold, Marilyn, *Willa Cather: A Reference Guide* (Boston, MA: G. K. Hall, 1986).
Crane, Joan, *Willa Cather: A Bibliography* (Lincoln, NE, and London: University of Nebraska Press, 1982).
March, John, *A Reader's Companion to the Fiction of Willa Cather*, ed. Marilyn Arnold with Debra Lynn Thornton (Westport, CT: Greenwood Press, 1993).
Meyering, Sheryl L., *A Reader's Guide to the Short Stories of Willa Cather* (New York: G. K. Hall, 1994).
O'Connor, Margaret Anne, ed., *Willa Cather: The Contemporary Reviews* (Cambridge: Cambridge University Press, 2001).

Biographies and archival resources

Regrettably, because of the strictures in Cather's will regarding publication of her letters, there is no published collection. Janis P. Stout's recent *A Calendar of the Letters of Willa Cather* (Lincoln, NE, and London: University of Nebraska Press, 2002) offers detailed summaries that are true to the tone and spirit of Cather's letters. The book is a meticulous work of scholarship that will be of immense value to a range of readers, but some will still need to consult the documents directly. Major repositories of Cather archival materials are the Willa Cather Historical Center in Red Cloud, Nebraska, and the Nebraska State Historical Society in Lincoln. The Houghton Library, Harvard University, has an extensive collection of letters pertaining to her relationship to her first publisher, Houghton Mifflin, and her literary mentor, Sarah Orne Jewett. The Harry Ransom Humanities Research Center at the University of Texas Library has material focused on her relationship with her second publisher, Alfred Knopf. The Lilly Library at Indiana University has letters to S. S. McClure. The William R. Perkins Library at Duke University has the important letters from the early 1890s that document Cather's tempestuous relationship with Louise Pound. Other significant repositories are the Bailey/Howe Library, University of Vermont; the Beinecke Rare Book and Manuscript Library, Yale University; the Huntington Library; and the Clifton Waller Barrett Library, University of Virginia.

Of the several biographies, Woodress gives the most thorough coverage of Cather's literary career. O'Brien's psychobiography ends with the publication of Cather's second novel, *O Pioneers!*, but it is still critically influential, particularly on issues related to gender and sexuality. Stout's is as much intellectual or cultural history as it is biography. Its virtue is in the dialog Stout sets up between Cather and her world. Lewis's is a memoir, written by Cather's domestic partner of more than forty years.

Bennett, Mildred R., *The World of Willa Cather* (Lincoln, NE: University of Nebraska Press, 1951).
Brown, E. K., and Leon, Edel, *Willa Cather: A Critical Biography* (New York: Knopf, 1953).
Lee, Hermione, *Willa Cather: Double Lives* (New York: Pantheon Books, 1990).
Lewis, Edith, *Willa Cather Living: A Personal Record* (New York: Knopf, 1953).
O'Brien, Sharon, *Willa Cather: The Emerging Voice* (New York and Oxford: Oxford University Press, 1987).
Stout, Janis P., *Willa Cather: The Writer and Her World* (Charlottesville and London: University Press of Virginia, 2000).
Woodress, James, *Willa Cather: A Literary Life* (Lincoln, NE, and London: University of Nebraska Press, 1987).

Critical studies

Abraham, Julie, *Are Girls Necessary? Lesbian Writing and Modern Histories* (New York and London: Routledge, 1996).
Acocella, Joan, "Cather and the Academy," *New Yorker*, 27 November 1995, pp. 56–71.
    Willa Cather and the Politics of Criticism (Lincoln, NE, and London: University of Nebraska Press, 2000).
Adams, Timothy Dow, "My Gay Ántonia: The Politics of Willa Cather's Lesbianism," in Monika Kehoe, ed. *Historical, Literary, and Erotic Aspects of Lesbianism* (New York: Harrington Park Press, 1986), pp. 89–98.
Ammons, Elizabeth, *Conflicting Stories: American Women Writers at the Turn into the Twentieth Century* (New York: Oxford University Press, 1991).
    "The Engineer as Cultural Hero and Willa Cather's First Novel, *Alexander's Bridge*," *American Quarterly* 38.5 (1986), pp. 746–60.

Anders, John P., *Willa Cather's Sexual Aesthetics and the Male Homosexual Literary Tradition* (Lincoln, NE, and London: University of Nebraska Press, 1999).

Arnold, Marilyn, *Willa Cather's Short Fiction* (Athens, OH: Ohio University Press, 1984).

Bruccoli, Matthew J., "'An Instance of Apparent Plagiarism': F. Scott Fitzgerald, Willa Cather, and the First *Gatsby* Manuscript," *The Princeton University Library Chronicle* 39 (1977–8), pp. 171–8.

Butler, Judith, "'Dangerous Crossing': Willa Cather's Masculine Names," in *Bodies that Matter: On the Discursive Limits of "Sex"* (New York and London: Routledge, 1993), pp. 143–66.

Carlin, Deborah, *Cather, Canon, and the Politics of Reading* (Amherst: University of Massachusetts Press, 1992).

Chown, Linda, "'It Came Closer than That': Willa Cather's *Lucy Gayheart*," *Cather Studies* 2 (1993), pp. 118–39.

Cramer, Timothy R., "Claude's Case: A Study of the Homosexual Temperament in Willa Cather's *One of Ours*," *South Dakota Review* 31.3 (Fall 1993), pp. 147–60.

Donovan, Josephine, *After the Fall: The Demeter-Persephone Myth in Wharton, Cather, and Glasgow* (University Park and London: The Pennsylvania State University Press, 1989).

Downs, M. Catherine, *Becoming Modern: Willa Cather's Journalism* (Selingsgrove, PA: Susquehanna University Press, 1999).

Fetterley, Judith, "*My Ántonia*, Jim Burden, and the Dilemma of the Lesbian Writer," in Karla Jay and Joanne Glasgow, eds., *Lesbian Texts and Contexts* (New York: New York University Press, 1990), pp. 145–63.

   "Willa Cather and the Fiction of Female Development," in Carol J. Singley and Susan Elizabeth Sweeney, eds., *Anxious Power: Reading, Writing, and Ambivalence in Narrative by Women* (Albany: State University of New York Press, 1993), pp. 221–34.

Fischer, Mike, "Pastoralism and Its Discontents: Willa Cather and the Burden of Imperialism," *Mosaic* 23 (1990), pp. 31–44.

Flannigan, John H., "Thea Kronborg's Vocal Transvestism: Willa Cather and the 'Voz Contralto,'" *Modern Fiction Studies* 40.4 (Winter 1994), pp. 737–63.

Fryer, Judith, *Felicitous Space: The Imaginative Structures of Edith Wharton and Willa Cather* (Chapel Hill and London: University of North Carolina Press, 1986).

Gelfant, Blanche, "The Forgotten Reaping-Hook: Sex in *My Ántonia*," in *Women Writing in America* [1971] (Hanover, NH: University Press of New England, 1984), pp. 94–116.

   "Movement and Melody: The Disembodiment of *Lucy Gayheart*, in *Women Writing in America* (see previous entry), pp. 119–43.

Gilbert, Sandra M., and Susan Gubar, *Sexchanges*. Vol. II of *No Man's Land: The Place of the Woman Writer in the Twentieth Century* (New Haven: Yale University Press, 1989).

Goldberg, Jonathan, *Willa Cather and Others* (Durham, NC, and London: Duke University Press, 2001).

Goldman, Anne E., *Continental Divides: Revisioning American Literature* (New York: Palgrave/St. Martin's Press, 2000).

Griffiths, Frederick, "The Woman Warrior: Willa Cather's *One of Ours*," *Women's Studies* 11 (1984), pp. 261–85.

Gustafson, Neil, "Getting Back to Cather's Text: The Shared Dream in *O Pioneers!*" *Western American Literature* 30.2 (1995), pp. 151–62.

Harrell, David, *From Mesa Verde to the Professor's House* (Albuquerque: University of New Mexico Press, 1992).

Harvey, Sally Peltier, *Redefining the American Dream: The Novels of Willa Cather* (Rutherford, NJ: Fairleigh Dickinson University Press, 1995).

Hilgart, John, "Death Comes for the Aesthete: Commodity Culture and the Artifact in Cather's *The Professor's House*," *Studies in the Novel* 30.3 (Fall 1998), pp. 377–404.

Irving, Katrina, "Displacing Homosexuality: The Use of Ethnicity in Willa Cather's *My Ántonia*," *Modern Fiction Studies* 36.1 (Spring 1990), pp. 91–11.

Lindemann, Marilee, *Willa Cather: Queering America* (New York: Columbia University Press, 1999).

McDonald, Joyce, *The Stuff of Our Forebears: Willa Cather's Southern Heritage* (Tuscaloosa: University of Alabama Press, 1998).

Michaels, Walter Benn, *Our America: Nativism, Modernism, and Pluralism* (Durham, NC, and London: Duke University Press, 1995).

Middleton, Jo Ann, *Willa Cather's Modernism: A Study of Style and Technique* (London and Toronto: Associated University Press; Rutherford, NJ: Fairleigh Dickinson University Press, 1990).

Millington, Richard, "Willa Cather and 'The Storyteller': Hostility to the Novel in *My Ántonia*," *American Literature* 66 (1994), pp. 689–717.

Morrison, Toni, *Playing in the Dark: Whiteness and the Literary Imagination* (New York: Vintage, 1993).

Murphy, John, ed., *Critical Essays on Willa Cather* (Boston, MA: G. K. Hall, 1983).

Nealon, Christopher, "Affect-Genealogy: Feeling and Affiliation in Willa Cather," *American Literature* 69.1 (March 1997), pp. 5–37.

Nettels, Elsa, *Language and Gender in American Fiction: Howells, James, Wharton, and Cather* (Charlottesville: University Press of Virginia, 1997).

O'Brien, Sharon, "Becoming Noncanonical: The Case against Willa Cather," in Cathy N. Davidson, ed., *Reading in America: Literature and Social History* (Baltimore: Johns Hopkins University Press, 1989), pp. 240–58. (First published in *American Quarterly* 40 [1988], pp. 110–26.)

"Combat Envy and Survivor Guilt: Willa Cather's 'Manly Battle Yarn,'" in Helen Cooper, Adrienne Munich, and Susan Squier, eds., *Arms and the Woman: War, Gender, and Literary Representation* (Chapel Hill: University of North Carolina Press, 1989), pp. 184–204.

ed., *New Essays on* My Ántonia (Cambridge: Cambridge University Press, 1997).

Petry, Alice Hall, "Harvey's Case: Notes on Cather's 'The Sculptor's Funeral,'" *South Dakota Review* 24.3 (Fall 1986), pp. 108–16.

Reynolds, Guy, *Willa Cather in Context: Progress, Race, Empire* (New York: St. Martin's Press, 1996).

ed., *Willa Cather: Critical Assessments*, 4 vols. (Robertsbridge, East Sussex: Helm Information, 2003).

Romines, Ann, *The Home Plot: Women, Writing, and Domestic Ritual* (Amherst: University of Massachusetts Press, 1992).

ed., *Willa Cather's Southern Connections: New Essays on Cather and the South* (Charlottesville: University Press of Virginia, 2000).

Rosowski, Susan J., ed., *Approaches to Teaching Cather's My Ántonia* (New York: Modern Language Association, 1989).

The Voyage Perilous: Willa Cather's Romanticism (Lincoln, NE, and London: University of Nebraska Press, 1986).

Rubin, Larry, "The Homosexual Motif in Willa Cather's 'Paul's Case,'" *Studies in Short Fiction* 12 (1975), pp. 127–31.

Russ, Joanna, "To Write 'Like a Woman': Transformations of Identity in the Work of Willa Cather," in Monika Kehoe, ed., *Historical, Literary, and Erotic Aspects of Lesbianism* (New York: Harrington Park Press, 1986), pp. 77–87.

Ryan, Maureen, "No Woman's Land: Gender in Willa Cather's *One of Ours*," *Studies in American Fiction* 18.1 (Spring 1990), pp. 65–75.

Schroeter, James, ed., *Willa Cather and Her Critics* (Ithaca, NY: Cornell University Press, 1967).

Schwind, Jean, "The 'Beautiful' War in *One of Ours*," *Modern Fiction Studies*. 30.1 (Spring 1984), pp. 53–71.

"The Benda Illustrations to *My Ántonia*: Cather's 'Silent' Supplement to Jim Burden's Narrative," *PMLA* 100.1 (January, 1985), pp. 51–67.

"This Is a Frame-Up: Mother Eve in *The Professor's House*," *Cather Studies* 2 (1993), pp. 72–91.

Sedgwick, Eve Kosofsky, "Across Gender, Across Sexuality: Willa Cather and Others," *South Atlantic Quarterly* 88.1 (Winter 1989), pp. 53–72.

Shaw, Patrick W., *Willa Cather and the Art of Conflict* (Troy, NY: Whitston, 1992).

Skaggs, Merrill Maguire, *After the World Broke in Two: The Later Novels of Willa Cather* (Charlottesville and London: University Press of Virginia, 1990).

ed., *Willa Cather's New York: New Essays on Cather in the City* (Madison, NJ: Fairleigh Dickinson University Press, 2000).

Stouck, David, *Willa Cather's Imagination* (Lincoln, NE: University of Nebraska Press, 1975).

Swift, John N., and Joseph R. Urgo, eds., *Willa Cather and the American Southwest* (Lincoln, NE, and London: University of Nebraska Press, 2002).

Summers, Claude J., "'A Losing Game in the End': Aestheticism and Homosexuality in Cather's 'Paul's Case,'" *Modern Fiction Studies* 36.1 (Spring 1990), pp. 103–19.

Trout, Steven, *Memorial Fictions: Willa Cather and the First World War* (Lincoln, NE, and London: University of Nebraska Press, 2002).

Urgo, Joseph R., *Willa Cather and the Myth of American Migration* (Urbana and Chicago: University of Illinois Press, 1995).

Wasserman, Loretta, "Cather's Semitism," in Susan J. Rosowski, ed., *Cather Studies* II (Lincoln, NE, and London: University of Nebraska Press, 1993).

Willa Cather: A Study of the Short Fiction (Boston, MA: Twayne, 1991).

Wiesenthal, C. Susan, "Female Sexuality in Willa Cather's *O Pioneers!* and the Era of Scientific Sexology: A Dialogue Between Frontiers," *Ariel* 21.1 (1990), pp. 41–63.

Williams, Deborah Lindsay, *Not in Sisterhood: Edith Wharton, Willa Cather, Zona Gale, and the Politics of Female Authorship* (New York: Palgrave, 2001).

INDEX

CAMBRIDGE COMPANIONS TO LITERATURE

CAMBRIDGE COMPANIONS TO CULTURE